Nobody's Girl

Inspired by Virginia Giuffre and the Women Who Found Strength to Speak the Truth

Tasse Monagle

A powerful and emotional World War II tale of love, bravery, and friendship amid the darkness and struggles of war.

Bound together by past tragedy, Meg and Clarrie have built a deep friendship that has finally brought them peace — but how strong is their bond, and how long can their happiness endure?

As war erupts, new challenges arise with the arrival of evacuees who soon become part of their home and hearts. Together, they must find the strength to stand united through the most difficult days of their lives.

Yet when a haunting figure from Meg's past returns, their courage and loyalty will be tested like never before.

A moving and unforgettable sequel to *Nobody's Girl*.

Table of Contents

One 1
   Summer 1939 1
Two 6
Three 10
Four 15
Five 22
Six 29
Seven 37
Eight 42
   Autumn 1939 42
Nine 48
Ten 56
   1940 56
Eleven 64
Twelve 70
Thirteen 73
Fourteen 78
Fifteen 84
Sixteen 87
Seventeen 90
   1941 90
Eighteen 95
Nineteen 102
Twenty 106
Twenty-One 111
Twenty-Two 117
Twenty-three 124
Twenty-Four 128
   1942 128
Twenty-Five 135
Twenty-Six 140

Twenty-Seven 144
   1943 144
Twenty-Eight 148
Twenty-Nine 152
   1944 152
Thirty 157
Thirty-One 164
Thirty-Two 167
   1945 167
Thirty-Three 171
Thirty-Four 175
   1946 175

One

Summer 1939

Raising her gaze from the patchwork she was working in the sewing room at Robin Hill House, Nana May Whitehead looked across at the slender, graceful figure at the window. Clarissa Stratfield-Whyte looked out across the fields that surrounded the long driveway; these fields had been used for sheep grazing but were now hay meadows. However, Nana May didn't think her mistress was really interested in the hay. The elderly woman dragged herself to her feet, put down her stitching, and picked up her stout walking stick that was leaning against her chair. She then moved her spectacles to the end of her nose and proceeded to join Clarissa at the window.

'What's caught your attention out there, Clarrie, dear?' she asked softly as she came up to the younger woman's shoulder.

Clarrie turned her head and smiled down serenely at the elderly lady. Oh, what a rock Nana May had been to her. She'd warmed to her immediately on that first day Wigmore had taken her home to meet his widowed mother, in the opulent London villa that had been the home to the wealthy, industrialist family since mid-Victorian times. May Whitehead had been engaged as nanny to Wigmore just before his birth, and had been part of the family ever since. Now the younger Mrs Stratfield-Whyte loved Nana May as much as everyone else did. Twenty-three years she'd been married to her dearest Wig, and the older woman had been part of every day, sharing every joy and tragedy.

'I was just thinking how happy Meg seems now,' Clarrie mused, turning her gaze back to the field at the front of the house where two young people were gathering in the hay. 'So different from the headstrong young lady who came to us, what? It can't be far off three years ago now. The way she blamed us for the accident. And now look at her.'

'Poor child was lost in grief,' Nana May said quietly. 'Can you imagine being not quite sixteen and losing both your parents in one fell swoop? At any age, grief can manifest itself in anger, but when you're that young… I know it was the chauffeur's fault, that despicable Nathaniel Green. But you and Wig were travelling in the car, so I can understand why she blamed you, too, at first. Green was put away, but you were accessible. But, you know, I was so proud of the way you insisted on standing by her. You gave her not just a home, but time and love to help her heal.'

'I'd like to think I did my best for her. But I'd rather not think about Green again!' Clarrie's voice rang with unaccustomed bitterness. 'After what he did to our poor Meg to try and get his revenge, if you can call it that, when it was his own fault he was sent to prison for dangerous driving, not hers. And then what he put poor Jane through, as well.'

'Well, at least he's back behind bars where he belongs. And that Esme Carter.'

...rrie sighed, thinking of the other girl she had once tried to help — the one who ...siding with Green. "I made a mistake taking her in all those years ago. I thought ...ng the right thing, adopting a child from an orphanage. But look how she repaid us."

"Maybe that was part of the problem," Nana May replied gently. "She'd never had anyone truly love her, so when that monster showed her attention, she clung to it completely. He manipulated her, and she let him drag her down."

Clarrie shook her head slowly. "Oh, Nana, you really are a wise old soul. But our dear Meg was orphaned in the worst way, and she never behaved like that. She lost her family and her home, yet when she came to us, she was always kind and respectful. She might have been hurting, but she carried herself with such grace. And now she's part of our family — just like you, Nana May."

The old nanny smiled softly and turned back to her mending. Yes, Meg Chandler truly was part of the family now. But Nana May still sensed something in her — a quiet waiting, as though Meg expected something more from life. Meg had lost the family farm because she was too young to take over after her parents' deaths, but she had proven herself wise beyond her years. With her farming skills, she had helped turn the struggling estate around when times were hard.

Nana May remembered clearly when the young girl had first arrived at Robin Hill House. Meg had insisted she didn't want to be a guest, as Clarrie intended, but a servant — just a roof over her head, no charity. She refused to live off her insurance money and asked instead that it be invested along with the small inheritance from her parents. Even at sixteen, she'd had a strong, sensible mind.

Perhaps Clarrie had forgotten that day, but Nana May never had. She knew Clarrie hoped Meg would stay with them forever — and with Meg now in love with Ralph, the head gardener, and he with her, that wish might just come true. Clarrie loved Meg deeply, though she tried to hide it, and Nana May understood why.

Still, no one could know what the future would bring. Hitler had already taken Austria and much of Czechoslovakia, and now, in March, he had invaded Prague and claimed the rest. Britain's Prime Minister, Neville Chamberlain, had warned him to stop his aggression, but Germany's ally, Italy, had already conquered Albania. At last, the British government was beginning to see that Winston Churchill had been right all along — that Hitler was dangerous and not to be trusted.

The new Military Training Act required all single men aged twenty to twenty-two to complete military service. Ralph and Bob, the estate's maintenance man, were just too old to be called up, but the future was uncertain. Meanwhile, Wigmore had begun working with Churchill, producing shell casings in his London factory just as he had during the Great War.

It seemed history was about to repeat itself — another war was coming.

As ever, Nana May kept her own counsel as she went back to her chair and lowered herself into it. If she were honest with herself, she secretly loved Meg as the grandchild she'd never had, and she, too, hoped the girl would stay at Robin Hill House. But one thing was certain. Everybody's life would be put on hold if what they all feared was coming indeed materialised. She only hoped her old bones – after all, she was in her eightieth year – would be strong enough to support Clarrie and Meg and all the Robin Hill family while this Hitler fellow was on the rampage.

Nana May's stomach steadily churned. The war that had taken so many lives, the war to end all wars, had failed. And another was surely on its way.

Unaware that she was being watched from the sewing-room window, Meg stopped the tractor at the end of the field and turned in the driving seat to look back over her shoulder. The previous month, they'd borrowed the machine to prepare the ground for the planting of the turnips and swedes that would feed the cows through the following autumn and winter. There wasn't enough land to warrant the expense of buying a tractor of their own. Some of the forty acres was, after all, taken up by the garden, the lake and woodland. But this year, Meg wanted to cultivate as much land as they possibly could, and a neighbouring farmer had been happy to lend them his tractor for a small fee.

Meg couldn't wait to learn to drive it the first time it had rattled up the front drive. She remembered fondly the teasing arguments she'd had with her father over acquiring a tractor. How far she'd come since then. She could look back now without pain, able to rekindle her memories of her beloved parents without tears. And all because of the love and support shown her by Wigmore and Clarissa – or Mr W and Mrs C as everyone called them – Nana May, and all the staff. And, of course, Ralph.

When she'd first arrived at Robin Hill House, it was Bob, the gentle, easy-going general handyman, who'd shown her most attention. Ralph, then the under-gardener and also acting chauffeur after Green's dismissal, she'd resented. Despised, almost. He'd been too involved with the aftermath of the accident that had left her orphaned. Always seemed to be there when things went wrong and in her agony, she needed someone to blame. But it was Ralph who'd searched all night when her beloved dog, Mercury, had gone missing, Ralph who'd made her first birthday at Robin Hill House into a turning point in her recovery from grief. Ralph it was who had presented her with the puppy after Mercury had been poisoned, to whom she had turned when Jane had been kidnapped. And when he had risked his own life to save the scullery maid, Meg had realised that he meant the world to her.

Now when she was with Ralph, her heart seemed to fly. His teasing banter was a challenge that set her mind on fire as she rose to meet him. He made her feel so *alive.*

'You two are meant for each other,' Bob had said wistfully to Ralph, since his good friend hadn't been unaware of his feelings for Meg. 'I've seen it coming for months, waiting for the pair of you to realise how you felt. So I want you both to be happy. And, to be honest, I'm getting on rather well with Sally.'

Indeed throughout the winter and spring, Ralph had watched the relationship between Bob and Sally, the replacement housemaid for the scheming Esme, grow and blossom. And he really felt that all the bad times for Meg were behind her now, and that together they could go forward and build a new life for themselves. And with the arrival of summer, they couldn't have been happier – except for the cloud that hung over the entire country. The previous week they'd borrowed the tractor again, and Meg had honed her driving skills preparing the ground for the flatpole seedlings they'd then planted by hand, working long into the light June evenings. Then it was time for the swedes, and now they were haymaking in the flat, eight-acre field to one side of the drive.

While the hay sweep gathered the turned and dried swaths into larger windrows, Ralph still had to fork the hay onto the small cart by hand. Meg watched him, her heart flipping over at his strong, pliant body bending as he worked. Inevitably, the tractor-drawn machine worked faster than Ralph could, and so every now and then, Meg would turn off the engine and jump down to help him catch up. She did so now, running back alongside the ridge of hay, a broad grin on her face.

'Come on, slowcoach, catch up,' she teased as she reached him.

'Cheeky monkey,' he grinned back and, throwing the pitchfork to the ground, caught Meg in his arms. 'Where's my kiss, then?'

'Greedy! You had one last time,' she giggled, trying to escape.

'Then it's time for another.'

She pretended to struggle, laughing hysterically until his mouth on hers silenced her. His lips were warm and moist, and Meg never ceased to be amazed how their touch sent ripples down her spine. She slid her arms about his neck, and his went about her waist, pulling her against him, and she felt the lean length of him pressed against her own body. A thrumming sound in the clear summer sky above them made them draw apart. The droning increased in volume, and as they both turned their eyes heavenwards, three small planes passed overhead and disappeared. A long sigh expired from Meg's lungs as her hand still rested on Ralph's arm.

'D'you know what they were?' she asked ruefully.

'Too high to see. But either spitfires or hurricanes, I think. Heading for Biggin Hill or one of the other aerodromes around, I guess. New ones are arriving every day.'

Meg's heart plummeted. 'There's definitely going to be a war, isn't there?' she murmured, her previous happiness fled. 'Mr W's designed some new machinery to make bomb cases faster, and the factory's been working flat out all year.'

'Yup,' Ralph answered, his mouth twisting. 'The government wouldn't have authorised that so early if they'd thought the Munich Agreement would hold.'

'Which it hasn't, of course. Hitler's already broken it once. But what makes me feel so guilty is to think you and I mightn't've had a roof over our heads without the threat of war. Mr W's factory was really beginning to struggle before it was recommissioned for making shell cases again, like it did in the Great War.'

'You mustn't think like that, Meg. It's not our fault Hitler marched into Prague and just took the rest of Czechoslovakia he didn't get in the Agreement. Or that his friend Mussolini walked in and took over Albania. No, Meg. Winston Churchill's right. We've *got* to be prepared. Hitler could have *us* in his sights next.'

Meg nodded slowly. 'I know. It's just… so horrible. My dad and his generation fought and died or were maimed just so that it'd never happen again. And now this.'

Ralph sucked in his lean cheeks. 'I know. So let's just enjoy the peace while it lasts, eh? Like Jane does.'

'Yes.' Meg had to smile. 'Eric, her policeman friend, came to pick her up again today. He's been so kind to her ever since that night. Only I'm sure there's more to it than that. They wouldn't still be seeing each other nine months later if there wasn't!'

'Silver linings and all that,' Ralph agreed. 'She'd maybe never have found a sweetheart else. And she's really blossomed since then, with Eric's attentions. So, perhaps being rescued from kidnappers did have a good side to it.'

'You were the one who really saved her from Green. Going in on your own like that before the police arrived.'

'Only because Green was starting to knock her about. But at least Green's been locked up for years and can't do anyone any more harm.'

'And Esme, too. Even if they were more lenient to her.'

'Well, I had to say what I saw. That she tried to stop Green hurting Jane. And it seemed he was using Esme all along, egging her on to find ways of getting back at you.'

'Oh, but she had a vicious streak of her own,' Meg snorted. 'It was her idea to poison Mercury, even if Green carried it out. I could never forgive her for that.'

'Well, they're both banged up for some years, so they both got what they deserved.'

'Not for long enough in my mind. But at least we can rest easy for some time. And Jane has Eric because of it.'

Ralph gave an amused grunt, and then his face sobered. 'Yes, funny how things work out. You don't... d'you ever think that if your parents hadn't died, we'd never have met?'

Meg stared at him, and saw the anguish etched on his beloved face. Her heart lurched. 'No,' she said firmly. 'My parents died because Green was driving dangerously. Not so that Fate could bring us together. And who knows, we might've met somehow anyway. And then perhaps I wouldn't have been so horrible to you.'

'And that, my darling, is all in the past.' Ralph drew her towards him again, and engaged her in a long, deep kiss that sent shivers of delight through her entire being.

'Mmm, that was very nice,' she said at last, pulling away, 'but we've got to get on with this haymaking before the weather changes. And we've only got the tractor until the end of the day, remember. But if we get it all finished, I'll let you have another kiss then.'

Ralph chuckled before turning back to his work. As Meg picked up the other pitchfork, the smile faded from her face as the distant sound of another aircraft engine reached her ears. Another war when the horrific memories of the last one were still so fresh in some people's minds. At least her parents had been spared that. But, although it was true what she'd said to Ralph, that she never felt that they died so that she and Ralph would meet, she'd give anything to have them back.

Two

"You can't say no this time; we'll be taking in evacuees," One Saturday night, when Wigmore had finally returned home from the factory for the weekend and had taken a seat on a deckchair on the patio, Clarrie made a clear statement. The greens and emeralds were gentle in the summer evening light, and the breathtaking vista over the Kent Weald was as serene and magnificent as ever. But Clarrie's heart was anything but at rest. She dreaded contradicting her loving husband, but back in the winter, he'd refused to take in any Jewish kid refugees from Germany. He had had his justifications, and they were valid. However, Clarrie wasn't going to accept no this time.

Wig raised his eyebrows to her as he sipped his whisky and soda. 'Indeed, we can't. We're in what's considered a safe area, and we have a large house. We had to fill in that form last year, remember? In preparation for a massive evacuation programme, should it be necessary. We'll be obliged to take in evacuees, whether we like it or not. But, as it happens,' and now he turned his loving smile on his wife's anxious face, 'this time, I utterly agree to it. These children will be on *our* side. Any old enough to understand will be happy that I help make armaments to use against the enemy, not hate me because I might make the very bomb that falls on their family trapped back home. So, yes, my darling. Open our doors as wide as you wish. I know you'll make them all feel safe and loved. And if there are any troublemakers, at least they'll speak English so we can deal with it.'

'Oh, Wig, I knew you'd agree!' Clarrie threw her arms about her husband's neck, and just missed spilling his drink. It was terrible that children from all the big cities and other places considered vulnerable to bombing should have to be uprooted from their homes and evacuated to the safety of the countryside. But she would move heaven and earth to make it a happy time for any who came to Robin Hill House.

'As I say, we don't have much choice,' Wig went on. 'And if it'll make you happy, take as many as you want.' He smiled indulgently now. 'But it mightn't be as easy going as you think. It'll be the first time many of them have been outside London, or whatever other city they might come from. And for most of them, the first time they've ever been away from their parents. They'll be upset, lonely, frightened—'

'Then it'll be our job to make them feel welcomed and loved,' Clarrie said emphatically.

'Even so, you might find some of them rebellious. Some of them might not even know how to hold a knife and fork.'

'Oh, surely not.'

Wig tipped his head at her. 'You'd be surprised. I've seen such things with my own eyes, with the factory being in the East End. They could find it a huge wrench coming somewhere like this. And their language mightn't be too savoury, either.'

Clarrie drew in a breath and held it for a moment, but she wasn't to be deterred. 'Well, we'll have to educate them, won't we?' she grinned. 'The important thing will be to keep them safe, though. And we can take some mothers and babies. Finding places to keep little families together won't be easy, and we've got the space.'

'Whatever you think, my dear,' Wig nodded, and went back to contemplating his drink. God, it was good to relax for a few hours before getting back to the responsibilities of the factory. It was running to full capacity again, with well over a thousand workers employed by him, with all that entailed. To say nothing of all the machinery and the demands from the government on his engineering skills. When he could get away, it would be bliss to come back to his tranquil country estate and have his wife to himself. But this war was going to be different from anything else the country had ever seen.

He just hoped his fragile wife was strong enough to cope with the demands she was putting on herself. What strain would the sight of young children, mothers with babies, put on her? Did she realise what it would mean to her? Getting emotionally involved? It was bad enough how she felt about Meg, even though she thought she'd kept it hidden from him. But this?

This was war though, wasn't it? And Clarrie had a heart as big as the ocean. He couldn't put a halt to her generosity. All he could do was hope and pray that the old wound wasn't reopened.

*

'Hopefully Ralph won't mind Bob moving in with him,' Clarrie frowned, thoughtfully sucking the end of her pencil as she contemplated the brand new notebook in her hand. It was totally blank apart from the neatly written title on the front page: Evacuees. 'He could go back to the cottage, but then Gabriel and Mary won't be able to take anyone. And besides, I'd like to have both him and Bob in the house in case we get billeted with any unruly young boys. So if he doesn't mind Bob being in with him, that'll free up Bob's room, and the other single up there is empty anyway. So that's the male staff quarters,' Clarrie went on, jotting something in her notebook. 'The female quarters are all full anyway, so that leaves the three guest rooms. And then, of course, the chauffeur's cottage has been empty since dear Vic was called up.'

'Oh, I do hope he's getting on all right,' Nana May frowned.

'Don't we all. And it was lucky Wig can do his own driving, although he's got enough on his plate as it is.' Clarrie paused, biting her lip. But then her face brightened as she looked down at her notebook again. 'Hmm, so let me work out how many we can take, then.'

Her mouth curved with satisfaction as she made her calculations. She was sitting out on the terrace in a circle made up of Nana May and all the female staff, enjoying the July sunshine. Below them on the levelled lawn, Topaz, the golden Labrador, and Trampas and Sunny, the two mongrels, all getting on in life now, were being encouraged into a game of chase by Meg's young collie, Thimble, while the old man of the pack, Patch the terrier, was lazily sunning himself on the upper terrace by his mistress's feet.

The women, however, didn't have the pleasure of being able to relax. Each of them had on her lap a huge length of heavy black material, cut to fit the large windows of Robin Hill House. They were hemming the edges to stop them fraying before Bob and Ralph stretched them over the frames Bob had made. He'd devised an ingenious method of fixing them tightly over the windows with relatively unobtrusive clips, and with rubber seals on the blackout frames, little damage would be done to the ornate window frames themselves.

Nana May rested her sewing in her lap. Working with the heavy material was hurting her arthritic fingers, and she needed to rest both them and her old eyes that struggled with close work nowadays, even with her glasses. She bent her head towards Clarrie, lowering her voice warily. 'What about the sewing room?' she whispered so quietly that it was only Clarrie who could hear her. 'The billeting officer might insist.'

Clarrie's eyes flew open and met Nana May's gentle gaze. 'No,' her voice trembled. 'Surely we'll be doing enough without that? Besides,' she went on, her tone stronger now, 'I think the sewing room's going to be extremely busy with all these young people in residence, don't you?'

The old lady nodded with a rueful smile. 'I'm sure you're right, my dear. But just be warned, eh?'

Clarrie raised her chin, filling her lungs with the pure country air, and then jerked her head before burying her nose in the notebook again, her lips moving silently. This was what she was good at, organising. It was what she'd thrown herself into after the tragedy that had very nearly destroyed her. And this was a chance to do what she had always hoped to at Robin Hill House: fill it with children.

Sitting opposite her, Meg glanced up from sewing the stiff material. When autumn arrived with its darkening evenings, it was going to feel like being in prison having to put up these monstrous things the moment they needed artificial light inside. But for a German bomber in the sky above, even a tiny flicker escaping from a window in the darkness could provide a target. That was assuming war broke out, of course. It was doubtless a vain hope, but perhaps it wouldn't come after all.

Mr W had already brought home reels of the sticky tape that would crisscross the windows to help prevent flying glass should a bomb explode anywhere near. But surely, being out in the countryside that wouldn't happen. That was precisely why it was planned to evacuate children and young mothers to the area, wasn't it?

It was such an outrageous thought that Hitler might well start dropping bombs on civilians, even if it was so-called collateral damage. There'd only been a handful of instances of that sort of atrocity in the previous war. But air power had been in its infancy then, and if what had happened in the recent Spanish conflict was anything to go by, whole towns and cities could be flattened in one air raid.

Meg's heart sickened at the thought. She was fundamentally a pacifist. But as Ralph had recently pointed out, you only needed to think of how Hitler was treating the Jews in his own country and the horrific events of the *Kristallnacht* in November of the previous year to wonder what he was capable of. How else could you deal with a demon like that if not by destroying him, even if it meant a terrible war?

'Nana and I had better go through all the bed linen,' Meg thought aloud, glad to have something practical to consider that would divert her thoughts. 'I think there's a few old double sheets that we can cut out the worn middles from, and sew the outer sides together to make singles. And if that doesn't give us enough and we can't buy any extra ready-made sheets, maybe we can get material and make them.'

'Who's going to do all the laundry is what I want to know,' Ada Phillips, the cook, grumbled. 'Louise and Sally just about manage it between them now, but with a complete houseful and doubtless lots of wet beds, how are we going to manage? And you'd better add rubber sheeting to your shopping list, if you don't mind my saying so, Mrs C.'

'What a good idea, Mrs Phillips.' Clarrie immediately jotted it down. 'Thank you.'

'And how am I supposed to cook for so many mouths?' Mrs Phillips went on. 'I've only got one pair of hands, and if Louise is going to be up to her elbows in smelly sheets all the time—'

'We'll just all have to pitch in together, Mrs Phillips, so don't worry.' Meg had to bite her lip. She knew the cook had a kind heart, but she still got agitated when she felt under pressure – even just the thought of it – so Meg was sure sparks would fly. But she went on to pacify her, 'If we can take a couple of mothers with tiny ones, they should be able to help. And if we have some older girls, they can help as well. Just think, you can teach them some of your wonderful culinary skills.'

Culinary. Now that was a word Meg wouldn't have used before she came to Robin Hill House. She mightn't even have known the word. She couldn't remember, it all seemed so long ago now. But Mrs Phillips was preening herself, so it had done the trick anyway.

'I'm not sure they'll all be used to anything fancy, though,' Clarrie added doubtfully. 'They'll just want good, solid English food, but I know you'll make it tastier than anything they've had before.'

'They do say most of them will be from poorer families,' Nana May put in. 'But whoever they are, we've got to remember they'll be away from home and frightened, so we must all do our best to welcome them. But I'd suggest, Clarrie dear, that you put all your best things into storage. I'm not suggesting anything might be stolen, but with a houseful of children, things could easily get broken.'

'Oh, my goodness, there's going to be such a lot to do.' Clarrie released a not unhappy sigh.

'And they're only allowed to bring one small case each, aren't they?' Meg said. 'And one small toy that fits in it? So perhaps we could do a collection in the village for clothes and toys?'

'What a wonderful idea! I'll organise something at the next village committee,' Clarrie exclaimed delightedly.

Meg glanced across at her, bitten with curiosity. The thought of impending war made her feel sick. Her father had been lucky to survive the last one unscathed, but the horrors he'd seen were so unimaginable that he'd never spoken of his experiences. And as if that wasn't bad enough, this war was likely to be different, involving civilians, or God forbid, invasion. Which was worse, Meg didn't know. Certainly Hitler wouldn't just let them get on with their lives. So, was she beginning to see Mr W's point of view after all when she'd questioned the morality of his making shell cases at the factory?

What she *did* know was that she was scared. Scared of bombs dropping on innocent people, although there were unlikely to be any in the Kent countryside. Scared for all the men who'd be fighting. Scared, more than anything she'd ever known, for Ralph. At twenty-three, he and Bob had both been too old for the six months of military training all twenty to twenty-two-year olds had been obliged to undertake. But if war broke out, conscription would follow. And Meg quaked at the very thought.

When she looked at Mrs C, though, the older woman seemed different. Meg had always detected a reserve about her, maybe even a sort of sadness, something Meg couldn't put her finger on. But the moment the billeting officer had come recently to discuss evacuees with her, Mrs C had appeared to come to life. While everyone else was enshrouded in gloom, she seemed to be in her element. How very strange, Meg considered, and got back to sewing her blackout blind.

Three

"Louise, could you please pass the biscuits?" Sally inquired as all the workers sat around the table in the servants' hall for their afternoon tea. "Did you create them?" They look pretty good.' The kitchen maid grinned happily and said, "Yes, I did." "Under the direction of Mrs. Phillips." "She has all the makings of a great chef." Mrs. Phillips smiled broadly, one of her rare grins. "She might as well, having studied under me for four years." Sally reassured them, "Well, at the last place I worked, you wouldn't find the cook passing on her skills to others." "I can't express to you how delighted I am here," she said slyly, grinning subtly at Bob, whose eyes, Meg saw, brightened in reply.
Yes, Meg thought to herself as she carefully poured the tea, one of the duties that had been assigned to her as parlourmaid. It had been pure chance as well as tragedy that had brought her to Robin Hill House. Before Fate had placed her in such dire straits, domestic service had never entered her head. She was a farmer through and through, and even if she enjoyed the privileges of being parlourmaid, looking after the animals and running the farming side of the small estate remained her passion. But, oh, yes, she appreciated how lucky she was to be part of such a liberal household that cared nothing for the old, rigid ways of such prestigious establishments. It was 1939. The Great War had changed many things, yet nevertheless, she knew that the way Robin Hill House was run was mainly down to the attitudes of its owners.
Meg passed a cup to Mrs Phillips first, and then the other cups were passed down the table to the other staff, so perhaps there was some protocol that was still adhered to. Sandwiches and biscuits were also passed around the table, everyone helping themselves. It was such a happy place, based on trust and mutual respect. But the tranquillity was about to be broken.
The door opened and Nana May walked into the room. For not the first time, Meg's heart sank to see that the old lady she had come to hold in such affection always used her walking stick even within the house nowadays. Chairs scraped on the old, wooden floor as everyone stood up out of love and deep respect rather than tradition, and both Ralph and Bob sprang forward to help Nana May into a chair. But she waved them away.
'Thank you, boys, but I'm not stopping.' Her face was grave as her eyes embraced everybody in the room. 'I've come with some news. You might've heard the telephone ring a few minutes ago. It was Mr W ringing from London. The news has just come through. Germany signed an agreement with Russia earlier today. Apparently it's all over London. Newspaper boys are calling it out in the streets, and it's going to be in the evening papers. But we thought you ought to know straightaway.'
A hushed silence settled on the room. Lips pursed and brows tightened. It was only as the old lady turned and Ralph went to hold the door open for her that murmurs began to break out and people sat down again, their minds distracted from the ample tea before them. Nana May's stick could be heard tapping on the terracotta tiles of the kitchen floor, and Ralph disappeared for a few moments, presumably to hold open the other doors for her. By the time he returned and sat back down at the table, lowered voices were muttering wary thoughts as stomachs quietly churned.

'It's coming closer, then.' Everyone turned as Mrs Phillips grasped the edge of the table with a resounding thud, her expression grim. Easily ruffled was Mrs Phillips, but just now her expression was one of calm, if bitter, acceptance.

'What is?' Jane piped up after a moment's silence. 'The war? I don't really understand.'

Mrs Phillips audibly drew in her breath. It was hard not to be exasperated by Jane's naivety, but then her simple, trusting nature was what made her such a joy.

Ralph had taken a mouthful of his tea, and met Meg's gaze across the table. She saw his Adam's apple move up and down as he swallowed. She just wanted to forget the world, to be locked in his arms, to kiss that little well at the base of his throat.

'Can you imagine a map of Europe?' he asked Jane patiently. 'With Russia out to the east?'

Jane gave a confused shake of her head, her eyes wide.

'I can get an atlas from the study,' Meg offered, shaking herself from her pleasant reverie. 'We'd have to clear everything away, mind, so we don't get anything on it.'

'No, don't worry. I'd want to draw on it, anyway. Mrs Phillips, do you have some paper and a pen or pencil handy?' Ralph asked.

'I can tear a page out of my notebook,' the cook offered. 'Anything to explain things to the poor kid,' she added under her breath, rolling her eyes to the heavens.

A few moments later, with Jane sitting close by his side, Ralph was sketching a map. Meg was about to start helping clear the table, but her attention was drawn by Ralph's strong, brown hand creating a near perfect replica of the outline of the British Isles. Apart from reading, drawing and watercolour painting had been her lifelong passion, but she had no idea that Ralph could reproduce such accurate maps from memory. She wasn't the only one who seemed fascinated, and they all crowded round to watch.

'Here's London,' he said to Jane, putting a large cross to mark the spot. 'And here's us to the south. And then here, down in Cornwall, that's where Mr Peregrine and his family live.'

'That's Mr W's brother, isn't it?' Sally asked. 'The famous artist? The one that Mr W and Mrs C and Nana May went to stay with at Easter?'

'That's right. You would've met Mr Peregrine and his family last Christmas. They were due to come up here, only they all went down with 'flu and had to cancel at the last minute. I expect they'll come this year instead, if they can. And believe me, you'll never forget them once you've met them,' Ralph chuckled fondly. 'But back to this, Jane,' he continued, dragging the pencil across the page. 'Now, this is the coast of France.'

'Blimey, it ain't far away, is it?' Jane's eyes nearly popped out of her head. 'Loads nearer than where Mr Peregrine lives.'

'Yes, worryingly, that's so. And then as we go up the coast, we have Belgium, and the Netherlands, both really quite small,' Ralph went on, talking slowly as he drew. 'And then to the east, we have Germany and his lordship, Herr Hitler. You can see how big it is by comparison, almost as big as France. But France is very agricultural, whereas Germany is much more industrial. And that means power. And Hitler's already taken Austria for himself, and also Czechoslovakia which is also rich in minerals and industry.'

'Yes, I remember you all talking about that,' Jane frowned. 'I didn't really understand, but now I do. But why is this thing today so important?'

'Well, it changes things even more. And not for the better,' Ralph said glumly. 'Now Hitler has his sights on Poland, which you can see here is wedged between Germany and Russia. But *we* have signed a pledge to help protect Poland, and we were hoping to get

Russia on our side as well. But we failed, and now they've signed this agreement with Germany instead. And you can see how enormous and powerful Russia is. So if Russia supports Germany from the east, like so,' Ralph concluded, drawing arrows across from Russia into Poland, 'and Germany attacks from the west,' this said breaking off to put more arrows, 'Poland won't stand a chance, and Hitler will add all its industrial strength to his pot of gold. And with Italy to the south, here, being friends with Germany, it'll leave Hitler free to invade west,' – more arrows – 'to the Netherlands, Belgium, France. And then us.'

Jane's eyes grew even wider, and her jaw dropped. 'Oh, Lordy love, it really is serious, ain't it?'

'Yes, sadly it is.' Ralph puffed out his cheeks. 'But at least you understand now.'

'Yes. Thanks, Ralph.' Jane frowned, and Meg wondered if she wasn't still a little puzzled. 'Can I keep the drawing?' she asked, brightening a little almost as if Ralph's map were a prize.

'Of course you can.'

'And I think we need to give Ralph a clap.' Meg forced a smile, trying to lighten the atmosphere, and everyone joined in a round of applause before slowly dispersing to return to work. 'That was brilliant,' she said to Ralph, raising her eyebrows in admiration. 'You should've been a teacher rather than a gardener. And I had no idea you could do maps like that.'

Ralph's mouth twisted in wry embarrassment. 'I've always been interested in maps. And you know how we've all been keeping abreast of what's been going on. But give me a garden over a schoolroom any day. And, well, I did feel a bit like the harbinger of doom just now.'

'You can't help what's happening, Ralph. And I bet you Jane wasn't the only one listening intently to what you were saying. Half the population probably don't understand all the ins and outs. Just that war seems very likely now. But I suppose with the factory, we feel more involved.'

'We're all going to be involved if you ask me.' Ralph released a rueful sigh, rubbing his hand over his chin. 'But nothing's going to stop what I feel for you. So, come here,' he teased, pulling her down onto his lap, 'and give me a kiss.'

Meg willingly obliged, trying to force all her fears to the back of her mind. In his arms, she felt protected, as if the world and all its troubles were blocked out. It seemed impossible that two people could love each other so much when whole countries were threatening to bomb each other to smithereens.

'I know!' She suddenly bounced up. 'Why don't we have a picnic down by the lake tomorrow? To cheer ourselves up? All of us. Mrs C and Nana May, your parents. I'll go and ask Mrs C now.'

Ralph couldn't help but laugh as Meg skipped out of the room before he had a chance to answer. She was a great one for planning, was his Meg. He'd never met anyone so mature for her age. That was why he'd been so struck by her the first time they'd met, the morning after her parents had been killed. There she was, all alone, coping with the family farm. Broken, defensive, and yet through it all, so dignified. He'd admired her, even if she'd been as sharp as a thorn with him. But that had been her grief talking. Now he knew her as intelligent, sensible, compassionate, and yet with a glorious sense of fun.

It was no wonder he loved her! But what this looming war was going to mean for them, God alone knew.

Meg dipped the wide brush in the little pot of water and, collecting a moss green tincture on it from the palette, stroked it across the paper beneath the grey wash of the lake. She'd already captured the azure sky streaked with hazy ribbons of dappled cloud, and the woods beyond the open fields on the far side of the lake. The verdant wash for the grass would complete the background, and then she would have to wait for it all to dry before she could start putting in the detail, the reeds by the water's edge, the ducks, the figures playing an impromptu game of rounders. They were all there, Ralph making her heart leap up inside her as he bowled gently to Jane who squealed with delight as she actually managed to hit the ball, Mrs Phillips presiding over the picnic set out on a tartan blanket, and Mrs C and Nana May reclining in deckchairs with Ralph's parents beside them. And of course, she mustn't forget the dogs! Meg could see it all in her mind's eye ready to add in later.

'Oh, Meg, dear, that's very good.'

Clarrie's voice at her shoulder made her jump. She'd been concentrating so hard on the painting that she hadn't heard her mistress come up behind her.

'Oh, it's just the beginning,' she answered. 'I wanted to capture a record of today. Something we can all look at and remember. I'm going to put everybody in there when it's dry, even Mr W and Jane's Eric, even if they're not actually here today. I want it to be a *friendship* painting. So that if there are hard times ahead, we can look at this and know that we're all going to help each other through.'

She watched as the tiny muscles in Mrs C's forehead twitched. 'I think that's a lovely idea. Just as this picnic is. We none of us know what's coming, after all. Life can be so cruel.' She broke off, and such an expression of distress darkened her features that Meg felt her mind still in confusion. Did Mrs C mean the *accident*? But it was Meg who'd lost her parents. Although Mrs C was so kind and compassionate that she could easily share someone else's grief. But then she felt the older woman's cool hand on her painty one, and she squeezed tightly. 'Whoever knew that you'd come into our lives, Meg? You've been such a joy to me, you know. To all of us.'

Her face was creased in earnest, and Meg frowned at her. What was she trying to say? Or was the emotion of uncertainty getting the better of her? After all, they were all mentally holding their breath. The whole world was.

'You were such a rebellious young thing when you came here,' Mrs C went on, her lips curved contentedly. 'No, not rebellious. Your behaviour was always impeccable. But you knew your own mind. So… I do hope you're happy with us now, Meg.'

Meg's face broke into a smile. 'Yes, I am, thank you, Mrs C,' she said sincerely, for it was indeed true. She'd only accepted the older woman's invitation to come and live at Robin Hill House with bitter reluctance, and because it had suited her. Back then, she'd merely been biding her time until she was twenty-one and could achieve legal independence. But she hadn't reckoned on finding such happiness there. On becoming so fond of Mr W and Mrs C and all the staff. On falling so deeply in love with Ralph. 'Good. Because I want you to be happy, Meg. Really I do.'

'Come on, Meg! Your turn to show us how it's done!' Ralph called, cutting through their conversation, and Meg's heart flipped over, the way he was grinning across at her.

'And there's someone else you mean so much to!' Mrs C suddenly grinned. 'Even if, I believe, you did give him such a hard time at first!'

Meg blinked at her. The strange moment was over, but as she put down the paintbrush and ran across to Ralph and he caught her deliciously about the waist, she couldn't help wondering exactly what Mrs C had meant. But perhaps it was best not to dwell on it. This was meant to be a happy interlude, after all. Her own idea. So she stretched up to brush a quick kiss on Ralph's cheek as she broke away from his side and ran over to pick up the rounder's bat.

'Right, let's see what I can do!' she laughed, and swung her arms towards the ball that was flying through the air.

'Are you sure you want to do this, Clarrie dear?'

Nana May's lined face wrinkled with concern as Clarrie turned the key in the old trunk, unopened for years, and lifted the lid. The trunk was full, and over the top was a double layer of tissue paper, yellowing and musty with age.

Clarrie turned to her dear friend and companion, eyes swimming with unshed tears. 'Yes,' she replied in a small voice. 'I've thought about it long and hard. There won't be any children of our own now, Nana. My body's long stopped working in that way. But, for a while at least, this house is going to sing with the sound of children, just as Wig and I had always meant it to. I know it's because there's going to be another war, and war is the most terrible thing. But if it means the house'll be full of children, even if they're not my own, then let me indulge myself.'

'Of course.' The old lady's voice rang with compassion as the vision of the beloved toddler dying in her mother's arms sprang into her mind so vividly even after so many years. 'But… Rosebud's toys? Her clothes?'

Clarrie removed the top layer of tissue paper, and then unwrapped a small, pink teddy bear. She tipped it this way and that, as if making it talk, and a rueful smile twitched at her lips. 'What's the use of them rotting here when the poor little mites coming to us will have so little?'

'Well, if you're sure. If you're ready. But none of them will be Rosebud.'

'I know.' Clarrie's words were barely audible. 'We can never replace her. I'd never want to.'

Nana May observed her for a moment, her hand trembling as she touched Clarrie's arm. 'And what about Meg?' She finally articulated the words she'd wanted to say for the past three years. 'She's always meant something very special to you, hasn't she? Far more than just being someone you wanted to help?'

Clarrie flicked her eyes towards Nana May without turning her head. 'How long've you known?' she croaked.

'Since the beginning. I think even without the coincidence of the name, you felt something for her. And she's a great girl. I feel myself that she's almost like a grandchild to me.'

'And she's like a daughter to me. Not a replacement for Rosebud, but another, a different daughter.'

'And does Wig know?' Nana May asked gently.

'At first, he thought it might be the case. He was worried I'd get hurt, but I think I managed to persuade him that I just wanted to help Meg out of human kindness. Not because she

makes me think of Rosebud. That's why I can't show Meg how I *really* feel, although I'm sure she knows I'm very fond of her. I hate deceiving Wig, but you won't tell him, will you?'
'My lips are sealed. But he might already have guessed. Anyway, let's see what we've got in this trunk, shall we?' And Nana May unfolded the tissue paper wrapped about what had been little Rosebud's favourite rag doll.

Four

The small girl tightened her grip on her mother's fingers as the sound of the rumbling London train station reverberated in her mind. A flurry of noise that left her lightheaded. Boys shouted in delight, instructors used megaphones to yell directions in rivalry with hefty ladies in WVS uniforms, newborns cried out for overdue food, toddlers screamed in fear and exhaustion, and voices grew louder and louder to be heard over the din. Swelling up and filling the lofty span of the Victorian glass ceiling was the booming fanfare of hundreds, perhaps thousands, of nervous, agitated people forced together in a chaotic hullabaloo. Steam and smoke hissing in a sulfurous, billowing cloud, porters trundling baggage carts, and train brakes screaming as they came to a grinding halt beside the platforms

Doris Sergeant was scared. She'd been to the station on many occasions with her mummy and daddy, skipping along happily between them because they were going to the seaside. It had been a good place to be, exciting as they found the right platform and went through the barrier, their nostrils filling with the smell of coal dust and hot engine oil. But today the fetidness of so many sweating, and in many cases unwashed, bodies, the rank taint of bad breath, dirty nappies and wet knickers, made Doris feel sick.

'Oh, you're a pretty young thing,' a voice blared from below a trilby hat. 'D'you mind if I take a picture of your daughter, madam? Doesn't matter about her red hair. It won't show in black and white. It's for the Ministry of Information. Look, here are my credentials. Just let go of your mummy for a minute. That's it. Now hold this dolly in one hand and your suitcase in the other. Excellent. Now smile at the camera.'

Doris blinked in terror as the searing light blasted into her eyes. Oh, no, she'd lost sight of her mummy! And the next instant, the doll was snatched from her, and the man moved off to assail another petrified child. 'Why didn't you smile, dear?'

Her mother's beloved face was bending over her, and Doris clamped her arms about her mummy's waist, burying her head against the thin, bony hips. Her mum had been smiling, but Doris had seen tears pooling in her eyes. Her own were dry and wide with fear and bewilderment.

'Right, time to say goodbye to your mothers,' a familiar voice stabbed into her misery. 'Our train's ready and we mustn't keep it waiting. All the trains have a very tight schedule to keep.'

Doris was nine years old and would have been about to start in her third year at junior school if it hadn't been for this wretched war that was supposed to be coming. 'You'll be safer in the countryside,' her mummy had told her. And Doris would never argue with her adored mother even though every fibre in her young body cried out in protest.

It had broken her little heart earlier that morning saying goodbye to her daddy who couldn't come to the station because he had to go to work. And to find when they got there that the school had decided it would be better for the children to be escorted by their teacher of the previous year, Mrs McCormack, rather than their new teacher who they scarcely knew, had been a bitter blow.

Mrs McCormack was a bully, and Doris hated the way she would always pick on her to come up with the answer, when all Doris wanted was to hide away in a corner. But it wasn't school she hated. It was Mrs McCormack. She'd been looking forward to the new term with the kindly Mrs Mitchell who didn't terrify her in the same way. Just the opposite, in fact. She'd loved the time when the dragon had been off sick for a fortnight, and she'd been one of those who'd been absorbed into Mrs Mitchell's class. So to find herself under the care of the witch amongst this seething, hostile, swarming multitude was the last straw.

Her mummy gently pulled her arms away and bent down so that her face was on the same level as her daughter's. 'Be a brave girl now, my darling,' she croaked, sounding anything but brave herself. 'We don't know exactly where you're going, but once you've arrived, write to us straightaway.'

'Of course, Mummy,' Doris gulped. 'And I'll do you some drawings, too.'

'That'll be lovely, poppet. But we'll see for ourselves soon. We know you should be staying somewhere in Kent, which isn't that far away, so we can come and visit you. So, we're lucky, really.' Mrs Sergeant forced a watery smile. 'Some children are going hundreds of miles away. To places like Wales or Cornwall.'

'I know.' Doris's young face screwed up in anguish. 'I just wish you and Daddy could come, too,' she moaned.

'Well, Daddy has work, and only mummies with little children can go, not big girls like you. And here,' she said, suddenly removing the brooch from her jacket lapel and pinning it on Doris's cardigan. 'This will keep you safe. Now you make us proud, and remember your manners at all times.'

It ripped at her heart to see the torment in her daughter's eyes, and she pulled her against her to kiss the top of her head. But a second later, she felt Doris being wrenched away from her, and they both found themselves staring into Mrs McCormack's irate face.

'Oh, there you are!' she snapped. 'Everyone else has gone through the barrier and I had to come back for *you*. The train won't wait for you, you know!'

With that, she dug her fingers into Doris's shoulder and dragged her away. The last thing Mrs Sergeant saw of her daughter before she was swallowed up in the crowd was the child's desperate, pleading eyes.

'Love you!' she yelled as loudly as she could, but whether or not Doris heard, she had no idea.

Doris's feet stumbled along as Mrs McCormack pushed and shoved a path through the bustling hoards. As they fought their way through to the barrier of the correct platform, Doris noticed several mothers in floods of tears, while others hurried away with their children, evidently having changed their minds at the last minute.

Doris wished as she'd never wished for anything else in her life before that she could be among them. That at any second, her mother would appear out of the crowd and snatch her back out of Mrs McCormack's clutches. But the next thing she knew, she'd been hauled through the barrier onto the platform where, up ahead, a monstrous black engine was spitting fire and steam in its impatience to be away, rattling down the track and spiriting hundreds of children to their doom.

Mrs McCormack pushed her way along the platform and panted up to an official-looking woman with a clipboard standing by the open door of a carriage compartment. 'Sorry, this is the missing child,' she said brusquely.
'Couldn't get her away from her mother.'
'She's the last of your lot, then?' the other woman asked just as brusquely. 'Doris Sergeant.' She pulled towards her the label hanging about the girl's neck, and then ticked something off on her board. 'Gas mask, suitcase. And here are your sandwiches for the journey,' she said, pushing a brown-paper bag into Doris's free hand. 'Right, in you get. Just in time. Train's leaving in two minutes.'
Mrs McCormack propelled Doris towards the open door, and Doris scrambled up, manoeuvring her little suitcase and feeling as if she was entering the gates of hell. Condemned to who knew what horrors.
'Ah, Dozey Doris, trust you to be last,' one of her classmates sneered, but his mouth soon shut when, to everyone's horror, including Doris's, Mrs McCormack climbed up behind her. The teacher did, however, come to Doris's assistance as she struggled to heave her case up into the luggage rack. But then she plonked herself down on the seat in the middle of everyone, and glared about her.
'Gary, get your head in from the window before you get it knocked off by another train,' she snarled. 'And I hope none of you have started your sandwiches yet. You won't be getting anything else until we arrive, so you've got to make them last. Doris, sit down here, or you'll fall over when the train starts.'
She indicated the place beside her and Doris looked about the compartment in dismay. It was indeed the only space left, and so, reluctantly, she wriggled herself into it, wedged between Mrs McCormack and Gary Wilson who was sitting by the window. He was all right, was Gary. As were most of the others of her travelling companions. They were all boys, though, apart from Annie Davies who was a bit snooty and clearly had her nose put out at being separated from her buddies.
Doris, too, resented not being with her friends, although it was her own fault for taking too much time saying goodbye to her mum. Not that she was close to anyone in particular. She was too shy for that. But it would have been better than travelling under Mrs McCormack's strict eye!
From outside came the bangs as the last doors were slammed shut, the guard's whistle blew and the train jerked as it edged forward, slowly at first as it pulled away from the platform and began to pick up speed. Doris felt a violent pain in her chest as if her heart was being yanked out and left behind in the station. But she wasn't going to cry. Her mummy had said she wanted to be proud of her, so she was determined to be strong.
Mrs McCormack's very presence kept them all silent as the train clackety-clacked through London's built-up areas, and Doris felt her despair deepen. As they rumbled and swayed out into the countryside, however, the atmosphere in the compartment lightened. Some of the children had never been beyond the capital before, and the sight of green fields basking in the late summer sunshine made them bubble with wonder and excitement. Mrs McCormack made them take turns to sit by the window, her eyes narrowing with anger if anyone disobeyed. But Doris wasn't bothered when it was her turn to watch the countryside flash past. She'd seen it before. All it made her think about were the happy times when she'd been speeding down to the seaside with her mum and dad. Now she had no idea when she'd see them again.

Glancing down, Doris fingered the brooch pinned to her cardigan as if it would give her strength.

She wondered miserably who she'd be billeted with. That was a new word she hadn't heard before. Would it be in a quiet, clean and tidy little house like she was used to, or a dirty cottage only fit for pigs? They'd been warned that some places in the country didn't have running water. Or that sometimes the only lavatory was a tiny wooden shack in the garden where the waste simply fell into a bucket filled with earth to absorb the smells. Even worse than the cold, outside toilet at her own house. At least that flushed when you pulled the chain!

The thought of an earth closet, as they'd been told they were called, filled Doris with horror. Worst of all, *who* would she be billeted with? A family with existing children who'd tease her about her bright red hair and pull her plaits? Or a resentful old woman who'd treat her as an enemy or even a slave? Would she be alone, or with any of her school friends? Would she be made to feel welcome, or teased and bullied from the start? Every turn of the carriage wheels, every mile they drew closer to their destination, made the dread rise up inside her and take her by the throat.

An hour or so later, they stopped at a station and everyone was told to go and use the lavatories. While she stood in the queue, Doris saw mothers with younger children for whom it had been too late. A little girl just behind her couldn't wait any longer and went just where she was standing. Her mother had no sympathy, and cuffed the little mite across the cheek.

Doris had to jump back so that the toddler's urine didn't splash on her own shoes. But she couldn't help but feel sorry for the child. She was pretty desperate for a wee herself. And she saw several little boys with tell-tale wet patches on their shorts, and other children who'd obviously been sick and had vomit down their fronts. Doris could understand that. She felt sick with anxiety herself, but she was so thankful she was travelling in a compartment with her peers who were old enough to control their bodily functions. They wouldn't dare do otherwise under Mrs McCormack's icy stare!

'You can open your sandwiches now,' the draconian teacher conceded once they were all back on the train, and were rumbling through the countryside again.

Everyone else dived into the contents of their paper bag. Doris took a nibble of one of her sandwiches, but it stuck in her throat and she nearly choked as she finally forced it down. She carefully replaced the rest of the sandwich in the bag and folded over the top of the paper.

'Not hungry, Doris?' Mrs McCormack demanded.

Doris recoiled into the seat, wishing she could disappear altogether. 'Not really, Miss,' she managed to croak in reply.

'Too nervous, eh?'

Doris lowered her eyes as she nodded. Oh, why had her mummy and daddy decided to send her away?

'Can I have her sandwiches if she don't want them?'

'No, you can't, Johnny Wight,' the dragon barked back. 'Doris might want them later when she's feeling better.' Then, she poked her head down so that Doris could see the individual fine hairs on the woman's upper lip. 'I'm sure it'll be all right. Most people will be very happy to have you if you behave. Did you hear that, Johnny? *If you behave*. But if you think you're being treated badly at all, you mustn't be afraid to report it to the billeting officer. They will come round to check on you occasionally, you know.'

Oh, crikey, Doris cringed, feeling even worse. If Mrs McCormack thought they could end up somewhere awful, it must be bad!

And then Mrs McCormack turned to her again, lowering her voice. 'You shouldn't worry about things so much, you know, Doris. You're the brightest child in the class, but you must try and come out of your shell and mix more with the others.'

Doris blinked at her, and managed to mumble a 'Yes, Miss,' with little conviction. The smile the teacher gave her was so fleeting that she nearly missed it. Perhaps Mrs McCormack wasn't so bad after all. And there must be a Mr McCormack, so someone must have liked her enough to marry her.

Doris spent the next hour conjuring up images of what the not quite such a dragon was like at home. Did she have children of her own? She was so ancient that if she did, they'd be grown up by now. She was the only married teacher in the school, so she must be considered good as married teachers were usually frowned upon. Or perhaps she'd bullied the headmistress into employing her! Doris could well imagine it. And then she wondered if Mrs McCormack wore a night cap in bed. The idea amused her, and she had to stifle a giggle.

A little while later, the train began to slow. Doris had occupied herself in imagining Mrs McCormack putting in her curlers and taking out her dentures at night – they had fangs! – or putting her voluminous bloomers through the mangle. But now she leant forward to see past Annie Davies and look out of the window. They were coming into a town. Doris wondered where, but as the train coasted into the station and lurched to a halt, she was none the wiser. The station signs had all been removed in case of invasion. Didn't want to help the enemy find their way around, did they?

Mrs McCormack pulled down the window on the platform side and stuck out her head. 'Is this it?' she bellowed, and a few moments later, turned back into the compartment. 'Right, we're here, children. Get your luggage down and then wait for me on the platform. Don't forget your gas masks, and don't leave anything else behind, either.'

Doris felt less frightened now of Mrs McCormack as the woman retrieved the luggage for those who couldn't reach. Certainly less frightened than of what was about to happen!

It was pandemonium on the platform, with a new set of WVS ladies checking labels. Mrs McCormack checked she had all of her class assembled from a total of three compartments, and then had them march in pairs to a line being formed towards the station exit. Organised chaos if ever there was, Doris considered ruefully.

Exactly where they were, Doris still didn't know. It was clearly a big town and she felt so lost as they were led through busy streets, a long snake of children of all ages, and mothers with tiny ones. Doris's class was led by a smiling young woman, with Mrs McCormack bringing up the rear.

The human crocodile eventually turned into a school, the various contingents being guided into different classrooms. Doris's class and the year above were lined up against the wall opposite a crowd of adults and families already waiting in the room. The young woman with the nice smile was pairing up hosts with evacuees, helped by someone in WVS uniform.

'Right, everyone else, listen, please!' she called, clapping her hands. 'The rest of you mingle together, and when you've palled up, come over to me. But please don't take too long. The buses are waiting to take you to your destinations.'

Doris sagged, her heart crumpling. How could she do that, mingle among strangers? Who would want her with her red hair and freckles? She hunched her shoulders and backed off into a corner, head down, hiding as the room thinned out. Perhaps if she wasn't picked, she could go home. Her stomach growled with hunger, but the thought of the sandwiches in her bag made her feel queasy. She felt faint, her head swimming. The room became quiet, a hundred miles away.

'Oh, we have someone left. What's your name, child?'

'Oh, no. Oh, Doris,' Mrs McCormack sighed. 'I thought everyone had gone.'

'Oh, dear, yes, Doris Sergeant,' the nice smile confirmed, consulting her list. 'I'm afraid we ended up with fewer hosts than we thought. Since registering with us, some people have already taken in relatives and don't have room anymore. Wait here, and I'll check there are no spare hosts anywhere else.'

The young woman scurried out of the room and Doris felt herself groan as Mrs McCormack pulled out two chairs from the desks that had been pushed to one side, and indicated that she should sit down beside her. Doris obeyed, wishing she could pinch herself and find it was all a nasty dream, but she knew it wasn't.

It seemed an age before the nice smile came back, time in which Doris felt she'd lived a whole lifetime. Mrs McCormack didn't say very much, for which Doris was grateful. She just wanted to curl up in her shell and escape.

'Right. I've found somewhere where there might be some spare places. But I'm afraid you need to get on the train back to Tunbridge Wells. Here are your passes. A billeting officer called Mrs Jenkins will meet you there. And then, Mrs McCormack, your ticket will take you back to London. But you need to hurry. Can you remember the way back to the station?'

'Oh, yes,' Mrs McCormack assured her with cool efficiency. 'Come along now, Doris. We mustn't miss the train.'

With that, she all but galloped out of the classroom and Doris had to run to catch her up, struggling with her little case. They scurried through the town, Mrs McCormack frequently having to stop and wait for her pupil, until she finally took the luggage from her. They panted into the station just before the train was about to leave, and the guard ushered them into a compartment and slammed the door as he blew his whistle.

Both teacher and pupil gasped. The reek in the compartment rasped at the back of their throats. The seats were damp with urine and on the floor was a splash of vomit they had to step over.

'Oh, dear God,' Mrs McCormack cried. 'And this is all your fault. If you hadn't hidden in the corner, I'd have been back on a proper train before this... this abomination. Now try and find a dry bit and sit down.'

Doris couldn't have felt more miserable. All her feelings that Mrs McCormack wasn't so bad after all dissipated into the stench about them. She perched on the edge of the seat, hoping it was a dry patch, as they rattled back through the countryside in silence. A vain hope began to unfurl in Doris's breast. Maybe they wouldn't be able to find a place for her after all. And she could be taken back home to London. To her mum and dad.

Mrs Jenkins proved to be not such a bad sort at all, and met them with a broad if weary smile. 'You must be Doris. I've come to collect you in my car. I do hope you were expecting me? So, say goodbye to your teacher, Mrs McCormack, isn't it? But I'm afraid I'll have to hurry you. My original group are all waiting in the village hall, and nothing can go ahead without me.'

In actual fact, it was a relief to Doris to bid Mrs McCormack a swift farewell. She knew that some teachers were going to stay with their pupils, but evidently that wasn't the plan for Mrs McCormack. And Doris supposed that someone had to stay behind to teach the children whose parents refused to let them be evacuated. She followed Mrs Jenkins out of the station, glancing back over her shoulder to see Mrs McCormack march out of her life for ever. She didn't know at that point that she was never to see her teacher again, nor any of her classmates.

'Well, Doris, welcome to Kent,' Mrs Jenkins said, starting up her car. 'Poor soul, you must be exhausted and feel as if you've been pushed from pillar to post. But never mind. It won't take us long to get there, and I'm pretty sure we'll find somewhere nice to billet you. You'll be out in the country in a village. D'you think you'll like that?'

Gazing out of the window, Doris saw that they had very quickly left the town which looked quite attractive in itself. Hardly the built-up, smoggy London she knew! Mrs Jenkins had advised her to wind down the car window a little as it was so warm, and she felt the fresh, sweet-smelling air waft against her face. What joy after the stinking compartment where she'd spent the last hour or so. And she'd visited the countryside with her parents before, and always loved it. She just hoped wherever she ended up would be welcoming and friendly.

'Yes, I think I will,' she answered, although her shy heart still thumped in her chest. For now she really had to face the prospect of a new home.

Five

'Can you eat them ones, miss?'

The boy tugged at Meg's sleeve as she led the motley procession along the lane from the village to Robin Hill House. It was Friday 1st September, and it had been a long day for the thousands of children who'd said goodbye to their mothers at London's main railway stations and at other major towns and cities throughout the country that were considered at risk from enemy attack.

Clarrie had pre-organised with Mrs Jenkins, the billeting officer, that she would take in two families with children not yet at school which was the age limit for when their mothers could be evacuated with them. She'd been told in advance that she'd been allocated families Durr and Higginbottom. One would take the chauffeur's cottage and would cater for themselves, while the other would occupy the largest guest room in the main house.

Putting her heart and soul into the organisation of the evacuees, Clarrie had anticipated that the walk from the village to the house would be far too long for these little families. So that Monday, instead of driving himself up to London, Wig had gone by train, staying during the week, as he had been for months now, at his club. Thus the motorcar was available to give the mothers and their small children a lift. Ralph was driving it since Wig's young chauffeur, Vic, had already been called up. And so Mrs Higginbottom with her five- and three-year-old sons and bouncing sixmonth-old baby daughter had been collected from the village hall in the Daimler.

'Flipping 'eck,' Mrs Higginbottom had declared, climbing into the back of the posh motorcar with her double chins and her equally chubby infant. 'Don't yer touch nuffing,' she'd commanded her two other offspring. 'Keep yer sticky fingers to yerselves.' And then she'd amused Meg by giving a regal wave as they were driven off.

The Durr family who were going to live in the chauffeur's cottage were going to have to wait for the car to return for them. Back inside the hall, the sour-faced mother was complaining, 'Don't see why they should go first. That brat'll probably be sick in the car and we'll have to put up with the smell.'

Meg rolled her eyes at the woman's moaning, but she supposed it had been a long and disconcerting day for everyone. 'Oh, I shouldn't think so, Mrs Durr,' she attempted to pacify her. 'It's just that with the baby, Mrs C thought it best we didn't keep them hanging around any longer. It isn't far, so the car will be back before you know it. Why don't you all have another sandwich while you're waiting?'

The two little girls' eyes lit up and they dived towards the table, scoffing as much into their mouths as they could. Mrs Durr huffily hitched up her bosom as she threw Meg a cold glance – but nevertheless filled herself a plate of scones and biscuits.

'Take your pick of the rest, Mrs Stratfield-Whyte,' Meg heard Mrs Jenkins tell Clarrie as she turned her attention back to the others in the hall. 'As you're taking so many, you can have first choice. Only please don't take too long. You can see there's a lot of other people waiting.'

Meg exchanged glances with Mrs C. She could tell the mistress was thinking exactly the same as she was. It was like a cattle market.

Clarrie blinked her eyes wide. How could you choose just like that? Her gaze passed bewilderedly along the line of children. She'd love to scoop them all into her arms, tell them how she'd take care of each and every one as if they were her own. Take them all into her house. But there simply wasn't enough room.

She was grateful when she felt Meg tap her on the shoulder.

'Mrs C, don't forget we need two boys for the attic rooms,' she whispered. 'How about those two?' Meg jabbed her head at a couple of boys so identical they had to be twins. She hated thinking that way, but they looked quite strong and with so many mouths to feed, they might be needed to work in the vegetable garden.

'Right,' Clarrie agreed. And then raising her voice, she went on, 'Mrs Jenkins, I'll take those two boys, please. They look like twins, so they can stay together.'

'Cor, thanks, missis,' one of them said, stepping forward confidently. 'Come on, Cyril.'

'Excellent, Mrs Stratfield-Whyte. Thank you.' Mrs Jenkins smiled efficiently. 'You boys must be Leslie and Cyril Langport,' she confirmed, comparing their labels with her list. 'Go and wait by the door. Mrs
Stratfield-Whyte has other choices to make.'

'Blimey, must be a big house,' Meg caught Leslie whispering to his twin as they obeyed at once, and she smothered an amused chuckle.

'If you'd like to help with keeping siblings together,' Mrs Jenkins had continued, turning back to Clarrie, 'may I suggest these two little girls, Joyce and Maureen Gregson? Aged, let me see, nine and ten.'

Clarrie and Meg both looked to where the billeting officer was indicating two girls dressed neatly in what passed for school uniform. The similarity between them was striking, and they were holding hands, gripping each other tightly, their young faces tense with anticipation. Meg wasn't at all surprised when Mrs C nodded without hesitation, and the sisters jumped up and down with relief at being billeted together.

Meg noticed that the billeting officer, too, looked relieved that Clarrie had made her choices so swiftly. 'Right, thank you, Mrs Stratfield-Whyte,' the woman said decisively. 'Two mothers with children under school age, the Langport twins and the Gregson girls. I'm sure we're all very grateful to you. Now, if we can move on, please. Who's next? Mr and Mrs Hillier?'

Joyce and Maureen stepped forward, both smiling nervously, but Meg saw their expressions relax as Mrs C gestured a warm welcome to them. They all began to move towards the doors of the hall so that Ralph's parents, Gabriel and Mary Hillier, could select an evacuee. With Ralph now living in the main house, they had a spare bedroom in the cottage and were more than happy to offer a home to an evacuated child.

Now, as the two sisters moved away from the band of children being selected like apples from a barrel, Meg thought bitterly, she noticed another young girl who'd been cowering behind them. The poor thing looked so miserable, shoulders hunched and white face crumpling as if she might burst into tears at any moment, that the idea of leaving her behind made Meg's heart sag. And she knew Gabriel and Mary were keen to offer a home to a boy rather than a girl so they were unlikely to choose her. They were used to a boy, Mary had explained. Having had Ralph so late in life, they were now both in their sixties, Gabriel nearer seventy, in fact. At that age, they felt they were getting too long in the tooth to learn new tricks. Besides, they had Ralph's old toys, and nothing for a girl to play with.

Meg felt a sudden rush of heat and touched her employer's arm. 'Mrs C, what about that little girl there? She looks terrified. We could look after her, too, couldn't we? If the two sisters don't mind sleeping in the double bed together, she could have the single room.'

Mrs C glanced back over her shoulder, and saw the forlorn specimen that Meg had noticed. Something about the child must have, what? Stirred a memory, struck a chord with Mrs C, as Meg noticed her jerk backwards. She stared at the little girl for a moment, and then seemed to gather her wits as she stepped forward again.

'Excuse me, Mrs Jenkins,' she said, lifting her voice. 'I think we can squeeze in one more if the sisters don't mind sharing a room. It only has a double bed, though, so they'd have to sleep together.'

'Oh, well, yes, that'd certainly be a help.' The billeting officer puffed out her cheeks. 'Girls, would you mind sharing?'

Joyce and Maureen exchanged glances – and bubbly smiles. 'We share a room at home, and we don't mind a double bed, do we?' the taller one answered. 'Keep each other warmer at night. They say it's colder in the country, don't they?'

'Well, thank you, girls. So, off you go, then, Doris,' Mrs Jenkins instructed. 'Told you we'd find you somewhere nice, didn't I? Poor Doris got separated from the rest of her school, you see.'

Doris picked up her little suitcase, her stomach still cramped with apprehension. There'd been more sandwiches and also cakes and lemonade when they'd finally arrived at the hall. She'd been thirsty, but still couldn't swallow a morsel of food, lost among the band of strange children, some of whom already appeared to know each other, which made matters worse. When they'd been asked to stand in a long row so that the hosts could pick from them, once again, she'd deliberately hidden behind the two girls who were evidently sisters, hoping she wouldn't be seen, and so would be sent home to her parents, after all.

Now, though, it was too late. Her plan had failed. She felt her legs wobbling as she silently followed – what were their names? Oh, yes, Joyce and Maureen. She'd heard them talking while they'd waited, and they seemed very nice. Her sort of people, and also her sort of age, so she hoped they could become friends. That would be something, at least. And the tall, smartly dressed lady had lovely, smiling cornflower blue eyes. And then there was the older girl accompanying her. Her daughter, perhaps. She looked nice and friendly, as well. Mind you, Doris wasn't sure whether to blame her for spotting her and destroying any chance she might have of going home, or to be grateful to her for getting her taken somewhere nice.

She prayed it would turn out to be the latter, but it looked as though she would soon find out!

*

'Oh, yes, you can eat those all right,' Meg answered Leslie's question as she showed the five young strangers the way along the lane to Robin Hill House. 'But there's an awful lot of berries that *are* poisonous, so never eat anything unless you're absolutely sure.'

Doris had been keeping up with the older girl, rather than lagging behind. She seemed really friendly and one of those people she instantly felt at ease with. Doris definitely felt more confident by her side than if she'd hung to the back on her own. And she certainly didn't want to get lost!

'They're blackberries, aren't they?' she surprised herself by venturing to ask.

'Indeed they are,' the older girl praised, making Doris feel a fraction more relaxed. 'Been to the countryside before, have you, Doris?'

Her question made Doris feel even better. 'Yes, with Mummy and Daddy. We used to bring a basket with jars in it, and fill them with blackberries. And then Mummy'd make them into jam when we got home.' Sadness pricked at Doris's heart at the thought of her parents, but picturing them all together, picking fruit from the hedgerows, also made her feel a little more a part of her new surroundings.

'That's exactly what we do, too,' Meg told her.

'Cor, do yer?' Leslie chipped in again, twisting his head about him as if he didn't want to miss a thing. 'We ain't never bin ter the country before, me and Cyril.'

'Really? Well, the blackberries are almost ready for picking,' Meg explained to him, 'especially if we get some rain in the next day or two to plump them up.'

'Ain't that stealing?' Leslie's frown was almost comical.

'Not if you just take them from the hedgerows. We can all go out together on a blackberry expedition if you like. It'll be great fun! We'll pick lots, and then Mrs Phillips'll turn them into jam, or maybe pies with apples from the orchard. That's our cook, Mrs Phillips.'

'Cor, you have a *cook*? Just like you see in some of them films?'

'Well, with so many of us to feed, we need a cook. And we all hope you're going to be very happy here. I know you'll still have to go to school, but other than that, it'll be like being on holiday, only not at the seaside.'

'Holiday? Never had one of them, have we, Cyril?'

He dug his twin playfully in the ribs, and Cyril, clearly the quieter of the two, muttered, 'No, we ain't.' But he, too, was gazing all about him, eager to take everything in.

'It was good of you to come with us, miss,' Doris said politely, warming to their guide even more. 'You could've just told us the way and gone in the car with your mother and that other family.'

Meg slowed her pace, frowning. Her mother? But her mother was dead, so… And then the penny dropped. 'Oh, no, she's not my mother,' she explained, pleasantly surprised that she hadn't found the girl's mistake upsetting. In fact, she found the idea that Mrs C could have been seen as her mother somewhat attractive. 'She's the mistress. Mrs Stratfield-Whyte. Only that's a bit of a mouthful, so we all call her Mrs C. Because her Christian name's Clarissa.'

'And presumably there's a Mr… Whatever-it-is Whyte?' Doris asked, for somehow she felt that getting all these strangers and their names fixed inside her head would give her more confidence.

'Oh, yes. He has a big factory in the East End, so he stays in London during the week. Usually he doesn't get home till Saturday afternoon, but he's hoping to get back tonight so he's got more time to get to know you all.'

'So, d'yer have a shortened name for him as well?' Leslie wanted to know.

'Ah, yes, we do.' Meg could already guess at the boy's reaction, and amusement tugged at her lips. 'Now don't laugh, but his name's Wigmore. But we call him Mr Wig or plain Mr W.'

She could see Leslie's face turn red as he tried to suppress his mirth. But he didn't succeed and exploded in a roar of laughter, dropping the pillowcase that served as his suitcase in order to lean his hands on his knees. 'He ain't… bald, is he?' he spluttered. 'And he don't have ter… wear a wig?' he guffawed. And his brother started to laugh, as well.

'Yes, I know,' Meg replied, unable to prevent her own giggle. 'I'd never heard of it before, either. But I think it's rather distinguished once you get used to it. And he's such a nice man. Of course, we all show them both utter respect, but they never put on airs and graces. We're like one big happy family, and I'm sure you'll all feel like that, too.'

They had all come to a halt, waiting for Leslie to bring his chortling under control. But hysterical tears were still coursing down his cheeks. Every time his merriment began to subside, it burst out afresh.

Meg couldn't be annoyed. They weren't in any hurry, and the boy's overreaction was probably a result of the day's tensions.

'Shall we have a rest?' she suggested, prompted by Leslie's pillowcase lying on the tarmac. 'It's not that far to the house now, but you have all got your luggage to carry. Come over here onto the verge and sit down. The ground's quite dry.'

There was a general rumble of agreement and the little tribe moved off the road to sit down on the verge.

'This could be a good opportunity for us all to introduce ourselves properly,' Meg suggested, beaming round at her charges. 'Now, Leslie and Cyril, I think you've already done so in your own way!' she laughed. 'So, Doris, you go first,' she encouraged. 'Tell us a bit about yourself.'

She watched as Doris bit nervously on her lower lip, and then took a deep breath. 'Well, I like school,' the child began, slowly gaining confidence. 'I don't have any brothers or sisters. Daddy works in an office, but Mummy doesn't go out to work. She keeps the house really nice. It's only small, but it shines like a new pin.'

'Wish we had a house,' Joyce, the elder of the two sisters, chimed in. 'Our dad's a baker and we live in the flat above. Mummy helps him in the shop, too. She makes fruit tarts and we often help her. That's how I knew about the blackberries, too. Maureen and me, we've only been to the country once. Couple of years ago.'

'Well, I hope you'll be very happy here,' Meg smiled.

'Think we will,' Joyce answered, and then she asked, 'So, who are you, then?'

Meg was pleased that everyone seemed to be more relaxed now. 'Oh, I should've said. I'm Meg. Meg Chandler. And I have two jobs at the house. I'm supposed to be parlourmaid. That means I'm supposed to clean the parlour, well, drawing room actually, and be around when we have visitors.

To open the door to them, serve at table, that sort of thing. Since the butler retired, that is. But don't worry. We don't really have those sort of visitors very often,' she added hastily, observing the suddenly worried expressions on their faces. 'But my main job is as farm manager.'

'So there's a farm as well?' Cyril's eyebrows shot up towards his hairline. 'But yer can't be a farmer. Yer a girl.'

'Ah, ha, you'd be surprised what girls can do, you know!' she gently chided him. 'I was training to be Mrs C's lady's maid, only we needed to make the farm pay, so I didn't have time to carry on training if I needed to concentrate on the farm. Ralph helps me. He was the one driving the car,' she explained, feeling a delicious warmth spreading through her as she thought of him. 'But his main job is as head gardener, growing all the fruit and vegetables we eat. Mr and Mrs Hillier who you might've seen at the hall just now, they're his parents. They live in a cottage in the grounds of the house.'

'Cor, yer blushing, miss,' Leslie teased, now that his own hysterical laughter had finally subsided. 'Is this Ralph yer sweetheart or something?

Then we'll have ter remember ter give yer some privacy, won't we?'

'Well, yes. As a matter of fact, he is.'

Meg caught her breath. She could feel the heat rising in her cheeks and was relieved when Leslie gave a light laugh.

'Don't worry. Only teasing,' he grinned. 'Does that a lot, I do. Tease. Don't mean nuffing by it. Just clout us round the ear if I go too far. Our dad hits me and Cyril all the time, so we're used ter it.'

Meg didn't know what to say. That sounded awful. But Mr W had warned them that some of the children would come from dreadful backgrounds, so she supposed it shouldn't have come as a surprise.

'Is everyone ready to go on?' she asked to diffuse the situation, and in reply, they all stood up again. Just as they were setting off on the last leg, Ralph's parents came round the bend with a little lad of about seven walking between them. He was holding Mary's hand, gazing up at her adoringly, almost as if she was his real-life granny, and chatting away nineteen to the dozen.

'This is young Ed,' Gabriel introduced him. 'Been explaining to him how we'll all be living together, even if he's officially at the cottage with us.'

'Hello, Ed,' Meg said, bending down to him and holding out her hand.

The boy frowned at her and then held out his own hand. 'Hello. Who are you, then?'

'I'm Meg. And I'm sure we'll all get to know each other very well.'

'I saw you were all sitting down,' Mary puffed. 'What a good idea. Shall we sit down, Ed, and have a rest? You can go on telling me all about your family, and we'll catch the others up in a bit.'

'Better go. Looks like my lot are anxious to get there. See you later.' Meg jerked her head towards the twins and the three girls who'd already set off again down the lane. She hurried after them, taking the suitcase from Maureen who was struggling with her luggage. And then Meg noticed with a secret smile that Cyril had given his pillowcase – which hardly appeared to have anything in it – to his brother, so that he could carry Joyce's and Doris's cases for them. Meg experienced a surge of relief. There might be some difficult moments ahead, due mainly to the children's differing backgrounds, but she felt it in her bones that all was going to turn out rather well.

They were just approaching the drive when the Daimler turned out of it.

Ralph stopped the car and wound down the window.

'I was just coming to pick up the stragglers, but I see I'm too late.'

'Your mum and dad were behind us, though,' Meg informed him. 'Nice little lad called Ed they've got. But your mum looked really tired.'

Ralph's face darkened. 'Yes, I know. Bit of a long walk for her on her poorly legs. I'll go and pick them up. See you later.' And he wound up the window again, just leaving a small gap at the top, and drove on.

'Right, this is it,' Meg called, indicating the ever-open gates.

All the voices hushed in awed excitement as they turned down the driveway, and the young faces peered to get a glimpse of their new home. It reminded Meg of that morning nearly three years previously when Ralph had driven her there. There'd been such rebellion in her heart that she'd never have dreamt that this house would come to be her home – or that the young man driving the van would come to mean the world to her.

'Cor blimey, miss, what's them?' Leslie demanded, pointing into one of the fields that had been used as grazing after the hay had been cut and the grass allowed to grow up again.

'The cows, you mean? And do call me Meg.'

'Them's cows?' Leslie's expression was incredulous. 'Blimey, ain't they whoppers? Only seen pictures of them in books, and they look about the size of dogs. And always black and white.'

'Oh, they come in all sorts of different colours and shapes. These are called Jerseys, and they give wonderful creamy milk.'

'Cor, that sounds good, don't it, Cyril?' Leslie dug his twin in the ribs once again. 'Can you teach us to milk them, miss? I mean Meg.'

'I don't see why not. Oh, here come the dogs to say hello.'

Meg's own young collie, Thimble, came cavorting down the drive with Mrs C's two mongrels and her golden Labrador following more sedately, while Patch, the elderly terrier, tottered a few yards before turning back into the house in aloof disdain. Meg noticed the two sisters squeal with delight as the dogs rushed up to them, poking their snouts into outstretched hands and licking fingers that still tasted of ham sandwiches. Cyril had put down the two suitcases and Leslie dropped their pillowcases on the ground, and both of them bent down to ruffle and stroke the animals that pranced around these interesting new arrivals. Cyril crouched down on his heels and threaded his arms about Topaz, who was probably the most docile of them all.

'Always wanted a dog, I did, miss. I mean Meg,' the quieter twin grinned up at her. 'Only our mum and dad was having none of it.' And then he fell over backwards, laughing as the Labrador licked his face. 'Oh, give over. I had a wash this morning. Honest I did.'

Well, that was someone who seemed happy, Meg thought to herself. But then she saw young Doris standing rigid, holding her clasped hands up to her face. The poor child looked petrified, and Meg hurried over.

'It's all right,' she assured her. 'There's no need to be frightened. They're all perfectly friendly.'

'Are… are you sure?' Doris stammered, wishing yet again that she was on the train back to London instead of being surrounded by furry monsters. 'I was bitten by a dog in the park once.'

'Really?' Meg said, full of sympathy. 'Oh, you poor thing. Well, I can understand you being afraid of dogs after that. But none of these will hurt you. They might try to lick you to death, but that's all.' She saw a reluctant half-smile twitch at Doris's lips, and gave her an encouraging look. 'Would you like me to introduce you slowly, so that you can get used to them gradually?' And when Doris nodded cautiously, Meg clicked her tongue, calling over the Labrador. 'Sorry, Cyril. But Doris is a bit nervous of dogs, and Topaz is the softest of them all. The other two are called Trampas and Sunny, but this is Topaz, Doris. He's an absolute angel. Topaz, sit. See how obedient he is? Now just hold out your hand and let him sniff at it. That's it. And give him a little stroke if you feel ready.'

Topaz sat still, as good as gold, big brown eyes gazing steadily at Doris whose hand had trembled as she reached out. But once her fingers felt the warm hairy coat, she smiled up at Meg with triumphant relief shining in her eyes. Meg made a mental note to spend some time with Doris to help her combat her nervousness with the dogs. It would be such a shame if the girl couldn't relish the companionship of man's best friend as she did herself. It could bring you such comfort.

'Cor blimey!' Leslie's amazed voice drew Meg's attention. 'Is all that one house?'

'It certainly is. Welcome, everyone, to Robin Hill House!'

'Blooming heck! Our whole tenement block's not as big as that! Me and Cyril and our mum and dad, we only have two rooms for all of us. Bedroom and kitchen. And we share an outside lav with three other flats. Don't suppose you have an indoor lav here, do you, by any chance?'

'Actually, we have five—'

'Five! Bloody hell—'

Meg was about to explain to him – quietly – that bad language wasn't acceptable here, but thought better of it. Best to let them all settle into their new surroundings first. It was like the first day at school, except that in the middle of the afternoon, they wouldn't be returning to their families. This was going to be *for the duration*. Meg's heart went out to them. Even though they would be well cared for, it would be a massive wrench for them all.

Doris was still looking a little apprehensive, so Meg stayed by her side as they continued down the drive towards the house. Five pairs of eyes opened wide in wonderment as the children surveyed the large building that was going to be their new home, the twins making no effort to conceal their dropping jaws. Meg sensed that she'd need to take Doris under her wing, but all the others looked as if they'd soon settle in. So, for now, it was quite a happy scene – except that across each and every shoulder was slung a cord, and hanging from that cord was a horrible cardboard box that smelt of rubber and disinfectant.

Six

'Right, I'm going to bed,' Nana May announced, snapping closed her spectacle case and putting her book to one side. 'Our first full day with our young guests and it's been a long one.'

'Certainly has, but a successful one, I think.' Clarrie watched the old lady haul herself to her feet. 'I'm going to turn in, too. Goodnight, Wig, love. Don't stay up too long.'

She stood up, and bending to give her husband an affectionate peck on the cheek, followed Nana May out of the drawing room. She might have stayed up a little longer, but it was a good excuse to see the former nanny safely up the main staircase of the house. Nana May wasn't as strong on her pins as she used to be, and Clarrie dreaded to think what might happen if she slipped on the stairs.

'I think it's all going to work out rather well,' Clarrie predicted with enthusiasm as they made their way slowly up the turning flights of steps, 'even if they do all come from differing backgrounds. The twins might be a bit rough round the edges, but they're good lads. And the girls aren't going to be an ounce of bother.'

'It's all quite new and exciting for them at the moment, mind,' Nana May warned. 'They might just be on their best behaviour to start with. And, Clarrie, you mustn't lose sight of the reason they're here.'

They had reached the landing, and she turned round to hold Clarrie's eyes steadily. She saw the little twitch at the corner of Clarrie's mouth, and her own heart contracted, for she couldn't bear to see the younger woman hurt.

'I know,' Clarrie muttered, meeting her gaze. 'They're here because we're about to go to war. Not to be substitutes for the children Wig and I never had.'

Nana May nodded, and then raised a wise eyebrow. 'Just like Meg.'

This time, Clarrie lowered her eyes. 'I know,' she repeated. 'I'll be taking my responsibilities very seriously. Their safety, their happiness, their education, it's all down to me now. I'm going to be the best guardian ever, and enjoy it. But I'm going to do my utmost not to get too emotionally attached. That part won't be easy. Especially with Doris with her red hair. Just like… Rosebud's. But with Meg, it's different, which is why it's so hard for me. You know how she's always been so close to my heart ever since we met her. Oh, Nana May, do you think she'll stay here now because of Ralph?'

She'd grasped the elderly woman's knobbly hand and was staring at her with her forehead bunched in anguish. Nana May could only shake her head with a profound sigh.

'Who knows?' she said sagely. 'It could be that she leaves, and Ralph leaves to go with her. Or they might not stay together. And none of us can make any plans for the future as things stand at the moment.'

'The war. Yes, of course.' Clarrie's voice was a mere whisper, and she had to drag her thoughts elsewhere. 'Oh, well, sleep tight, Nana.'

'And you, dear.'

But somehow, Clarrie couldn't leave it at that. 'We must make the most of every day, mustn't we?' she went on. 'And Mrs Higginbottom will cheer us all up, I'm sure. She's quite a scream, isn't she?'

'Indeed she is. Nice woman, though. Goodnight, then, Clarrie. See you in the morning.'

'I'm just going to check on the girls before I go to bed. Not the boys, though. They might think I'm fussing,' she chuckled. 'So, sleep well, Nana.'

Nana May sensed that Clarrie was still so excited that she could talk all night about her new charges. But Nana May really was tired. She, too, had enjoyed the day, getting to know their young guests, but it had worn her out. As Clarrie almost skipped along the corridor, Nana May plodded to her modest room in the older, central part of the house. She shook her head as she passed the sewing room, her thoughts prompted by her conversation with Clarrie just now. Ah. Only she and Wig and Clarrie knew that it had originally been designated as the nursery. Mrs Phillips was the longestserving member of the staff, but even she had arrived when Wig and Clarrie had long given up hope of having another child, and it had already become known as the sewing room, all the baby furniture and equipment having been removed. Gone. And the room had kept its secret ever since. A few minutes later as Nana May was unhooking her corset, she heard Clarrie walking back towards the master bedroom. Despite Clarrie's reassurances, Nana May knew she would become involved to some extent, but hopefully she would be sensible about it. Nana May felt she needn't be too worried. Not at this stage, leastways. She wasn't going to lie awake worrying, and was soon so soundly asleep that she didn't hear Meg and Ralph reach the top of the servants' stairs next to her room.

*

Just like Mercury before her, Thimble slept with Meg in the room she shared with Jane, and had loped up the stairs behind her mistress. Being alone, Ralph swept Meg into his arms, and pleasurable waves rippled through her as his mouth found hers in a delicious kiss. She laced her arms about his neck, fingers entwining in the hair above his collar. And when the kiss was over, her body melted against his as he held her close.

'We'll get even less privacy now we've got a houseful,' he complained.

Meg pulled away to look up at him with a grin. 'And you're going to have your work cut out growing food to feed them all.'

'Huh, fat chance of that, especially with Dad not being up to so much nowadays. And have you seen what an appetite that Mrs Higginbottom has?'

'She makes me laugh, though. Ah, well, I'll just do my duty and check on the girls before I go to bed.'

'And I'll look in on the boys, but I reckon they're as happy as Larry here. Goodnight, then, love.'

He kissed her again, letting her go with a deep sigh of reluctance. Together they took the few steps along the corridor to the east wing, and as Meg silently opened the door to the first bedroom that Joyce and Maureen were sharing, she saw Ralph blow her a kiss as he disappeared up the narrow staircase to the male servants' rooms above.

Meg popped her head round the bedroom door. The light from the corridor was just enough for her to make out the sisters sleeping peacefully in the double bed, so she quietly closed the door again, feeling happily satisfied. The two girls evidently seemed quite at home in their new surroundings.

'Oo, I do think it's lovely here,' Joyce had declared that morning as Meg had led all the newcomers on a walk around the grounds and the farm. It was their first full day at Robin Hill House, and after all the turmoil and uncertainty of the previous day when none of the evacuees had known where they would end up, everyone was relaxed and in high spirits.

'I just wish Mummy and Daddy were here to see it all,' Joyce went on.

'Well, they're welcome to come and visit,' Meg reminded her.

'I know. Which is great. But I wish they were here so that they could be safe, too.'

Meg saw the distress on the girl's face, and recalled her own first day at Robin Hill House. Her parents had been dead for little over a month. Shock, and the anger of grief, had made her want to hate everything about Robin Hill House and its occupants. But Nana May, more agile then, had been so kind as she'd shown Meg around the house and estate, just as Meg was showing the evacuees now, that her anguish had eased. It wasn't quite the same, but she could understand how the new arrivals must feel. Nervous and upset at leaving their homes and their parents behind. But Robin Hill house was such a beautiful place that you couldn't help but be soothed by it.

'Well, this evacuation lark will probably turn out to be just an unnecessary precaution,' she said to Joyce, trying to set her mind at rest.

'Yeah, I expect it will,' Penelope Higginbottom puffed as she waddled along beside them. 'But I don't mind being 'ere one scrap. Like an 'oliday, it is. And my Archie's eyes'll pop out of 'is 'ead when 'e comes ter visit. 'E's on the railways, see, and they say that's gonna be a reserved occupation so 'e'll be able ter visit sometimes. And I can tell yer, Nana May keeping an eye on Bella and Johnny fer us so I can come wiv yer ter see all this place proper is giving us a nice break,' she concluded, beaming down at her eldest, Sammy, who was deep in some conversation with Ed, who never seemed to be short of something to talk about.

Chuckling to herself, Meg turned her attention to the three girls who'd stayed by her side all the way. Apart from old Patch, all the dogs had come with them, and Doris had held Meg's hand tightly. But Meg had noticed that the child's confidence was already growing, and she no longer shrank against her when one of the animals bounded up to them.

Meg had begun the tour with the walled rose garden at the eastern side of the house, and then she'd shown them the fields on that side of the estate. 'Nowadays we only have the cows to graze the land,' she explained to just Mrs Higginbottom and the older children since Ed and Sammy seemed engrossed in watching a long worm slithering among the grass, and were too young to understand anyway. 'But we grow as much fodder as we can for them so that we have as little winter feed to buy in as possible. We rotate the fields so that we put back into the soil the nutrients we've taken out. You saw yesterday as we came up the drive that we keep three cows at different stages so that we've always got at least one of them in milk. We wean each calf as soon as possible and then sell it on, and if we're going through a stage where we have too much milk, we sell it to the local dairy. I don't suppose we'll have any spare with all of you here, mind.'

She paused, not quite sure how much they'd taken in. All five children nodded solemnly, but Mrs Higginbottom still looked baffled at her explanation.

'So how come yer know so much about all this?' Leslie wanted to know.

Meg had mentally caught her breath. She didn't blame him for asking, but she wasn't sure she was ready to share her past with these young strangers just yet.

'I was brought up on a farm,' she answered, hoping that was enough to satisfy the boy's curiosity for now, at least. And she was grateful when his brother chipped in with another question.

'Are them cows the only animals, then?'

'Oh, no, we've got a few pigs. Oh, and the hens, of course. They're kept in the farmyard on the other side. Behind the two cottages. Come on, I'll show you.'

'Ooph, I fink I'd better stay 'ere and catch me breath,' Mrs Higginbottom panted. 'I'll keep an eye on these two little tykes. They can see the uvver animals later.'

'Of course,' Meg assured her. Mrs Higginbottom was a lovely lady but she was obviously very unfit and most definitely needed to lose some weight! But perhaps staying at Robin Hill House would do her the world of good.

Leaving her to recover and make sure Sammy and Ed didn't get into any trouble, Meg led the others across the wild grass at the back of the house. At the bottom of the little valley was the lake, with open fields and more rough grass petering out into the woods beyond. On the near side, the land inclined gently up towards the house and the retaining wall for the flat, lawned area below the terrace. To Meg, it was still idyllic, even if the farm was a lot smaller than she'd been brought up with.

'Hey, Meg, can me and Cyril learn to swim in the lake?'

'Oh, heavens, no!' Meg was horrified. 'It's not a big lake, but it is quite deep. And it's full of weeds and things. You could get tangled up in them and drown. So you must promise me you'll never go in it.'

'Yeah, OK, we promise, don't we, Cyril? But can we play in the woods, make dens and things?'

'Yes, of course,' Meg had chuckled. 'Only no camp fires, and be careful if you climb any trees. Some of them have dead branches that'll snap under your weight, and I don't suppose your parents'd be very pleased if either of you had an accident.'

'Huh, don't suppose they'd care too much. Come on, Cyril, let's go and explore.'

'Nah, I want to see the other animals first.'

'Oh. Oh, OK, then.' Leslie looked so crestfallen that Meg wanted to laugh.

'Look, as we go through the orchard, pick up any apples that've fallen on the ground,' she instructed, 'and you can feed them to the pigs.'

'Cor, can we?' Cyril's eyes shone like stars and he ran ahead, his brother and the two sisters in hot pursuit.

Doris glanced timidly up at Meg. 'Are they… behind a fence or something? The pigs?'

'Don't worry, you won't have to go in among—'

'Oh, I'm glad I've found one of you!' an irate voice launched itself at them, and Meg turned to see Mrs Durr emerging from the chauffeur's cottage with her two little girls in tow. Earlier she'd declined Meg's invite to be shown about the grounds with a frosty glare. 'How the devil am I supposed to cook on that thing in there?' she demanded now, poking her face belligerently into Meg's.

Meg blinked at her, raising her eyebrows in affronted surprise. 'The range, you mean? But we left you a supply of coal.'

'Yes, but the blessed thing won't light. I demand a gas oven!'

Meg had to stop herself from laughing at the woman's stupidity. 'Well, I'm sorry, but there isn't any gas. We're miles from the nearest gas main.'

'What!'

'Look,' Meg said, trying to calm her down. 'Would you like me to show you?'

'Well, someone better had!'

'Doris, you catch the others up,' Meg told her young charge. 'The farmyard's just there, beyond the other cottage. Only make sure nobody lets the pigs out. They're devils to catch!'

Some twenty minutes later, having got the range lit again, Meg was grateful to join her young charges in the farmyard. Mrs Durr seemed like a woman never to be satisfied and even when Meg had left, had still been complaining. So Meg was relieved to catch up with the others again. To her delight, Doris was leaning over the wall of the pigsty with the others, laughing at the pigs as they snuffled noisily at the heap of fallen apples. Apart from the Durr family, everyone seemed to be getting on so well, settling in nicely. And when all the children had eventually gone to bed that evening, they had done so with reluctance, they were all enjoying themselves so much.

Now as Meg cocked an ear along the landing, not a sound came from the spacious room at the far end where the copious Mrs Higginbottom was asleep with her three little ones. All was indeed so peaceful as Meg went to cross back along the corridor in the central part of the house and climb the stairs to the female servants' quarters in the west wing.

Something, though, made her pause as she padded along the corridor. She just caught a tiny, faint whimper, so low that at first, she thought she was mistaken. But then she heard it again. Oh, dear. Poor little Doris was crying.

Meg tapped lightly on the door, and when she didn't get an answer, she gently pushed it open just enough to slip inside and tiptoe across to the bed. Unlike the sisters who'd evidently felt relaxed enough to sleep in total darkness, Doris had left on the bedside lamp. Meg could see she was curled up under the covers, sobbing quietly into the pillow. She didn't seem to have noticed Meg enter the room, but when Meg called out softly, 'You all right, Doris?' the child's sobs instantly ceased, although she didn't move a muscle.

'Yes,' her muffled young voice croaked in a whisper.

Meg bit on her bottom lip. What a stupid question. Of course Doris wasn't all right.

'Is there anything I can do, sweetheart?' she asked, her words soft with compassion. 'Has anyone said anything to upset you?'

Doris shook her head without shifting her face from the pillow. 'No, nothing like that,' she muttered.

'Then, what, love?' Meg perched on the edge of the bed and hooking the girl's bouncing halo of red curls back from her face, she heard Doris give a big sniff.

'I just miss Mummy and Daddy,' Doris managed to gulp. 'And I don't know when I'll see them again.'

'Oh, Doris.' Meg's sigh was heartfelt, and she stroked Doris's shoulder. The child couldn't resist the sympathetic gesture and scrambled up to fling her arms about Meg's neck and bury her head against her.

Meg lifted her chin, closing her eyes as the constriction tore at her throat. It brought everything back to her, her own first days at Robin Hill House when she'd felt so desperate and alone, despite everyone's kindness – apart from Esme Carter who'd been spiteful towards her from the start.

'I know, I know,' she crooned, rocking Doris back and forth. 'I know what it's like to miss your mum and dad.'

She wasn't sure whether she'd actually spoken the words. They were more locked inside her head. If she had said them, she was relieved when Doris didn't appear to have heard. But then the girl pulled back and gazed up at her.

'Where are your mum and dad, then?' she asked through her tears.

Meg felt her heart twist in pain. How could she tell Doris that she herself had suffered what the child feared so terribly? Yet if she made up some story and the truth came out later, it would destroy the trust Doris seemed to have found in her.

'They died a few years ago,' she muttered hesitantly, dreading the effect it might have on the child. 'So I really do understand how you feel.'

Doris sniffed again and stared at her with eyes widened as she tried to stem her tears. She said nothing, but nodded and used her fingers to wipe her wet cheeks. She seemed calmer now, though, and she didn't even seem to mind that Thimble had followed Meg into the room and was lying patiently on the rug by the bed. But Meg didn't think she should leave Doris quite yet. And then she spied the cuddly toy tucked into the bedclothes.

'D'you like the teddy bear? We knew you wouldn't be allowed to bring much with you, so Mrs C made a collection around the village from people who wouldn't be able to take any children. But she gave them all to the less well-off host families, and bought new ones for all of you. Wasn't that kind of her?'

Doris gave a final sniff and nodded again, the hint of a smile on her face. Feeling encouraged, Meg went on, 'And what sort of games d'you like to play?'

'Oh, well, all sorts, really.' Doris was talking normally again now. 'Skipping, and doing cat's cradle and French knitting and that sort of thing. And I like painting and drawing, but I'm not very good.'

'Oh, I expect you are. I like art, as well. Watercolour mainly. I've got lots of paints and everything. Mr W's brother's a famous artist, and he gave me some. We'll have to do some painting together, won't we? Would you like that?'

'Oh, yes, please.' Doris looked much happier now.

'You can do some paintings of the house and the gardens, and give them to your mummy and daddy when they come to visit, can't you? But for now, I think you should get some sleep or you won't enjoy tomorrow. And school starts in just a few days. They've said it might have to be on a rota system to take in all the new children in the village, but we'll have to see. Now, snuggle down. Shall I leave the light on, or shall I turn it off for you, and leave the door open a little bit? We're going to leave a light on in the corridor overnight.'

'Yes, do that, please. Leave the door open.'

'Yes, OK.' Meg stood up, turning off the bedside lamp. 'I'm afraid I sleep up in the attic on the other side, but if you get scared in the night again, Nana May's in the next room on the other side of the narrow stairs. She might be getting on, but she was a proper nanny in her time, and she'll look after you.'

'Thanks, Meg,' Doris said, wriggling herself comfortable and closing her eyes.

'Sleep tight, then.'

Meg couldn't resist bending down and kissing the child's hair before she padded out of the room, Thimble at her heels. She felt such affinity with Doris. And with her fears. Of course, virtually every evacuated child old enough to understand would feel the same, and many wouldn't have ended up in such a safe, peaceful haven as Robin Hill House, poor mites.

Oh, this horrible, *horrible* war. And it hadn't even started yet. Everybody was going to be living in mortal fear of losing someone they loved. Despite herself, Meg had eventually found, if not a cure for her grief, then at least some sort of reason to go on after her parents' deaths. But now the fear had taken a stranglehold on her throat once again. What if Ralph had to go and fight? What if she lost him, too? Surely she couldn't go on without him. She needed him to breathe, to wake up in the morning and know he'd be there. Oh, no, she couldn't go through all that again. It would kill her.

She dragged herself along the corridor and up the stairs to the attic room she shared with Jane. The country was expecting news in the morning. And it was likely to be of the worst sort.

'Quickly, everyone,' Wig urged, ushering everyone into the drawing room.

The following morning, Sunday 3rd September, Meg had been sent to round everyone up as the appointed hour approached. Wig and Clarrie had only just got back from church with the three girls, who were the only evacuees with a religious upbringing. Everyone was to congregate in the drawing room. Normally it was to be out of bounds to the house guests, but it was the only room that had a radio and was large enough to accommodate them all. There was no point excluding the children. The older ones knew perfectly well what was going on, and the news would go over the heads of those too young to understand.

As Meg counted everyone into the room, she felt her pulse quicken — a heavy sense of dread coursing through her veins. Deep down, she knew what was coming, though part of her still clung desperately to denial. It felt just like the other moments that had shattered her life — losing her parents, losing the farm, and the day Ralph had come out of the woods carrying Mercury's lifeless body.

Old grief rushed back in waves. But this time, Meg wasn't alone in her fear. Whatever the Prime Minister was about to announce would change life for everyone in that room — every staff member, every guest, even Gabriel, Mary, and Ed, listening on their own radio elsewhere. In this moment, strangers and friends alike needed each other's comfort.

Wig switched on the radio. The static crackled and hissed as he adjusted the dial, and a tense silence spread through the room. The air felt charged — filled with quiet sorrow and nervous energy. Wig finally caught a clear signal and checked his watch: **eleven twelve**. Little Bella Higginbottom began to cry. Her mother gently bounced her, but the baby only wailed louder. Calmly, Penelope bared her breast and began to feed her child. No one reacted; the moment was too grave. Only Mrs. Durr let out a disapproving *tut*, unable to contain herself even now.

Then the broadcast began. Meg held her breath. She felt Ralph's hand find hers, but couldn't bring herself to meet his eyes. All she could do was stare at the radio as Neville Chamberlain's voice — clear, deliberate, and grave — filled the room. He didn't delay or soften the truth. In just a few words, he confirmed what everyone had already feared: **Britain was at war with Germany.**

No one gasped. No one cried. The silence was complete, broken only by the faint sound of baby Bella nursing. When the speech ended, Mrs. C looked up at her husband, her eyes saying everything: *Not again.*

Leslie, usually the loudest of them all, whispered, "That's it, then, isn't it?" His voice, though quiet, seemed to release the room from its paralysis. People began to murmur, move, or sit lost in thought.

Then Mrs. Phillips suddenly stood, her voice brisk and defiant. "Well, I'm not going to let Hitler ruin our first Sunday roast together! We'll show him we British still have our standards. Come on, Jane, Louise — back to work!"

Meg sat frozen for a moment, the weight of the news pressing on her. When Ralph finally rose, she followed, taking Doris's trembling hand. Together, everyone drifted out to the terrace, dazed and quiet.

Meg looked up at the cloudless blue sky and whispered, "It doesn't seem right, does it — such a beautiful day?"

'Cor, look at that!' Leslie shrieked, pointing vigorously.

'That's London, ain't it?' Cyril piped up.

All eyes turned towards the capital. Far away, above the distant skyline, dozens of barrage balloons were floating upwards like silver cigars.

'What are those things?' Ed asked, his face a strange mixture of fear and awe.

'Them's to help stop enemy planes,' Cyril told him. 'Part full of gas to make 'em float, and held ter the ground with metal cables. Yer don't want ter fly inter that!'

Ed's little face had hardly had time to register his reaction when a haunting, bone-chilling wail came from the siren in the village and everyone froze in mid sentence, mid step, mid thought. The ghostly sound turned every stomach. Terrified, bewildered looks flew from one face to the other.

It was Clarrie who galvanised everyone into action. 'Oh, dear God, not so soon!' she cried.

'Quickly, down the shelters!' Wig took command. 'Just as we rehearsed yesterday.'

They all immediately hurried down to the three shelters Ralph and Bob had dug out in the grounds. No one had ever dreamt they'd be needed so soon. Meg called to the dogs and counted in the five evacuees and the female staff, as was the plan. The two families were to go in the second shelter, and Mrs C, Nana May, and Ralph's parents with Ed in the third, smaller one. Each person had their allocated role to play so that everyone was safely inside.

Meg hesitated by the door.

'Go on, in you go, and put the sandbags up behind the door.' Meg stared, motionless, into Ralph's beloved face.

'But… you…'

'You know Mr W and Bob and I will be on ARP duty when there's a raid. And look, Mr W's waiting.'

'Ralph, take care!' she squealed as she dragged herself inside, and Leslie and Cyril took delight in piling up the sandbags on the inside of the closed door. The two storm lamps had been lit, casting an eerie glow on the ashen faces of the three little girls, while Jane, Louise and Sally huddled together in the shadows.

'If my roast dinner burns because of that blooming Hitler, I'll give him what for if I ever meet him!' Mrs Phillips declared.

Seven

"Have you always lived here, Mrs. C?" Joyce asked as the group made their way down the lane toward the village.

It was Wednesday morning, and Clarrie had decided to join Meg in escorting the children to school. Until they knew exactly how classes would be organized and how many pupils the classrooms — and air raid shelters — could safely hold, she wasn't about to let them make the journey alone. One of the teachers from the twins' London school was also staying in the village to help keep lessons going, but the schedule was still uncertain.

Once everything was properly arranged, and if the twins' walk to school matched the younger children's, they would be allowed to go without an adult. But until then, Clarrie was determined to walk with them every day.

"The exercise will do me good," she had told Nana May when she caught her disapproving look.

But Nana May wasn't fooled. She knew Clarrie was enjoying the chance to play mother to the children. Life had denied her that role with one of her own, but now she had a chance to experience it — and she was embracing it wholeheartedly.

"No, we used to live in London," Clarrie replied to Joyce's question. "But that was a long time ago."

"Really? What part?"

"Knightsbridge."

"Cor, posh, then!" Joyce said, impressed. "No wonder you've got such a big house here. So why'd you move if Mr. W still has his factory there?"

Clarrie felt a small pang in her chest but didn't blame Joyce for asking. The girl was curious and bold — the sort who always spoke her mind. But Clarrie couldn't tell her the real reason they'd left London all those years ago — the little red-haired girl who still haunted her memory.

"Oh, we just decided we'd had enough of city life," she answered, forcing a light tone to mask the ache beneath. "I've always loved the countryside, so we made a fresh start here. It's been nearly twenty years now."

"That's ages! So you must know everyone in the village then? We know all our neighbours — always popping in and out of each other's houses, borrowing sugar and that. Mum gets a bit cross, though. Some people think that just because we've got a shop, they don't have to pay us back," Joyce said with a laugh.

"Oh, that must be annoying," Clarrie smiled. "Yes, I know most people here. I'm on the village committee — which is how I managed to find a pram for little Bella, so Mrs. Higginbottom doesn't have to carry her everywhere."

Joyce giggled. "She's the fattest baby I've ever seen — though I'd never say it, of course! And her mum's nearly as big — and just as funny!"

Walking a few steps behind with Doris and Maureen, Meg overheard and couldn't help chuckling. The two girls giggled too, Doris covering her mouth. Thankfully, the twins were further back with Ed and young Sammy Higginbottom — otherwise Leslie might have blurted out something far less polite about Mrs. Higginbottom's size.

Then Cyril suddenly pointed to the hedgerow. "Cor, is that bird real?" he exclaimed, running up beside Meg.

"Yes," she smiled. "That's a robin — like the ones you see on Christmas cards."

"Blimey! I thought they just painted them red for Christmas. Never knew they were real! The only birds we see in London are pigeons — and all they do is splatter everywhere!"

Meg laughed. "Yes, they do make quite a mess, don't they? But surely you have more than just pigeons in London?"

"What, you've *never* been to the Big Smoke?" Cyril gasped, eyes wide with disbelief.

'No, even though we're so close just here. I've been to the seaside, though. But only twice, and only for the day. Not for a holiday or anything. Just like Leslie said the day you arrived, I've never had a holiday, either. But I never felt I needed one, living here.'

'Yeah, I can see that. If I lived here, I don't think I'd ever want ter go anywhere else. Some of our friends've been hop-picking in Kent for a holiday,' Cyril volunteered. 'But we never have. Our mum and dad could never be bothered. So where's the hops round here? I ain't seen none. Me friends said they grow right up high on wires, and men go round on stilts ter get the top ones.'

'Well, there's not so many hop gardens round here as there used to be,' Meg explained. 'Nowadays you find them mainly in the central part of Kent. But we're right on the edge of the county here, almost on the border with Kent and Sussex.'

'Oh, are we?' Doris asked in surprise. 'I didn't realise. I'll tell Mummy and Daddy in my next letter.'

'I'll show you on a map when you get home tonight. Or maybe they'll show you at school, although I wouldn't think so today. I think it'll be pretty chaotic the first couple of days while they sort everything out. Ah, look, we're nearly there. I expect you remember the village from Friday?'

As they came into the village, the older children were all eyes. Meg pointed out the handful of shops, although the only one they were interested in was the tiny sweetshop. On the other side of the extensive green stood the vicarage and the church, and beside it, the village hall and the school. Children were arriving from all different directions, gas masks hanging from their shoulders. How on earth the school was going to cope with this new influx, Meg had no idea.

She felt Doris grip her hand nervously at the sight of all these strangers, and Meg's heart went out to her. Poor girl was so timid, and yet she wouldn't know a soul as she'd got separated from her school in the evacuation. Thank goodness she'd be in the same class as Maureen, and maybe Joyce as well if different years had to amalgamate, and both sisters were very friendly. Nevertheless, Meg was determined to see Doris settled before she went home.

'Meg, can yer look after Ed and Sammy now?' Leslie asked, running up behind her and almost shoving the two little boys forward. 'I can see some of our mates over there.'

Without waiting for an answer, he ran across to some other boys who were equally tattily attired, and a second later, Cyril joined him, throwing Meg a half-apologetic look as he scampered away. Meg took little Sammy's hand in her free one. He'd only recently turned five and this was going to be his very first day at school. Meg must hang onto him in the milling crowd, and she had Ed as well, not forgetting Doris whose hand she could feel was shaking.

Meg was swamped with relief when Mrs C, who'd been walking ahead with Joyce, gestured for the two younger girls to go with her.

'Maureen, Doris, why don't you come with me?' she encouraged them, holding out her hands. 'I'll find out what's going on. I know the headmistress, Miss Wingfield. She's on the village committee. Meg, can you hang onto Ed and Sammy for a minute longer? I think the twins can take care of themselves, mind,' she chuckled, glancing over to where Leslie and Cyril were racing round playing a game of tag with their old school friends. Meg felt Doris let go of her hand and she saw her clutch one of Mrs C's instead. And then, curiously, Meg noticed Mrs C give Doris such an affectionate smile that it set her wondering. But only for an instant. She had Ed and little Sammy to sort out. Although she did notice Mrs C seek out Miss Wingfield, the headmistress, who Meg recognised from some of the village events she'd been to over the past three years she'd been living at Robin Hill House. Mrs C passed Doris and the sisters into her care, and Meg was pleased as it meant Doris would feel less at sea among the chaos!

In the end, it was decided that the eleven- to fourteen-year-olds would attend an extra-long school day on Mondays and Tuesdays, and also on Wednesday afternoons, so that overall they wouldn't miss too much time in the classroom. Five- to ten-year-olds, whose education wasn't considered quite so important, would go to school on Wednesday mornings, and a normal-length day on Thursdays and Fridays.

'Well, I think the girls are too young to be expected to walk Ed and little Sammy to school and back,' Mrs C decided when they finally set off home. It had taken so long to sort everything out that it had been decided it wasn't worth starting classes that morning, so the younger children were heading back to Robin Hill House, leaving just the twins for their first afternoon.

'So I'll be happy to go with them.'

Meg couldn't help feeling that Mrs C was delighted with this new responsibility. It wasn't unheard of for her to walk into the village by herself, but Meg was surprised how eager she seemed to do so, there and back, twice a day, three times a week. Mind you, she could probably visit one of her friends or other committee members in the village on

Wednesday mornings so that she only had to do it once on that day. Meg was relieved, though, that the task wouldn't fall on her shoulders. She really didn't have time, what with her other duties and the farm and the animals to take care of.

'Perhaps Mrs Higginbottom could do some of it,' she suggested, 'especially once we pick up this pram, and she can take Bella with her. And there'll probably be room for little Johnny in it, too. After all, she'd have had to do it if she'd been at home in London.'

'Well, maybe she might,' Mrs C replied, almost reluctantly, it seemed. 'But I really don't mind.'

Meg mentally shrugged, but a little frown pinched her forehead. She'd witnessed how good Mrs C was at organising things with the Coronation Tea and other village events. But the older woman seemed to have thrown herself gleefully into everything to do with the evacuees. Nana May had confided in Meg a long time ago that Mr W and Mrs C had wanted children but they'd never come, but Mrs C's zeal over her young charges really seemed to have given her a new and fulfilling purpose in life. So perhaps she was just deriving as much pleasure as she could from her role as surrogate mother while the opportunity lasted.

*

'Blooming battleaxe!' Mrs Higginbottom grumbled in a deliberately loud voice as she shouldered her way into the kitchen with Bella screaming in her arms and Johnny snivelling about her skirts. 'Putting on airs and graces just 'cos she's an *Enumerating Officer* or some such! Well, I told her straight. No one bullies Penelope Higginbottom. It ain't my fault Bella decided she was hungry just as we went in. And she frightened poor Johnny and made him cry, too. Coming in here, throwing her weight around and upsetting everyone, just when we was all settling in so nicely!'

Mrs Higginbottom, or Penny as she wanted to be known, plonked herself down in a chair and unbuttoned her blouse to feed her yelling daughter. She never seemed to worry whether or not there were any men present, although in fact at that moment, there weren't. 'Oh, and she said ter send the next one in,' she remembered in an afterthought.

Meg glanced about the room. Penny was absolutely right that the last few weeks had gone smoothly and that everyone was getting along like one big, happy family, apart from the Durrs who continued to keep to themselves. Today was 29th September, National Registration Day, and every man, woman and child had to be entered on the register, just like a census. It was all to do with identity cards, ration books and conscription for those eligible when the time came. And any other planning the authorities might need to do.

The occupants of Robin Hill House had been allocated to a Mrs Blagden who had marched in and taken over Wig's study for the hour or so it would take to register everyone who lived there. Being a Friday, the children who should have been at school had been given the day off for the purposes of registration, although Clarrie had sat in on each of their interviews to make sure there were no mistakes. But now it was the turn of everyone else.

Meg supposed she ought to go next as Jane was cowering in the corner, and even the ebullient Sally looked a bit reluctant. When it had been her turn, Mrs Phillips had come out complaining that Mrs Blagden hadn't liked the fact that although she was the cook, she lived in her own little house in the village. The enumerator had already started filling out the form before she'd given Mrs Phillips the chance to tell her, and she was somewhat put out when she had to start afresh.

'OK, I'll go next,' Meg offered. She wasn't going to be bossed around, either!

'Good luck, then,' Mrs Phillips and Penny chorused, and everyone laughed since the two women of totally different character seemed to think so very similarly.

Meg nodded, and strode confidently out into the corridor. She nevertheless knocked politely on the study door. After all, you had to admit that this Mrs Blagden would have several other houses to visit during the day as well.

'Take a seat,' the officious woman said without looking up as Meg went into the room. 'Now, full name, please.'

'Meg Chandler,' Meg replied, and then added quickly, 'No, I'm sorry. My proper name is Marguerite Rose Chandler. I've always been Meg, so I forget sometimes.'

Mrs Blagden gave her a sour look as she wrote on a form. 'And I suppose you're another maid, though why it takes so many servants to look after one house, I don't know.'

'No, actually I'm not.' Meg kept her voice steady, suppressing her own anger at the woman. 'I mean, I do help out in the house. Five evacuees need a lot of looking after if you're to make them feel at home, on top of all the extra cooking and washing and ironing. But I'm actually the estate manager.

A farmer.'

She saw Mrs Blagden look up sharply. 'But... you're—'

'I know. A girl. But I'm still a farmer.'

'Oh.' Mrs Blagden pursed her lips as she crossed out the letter M – for maid, Meg imagined – that she'd started writing, and put farmer instead. She then took further details from Meg before writing out an identity card for her. 'There you are. Carry it with you at all times, just like your gas mask. Guard it with your life. And if you're stupid enough to lose it, you must report it at once.'

'Of course. And by the way, just to warn you, if you speak to Jane like that, you'll frighten her so much she won't even be able to remember her own name.'

Mrs Blagden's face turned puce as Meg spun on her heel and walked out of the room, head held high. The woman had got her gander up right and proper! It reminded her of the time after the accident when the whole world seemed to be against her, and everyone was trying to tell her what to do. She took a deep breath to calm herself down, and stepped through the kitchen door.

'Right, I'm done,' she called. 'Next one. I'll go and round up everyone else.'

It was good to escape outside, and she drew deeply on the fresh air. She hurried across to Gabriel and Mary's cottage where she knew they'd be waiting to be called together with young Ed, and then she went in search of Ralph and Bob. She found Ralph first, digging manure into a patch in the walled kitchen garden.

'She's a right old tartar,' she told him as he spiked his garden fork into the ground.

'Well, I suppose she's got a lot to get through today,' Ralph reasoned. 'And everything's got to be accurate. I mean, people are going to be conscripted from this register, so they've got to get it right. And,' he hesitated, seeing the angst on her face, 'they say there's going to be a whole range of reserved occupations. Men in specially skilled industrial jobs, all sorts. Including farmers and professional gardeners producing food. Only... there'll be age limits within that. I was too old for the military training that took Vic away, but I'll be below the age limit for gardeners. So, my darling, I *will* be called up. You know that, don't you?'

He took Meg's hands in his, ignoring the dirt on them, and his soft brown eyes gazed into her sapphire ones. He could see the fear and the sorrow collecting along her lower lids, deep pools of anguish. She had been through so much in her young life, and now this horror had come to ruin the peace she had eventually found. He pulled her against him, tucking her head beneath his chin. He loved her so much, his heart ached. No matter what happened, he *had* to survive. They both needed to survive whatever was coming. They had to be together in the end. Or life would have no meaning.

But all either of them could do was hope and pray. And have faith.

Eight

Autumn 1939

Cyril Langport leaned on his spade, squinting up at two small planes streaking through the clear autumn sky. "What d'you make of this phoney war, then, eh, Meg? Nothin's been happening! Even that first air raid was just a false alarm."

Meg frowned, brushing soil from her hands. "The longer it stays quiet, the better. Gives us time to build up our weapons and defences."

"Yeah," Cyril agreed, nodding toward the sky. "Like them planes — just like that Churchill bloke said we'd need."

Meg smiled faintly at his phrasing. "Yes, Mr. W thinks the government should've listened to Churchill sooner. Everything he warned about Hitler has turned out true."

"Churchill's running the navy again now, ain't he? Like he did donkey's years ago."

"That's right," Meg said, impressed. "And he's moved into Admiralty House too, from what I've heard. But talking won't get our work done, will it? You managing all right there?"

"Yeah, Meggy, I'm fine with these old girls." Cyril grinned, patting the rough hide of one of the sows rooting around near his boots.

"So I can leave you to finish mucking out the sties, then?"

"'Course you can. Don't worry about me."

Meg smiled and left the yard, heading back toward the house. She was amazed by how well the twins had adapted to country life — even thrived in it. Cyril, especially, had found a real fondness for the animals, and he'd learned to hand-milk the cows like he'd been born to it. Leslie, on the other hand, still struggled and — though he'd never admit it — Meg suspected he was a bit afraid of the creatures. He'd probably be in the vegetable garden now, working with Ralph and Gabriel.

Still, their brief talk had unsettled her. Everyone knew the waiting couldn't last forever — the calm before the storm. No one knew what would come next, only that it was inevitable. But as she crossed the lawn, her spirits lifted. It was half-term, and Ed's parents had come to visit. Down by the lake, they were playing a wild game of tag with their son. Clarrie, the three girls, and little Sammy Higginbottom had joined in too, laughter echoing across the water. The sight brought a smile to Meg's face.

There were fewer children now, though. The family in the chauffeur's cottage had decided to return to London. Meg remembered the day Mrs. Durr had come storming into the kitchen, her two daughters in tow.

"Where's Mrs. Stratfield-Whyte?" she demanded.

Everyone in the room exchanged wary glances. Mrs. Durr was clearly in one of her moods again.

"I'll fetch her for you," Meg said politely. "Would you like to wait here?"

"Huh, don't mind if I do. And give my girls some of that cake while we're here," Mrs. Durr ordered, "seeing as I can't cook a thing on that blessed range."

Meg nearly laughed but managed to hold it in when she caught Penny Higginbottom's offended expression. Meg knew exactly what Penny was thinking — that cake was meant for the children living in the house, not for Mrs. Durr's greedy pair.

Meg hurried off to find Mrs. C, who she discovered in the drawing room.

"Oh dear, what does she want this time?" Clarrie sighed as they headed back to the kitchen. "Everyone else has tried to fit in so well, but that woman hasn't been content since the day she arrived."

"I know," Meg agreed with a weary smile. "She's got a lovely cottage and good company here. Some people are never satisfied, are they?"

Clarrie gave her a knowing look as they stepped back into the kitchen — where Mrs. Durr's girls were already cramming their mouths full of cake as if they hadn't eaten in days.

'Now what can I do for you, Mrs Durr?' Mrs C asked in her most friendly tone.

'I've come to tell you we're not spending another day in that place,' Mrs Durr announced fiercely, crossing her arms over her chest. 'Out here in the back of beyond, with nothing to do but wash the mud off your shoes. And that wretched range going out every five minutes. And it's not as if there's any bombs falling on London! Waste of time and effort. So, we're packing up and I want a lift into the village to catch the afternoon bus.'

The woman stood there, glaring at Clarrie, whose eyebrows had slowly reached heavenwards during the tirade.

'Well, I'm very sorry, Mrs Durr,' she said slowly and deliberately, 'but that simply isn't possible. My husband has the car up in London during the week, as you know. He might be home tomorrow night, but it's usually not until Saturday afternoon that he manages to get away. Of course, we can drop you in the van, but the girls would have to go in the back, and that's none too clean. And it all depends on whether there's enough petrol to spare from the month's ration. But I can try and get you a taxi if you like. It might cost you a bit, of course. It would have to come all the way from Tunbridge Wells.'

Mrs Durr's lips contracted into a tight little knot, and she grabbed each of her daughters by the collar. 'Come along, girls. We'll have to wait till the weekend.' And she marched the two bewildered little souls out of the kitchen and back to the cottage.

As soon as they were out of earshot, Penny burst out in a guffaw of mirth. It was so infectious that in a few seconds, everyone else joined in the laughter. Meg was glad it was Thursday morning and while the younger children were at school, the twins were helping in the kitchen garden. She could just imagine Leslie mimicking Mrs Durr before she was even out of the door!

As the merriment subsided, however, Meg saw Mrs C shake her head. 'I can't say I'll be sorry to see her go,' she sighed. 'But I hope she knows what she's doing. It hasn't been long. Hitler could be biding his time. I'd hate to think of those little girls caught in a raid. Or worse.'

The jolly atmosphere at once turned sombre. None of them wanted to think about such horrendous possibilities.

'Well, we can't make up her mind for her,' Penny said, bouncing her head up and down. 'It's up ter us ter keep our heads high, and show Herr Hitler he can't keep us Brits down.'

Her words seemed to inspire everyone to go back to whatever they were doing before the interruption. Meg met Mrs C's wistful eye as the older woman turned back towards the drawing room. Each knew exactly what the other was thinking. Was this just the calm before the storm? Would Wig be in danger at the factory? Whichever force he went into, would Ralph, or Bob or Vic for that matter, be safe? The parents of their charges, Penny's husband who worked on the railways? It didn't bear thinking about.

Mrs Durr and her two little girls had departed at the weekend, and the remaining children had been enjoying their half-term from school. That day, the weather was mild, and as Mrs C and Ed's parents played joyfully with the children down near the lake, hoots of laughter wafted up to the terrace. *You'd think that all was well with the world*, Meg considered as she headed indoors. Certainly Mrs C seemed to adore taking charge of the children and racing around the grounds with them at any opportunity. And Doris seemed quite at home with all the dogs now. The four bigger ones were joining in the game, barking their heads off. Patch was no doubt toasting himself by the range back in the kitchen.

Meg waved cheerily and went to cross the terrace, but seeing her, Doris called out and raced up to her.

'You know Mummy and Daddy are coming to visit on Saturday?' she asked excitedly, eyes shining. 'Can you help me finish off my painting later on? I want it to be perfect for them to take back with them.'

'Yes, of course I can,' Meg grinned at her. 'I know how excited you are. Erm, I reckon I can leave Cyril to milk the cows on his own. We could do it then.'

'Oh, thanks, Meg!' Doris flung her arms about Meg, and then flew back down to rejoin the fun down by the lake. Meg watched her go. In the few weeks she'd been there, the girl had grown in confidence. What a change her parents were going to see in her!

As she turned down the side of the house and went in through the servants' entrance, Meg thought about the changes in the house as well. Mr W and Mrs C had never stood on ceremony, but everything was definitely more relaxed nowadays, and there was no longer any need for the formalities of a parlourmaid. Indeed, the very idea would appear somewhat ludicrous now. Instead, Meg just pitched in wherever she was needed. 'How much sugar did yer say ter put in this, Ada?'

Penny Higginbottom's voice boomed through the doorway as Meg entered the kitchen. She couldn't believe how the loud, overweight woman had blustered her way into everyone's affections, but particularly those of Ada Phillips. Under Penny's influence, the cook was even happy to be addressed by her Christian name by everyone nowadays. The two women had become as thick as thieves. Penny was so open-minded about everything, and it was rubbing off on the cook. She was also a hard worker, and seemed to be able to peel vegetables and chop onions with baby Bella tucked under one arm.

'We're making double quantities, so eight ounces,' Ada replied. 'And here you are, Johnny,' she said to Penny's middle child who was seated at one end of the vast table. 'A bit of pastry for you to play with.'

The kitchen was in utter chaos. Louise, who'd been a quiet, diligent member of the staff since before Meg had come to the house, was tackling a pile of carrots and cabbages, Penny was making a terrible mess but certainly powering through the tasks Ada gave her, Jane was running around collecting up all the dirty utensils and pans to wash in the sink, and Nana May was dandling baby Bella up and down on her lap. All was in alien disorder, but, as ever, Meg knew that the meal would arrive on time and every hungry mouth would be satisfied.

Meg lingered a moment on the threshold. It had always been a happy household, but now it exuded jollity and friendship. How strange that war could have such an effect on people's lives. But Meg prayed to God that this phoney war never developed into anything else.

*

'No, we don't want ter go back ter smoky old London, do we, Cyril?' Leslie retorted defiantly, flinging his arm around his brother's shoulder, though Meg suspected it was more for moral support.

'Yer'll do as yer bloody well told!'

Mr Langport raised his mean fist, but seemed to think better of it when Ralph and Gabriel stepped forward in unison. He'd found his sons in the kitchen garden, helping their two new heroes. Langport had already judged that the younger man, though slender of waist, was broad-shouldered and looked fit and strong. Even the elderly chap was tall when he straightened up, and was wielding a garden fork that looked decidedly menacing.

Langport changed tack. 'Me and yer muvver've come all this way ter fetch yer,' he went on, cajolingly now. 'She really misses yer, and she'll be right upset if yer don't come back wiv us.'

'So where's she now, then?'

'Having a cuppa and some cake in the kitchen—'

'If she's so anxious ter see us, then why didn't she come straight out?'

'Yer cheeky devil!' Langport roared, and then his face moved into a sneer. 'Is it that yer've gone chicken since yer've been here? Well, there ain't no bombs falling on London, so yer've no need ter be so soft.'

'I'm not frightened of no bombs,' Leslie challenged him, 'and I'm not frightened of you, neither. So we're not coming.' 'Prefer ter be wiv yer new hoity-toity friends, do yer?' 'Mr Langport, I really think—' Ralph tried to put in.

'Yeah, as a matter of fact, I do!' Leslie squared his young shoulders bravely. 'I don't want ter be like you, Dad, going from one odd job ter the next, never knowing where the next meal'll come from. I want ter make somefing of meself.'

'And how does me little Mr High and Mighty propose ter do that?' Langport mocked, crossing his arms over his chest.

'I'm gonna be a gardener. Ralph and Mr Gabriel's gonna teach me. When I leave school, I can do an apprenticeship,' he nodded triumphantly, 'and it won't cost yer nuffing.'

'Oh, yeah? Who says?'

'The boy shows promise,' Ralph attempted again.

'And what about you, Cyril?' his father jeered. 'Suppose you want ter be one, and all.'

'No. I want ter be a farmer.' Cyril's face was set determinedly, even though Meg thought he looked to be on the verge of tears. 'At least, I want ter work on a farm, even if I don't know enough ter have me own tenancy.'

Langport roared with laughter. 'Yer own *what*, Gaud help us?'

Meg had heard enough. Even though Ralph shot her a warning glance, she stepped in front of the obnoxious bully. 'Look, Mr Langport, I can understand you and your wife missing the boys. But don't you want them to do well? By the look of you, you're young enough to be conscripted. What if you have to go and fight, and… and something happens? Wouldn't you want to… to *go,* knowing your boys had a future?'

'Nah, this war's not going nowhere—'

'Well, I think you're wrong there. But be that as it may, wouldn't you want your boys to have the best chance in life?'

Langport glowered at her, and Meg saw that Ralph, bless him, was coiled ready to spring, fist bunched, if there was any trouble. But Langport seemed to reconsider, rubbing his stubbly chin.

'Well, I suppose put like that…'

'You and your wife can come and visit whenever you like,' Meg got in quickly – not that she hoped they would.

'And who's gonna pay our fares, then? I suppose that nice Mrs Stratfield what's-her-name wouldn't help us out occasionally?'

Meg felt sickened. The brute had changed his tune when he thought there might be something in it for him! A free day out for him and his wife. And she didn't suppose they'd be too worried about seeing their sons!

'I don't know about that,' Meg murmured evasively. 'You'd have to ask her yourself.'

'Oh, right.' Langport's face fell a little, but instantly brightened again. 'Here, yer couldn't spare some of them spuds, could yer?' he asked, eyeing the wheelbarrow full of potatoes his sons had been helping the men to dig up. 'And a few carrots and onions wouldn't come amiss, neither.'

Meg saw Ralph bite the inside of his cheek to stifle his anger. 'Go and see your mum,' he said quietly to the twins. 'And when you come back, ask Mrs Phillips for a *small* paper bag.'

'Thanks, Ralph,' the twins chorused, and started for the house at a run, their father scurrying on behind, looking very pleased with himself.

Ralph watched them, puffing out his cheeks. 'Phew, I didn't think that was going to end so well. I was worried he was going to thump you.' 'I saw you were ready to protect me,' Meg grinned.

'Just don't you ever do anything like that again.'

Meg's smile slackened. 'Who knows what any of us might do if the war gets going.'

'Better make that *when,* girl,' Gabriel said glumly.

Meg gazed across at the old man, and her stomach turned over.

*

Doris was positively bouncing along the lane as she walked into the village with Clarrie and Meg on the Saturday. Her parents would be arriving on the mid-morning bus, and she wanted to be waiting for them at the bus stop. The child was brimming with excitement. Oh, she couldn't wait to see her mummy and daddy again, and to show them the wonderful place where she was living and introduce them to all her new friends.

'Mrs C, is it all right if I take them up to my room?' she asked as she skipped along, unable to contain her happiness.

'Of course, my dear. I'm sure they'll want to know everything about where you're staying.'

'And can I show them all the gardens and the woods? And Meg, can I show them all the animals, too?'

Meg chuckled as she nodded. What a difference in Doris those couple of months had made. Instead of being terrified of the dogs, she was now totally at ease with them. Topaz had even become her constant companion, and she'd even asked if she could bring the Labrador into the village to meet her parents off the bus.

'And they're going to love the painting you helped me do for them,' she chattered on. 'Oh, what's the time? We're not going to be late, are we?'

Clarrie shook her head in bemusement. What had happened to the shy little girl who'd arrived at the start of September? To the child with the bright red curls, just like Rosebud? Fate could play such strange tricks. First Meg had come to them as the result of a tragic accident, and now Doris had arrived because of the fears of war. No bombs had fallen on British soil as yet, and pray God they never would. But if that fear had brought so many young people under her care, Clarrie hoped that they would stay for as long as possible, and at least until the conflict was totally resolved, unlike the Durr Family. In such a short time, Clarrie had become so fond of all her charges. But if she were honest, Doris was probably her favourite. And she knew why.

She waited by the bus stop with Doris while Meg went off to buy a few items Ada wanted from the grocer's. Doris was hopping up and down, and Topaz, at the end of his lead, kept standing up and sitting down again, not sure what was going on. When the bus trundled round the corner, Doris nearly took wing with uncontained joy.

A few moments later, she was crushed in her mother's embrace, and then her father might have tossed her in the air had he not noticed she was holding the lead of the big, golden dog by her side. So he just lifted her off her feet instead. Doris's heart was bursting and she grinned up at both her parents, not knowing which one to hug again next.

'And you must be Mrs Stratfield-Whyte?' Jeremy Sergeant said, holding out his hand. 'Doris has told us so much about you in her letters.'

'Oh, do please call me Mrs C. Everyone else does.'

'Well, Mrs C, we can't thank you enough for making our daughter so happy, even if we do miss her dreadfully.'

'It truly is my pleasure,' Clarrie beamed back.

'And who have we here?' Mrs Sergeant asked, nervously eyeing Topaz.

'Oh, Mummy, there's no need to be frightened of dogs anymore.' Doris's voice rang with confidence as she scratched Topaz behind the ear and the animal turned his head to push against her hand. 'Not most dogs, anyway. You know I told you there's five of them at the house. This one's called Topaz and he's a real softy. Well, they all are, but Topaz is extra soft because of his breed, and he's so obedient. Oh, and this is Meg I've told you about. She's the one who taught me not to be frightened of dogs.'

Meg took Mr Sergeant's proffered hand as she came up to the little group by the bus stop. 'A pleasure to meet you, Meg. We've heard so much about you. You're in charge of all the animals, I believe.'

'And you've been helping her to improve her painting, too, a little bird told me,' Mrs Sergeant put in with a wink. 'We're really grateful to all of you for taking such good care of Doris. We have heard of some children ending up in some awful places.'

'We have a little surprise for you later on, don't we, Meg?' Doris grinned, her eyes shining like stars. 'And you've got to meet everyone else, too. Joyce and Maureen. They're sisters, and their mum and dad are coming to see them tomorrow. That's because they run a baker's shop and so Sunday's their only day off. Maureen's the same age as me, but Joyce is a year older. But we're in the same class at school because we have to double up to fit in all the evacuees from around the village. And then there's the twins, and Mrs Higginbottom with her three little ones. We just call her Penny, though. She's ever so funny! And then there's Mr and Mrs Hillier's Ed, and Mrs Phillips, or rather Ada, the cook, and—'

'Whoa!' her father laughed. 'Slow down! I know you've told us about them all in your letters, but maybe we'd better wait until we get there.'

'Yes, I've never known you to chatter on like this,' Mrs Sergeant laughed.

'Well, come along, then!' Doris grabbed her mother's hand. 'It's this way. About half an hour. We have to walk because Mr W won't be back from London with the car until this afternoon. And anyway, his petrol ration's only enough for himself and his work.'

Meg and Mrs C shared a look as Doris pulled her mother along, still holding Topaz's lead in her other hand. Mr Sergeant hurried along beside them, adoration gleaming in his eyes. They were clearly a close-knit family, and it was lovely to watch them together.

Clarrie and Meg instinctively hung back. Later, perhaps, the Sergeant family would have lunch with all the residents of Robin Hill House, and see everything that went on within its walls and outside in the grounds. But for now it was time for the little family to be alone. To relish each other's company. For the day would pass far too quickly for them, and Mr and Mrs Sergeant would be returning on the late bus. And who knew when they might be able to see each other again after that? And besides, Clarrie thought as they let the gap between them lengthen, she could have Meg all to herself again on the long walk home.

Nine

"Meg? Oh, Meg, thank goodness I've found you!"

It was a cold, grey Friday morning in November. The younger children were off at school for the day, and the twins were helping Ralph and Gabriel in one of the greenhouses — the dreary weather making outdoor work impossible. That left Meg free to keep working on the new shirts she was sewing for the Langport boys, whose clothes had been little more than rags when they'd first arrived at Robin Hill House. They were growing so quickly that new outfits were needed before winter fully set in. Meg had already finished a pair of trousers for each of them, while Nana May had knitted several pairs of warm socks.

Now, Meg sat upstairs in the sewing room, needle flashing through fabric, while Nana May's knitting needles clicked rhythmically beside her. The older woman found knitting easier on her stiff, aching fingers than sewing, and she could work without even glancing at her needles — something that always amazed Meg. The two had been chatting quietly as they worked, unaware of the hurried footsteps approaching down the hall.

The door burst open. "Oh, hello, Mrs. C," Meg said cheerfully, looking up. "What can I—?" But her words faltered at the sight of Clarrie's pale, stricken face.

"Oh, Meg, dear, come quickly! It's Patch! I think—oh God, I hope not, but…"

Meg's heart gave a painful jolt. Patch — the little cairn terrier who had been Clarrie's first and most beloved pet — was thirteen now, and age had clearly been catching up with him. Still, the thought of losing him made Meg's stomach clench. She jumped to her feet at once.

"Where is he?"

"In the study. I was doing the accounts…" Clarrie's voice wavered.

Meg hurried after her, Thimble — the younger dog — stretching lazily before trotting close behind. Meg didn't have the heart to tell her to stay. The two women took the back stairs, the quickest way down to the study.

The room was dim but warm from the radiator. The fire hadn't been lit, yet the air was still comfortable. Patch lay on his side on the rug, his legs stretched out as though in one of his usual naps — but this time, something was terribly different.

Meg dropped to her knees beside him. His little body looked so still, too still. She watched closely, searching for the faint rise and fall of breath, but saw none. Gently, she placed her hand against his side. He was still warm — though not quite warm enough.

She looked up, catching the despair in Clarrie's face just as Nana May appeared quietly in the doorway.

"Pass me that small photo frame," Meg said softly. Clarrie, confused but obedient, handed it over. Meg held the glass near Patch's nose, praying it would fog with breath. Nothing. The glass stayed clear.

Meg lowered her head, pressing her ear against the terrier's chest, listening — hoping. But there was only silence. She opened one of his eyes, willing for a flicker of life, but the dull, motionless third eyelid told her everything.

A chill hollow spread through her chest. Patch was gone. Peacefully, yes — but gone all the same.

Her heart ached for Clarrie. She knew too well what it was to lose a loyal friend, the kind who asked for nothing and gave everything. Taking a steadying breath, Meg looked up at the trembling woman before her. There was no easy way to say it. Patch had simply reached his time — a small, gentle soul who had slipped quietly away.

But she knew that for Clarrie, this loss would cut deep. Strong as she seemed, there was a softness beneath her composure — and this was going to break her heart.

'I'm so sorry, Mrs C,' she said gently, fighting the lump that suddenly grew in her own throat. 'I'm afraid I can't find any signs of life.'

She watched as Mrs C's face twisted horribly and then she heard a suppressed howl as the woman sank on her knees. Mrs C's trembling hand stretched out towards Patch, and then recoiled, as if she was too afraid to touch him. It was as if there was more to it than the death of a beloved pet.

Slowly, carefully, with the utmost respect, Meg lifted Patch's lifeless body and slid him into Mrs C's arms. She bit back her own tears as Mrs C cradled Patch against her chest, her shoulders heaving as she sobbed. Nana May had stepped forward and placed her hand on Mrs C's shoulder, and Meg bit on her lip. She'd have liked to put her arms about

Mrs C. To offer her comfort. But it wasn't her place. Perhaps Mrs C would be better left to grieve alone with Nana May who'd been her dearest companion for so many years, especially since Mr W was, of course, at the factory.

So, quietly, Meg went to get up and leave the two older women alone together. 'I'll try and get through to Mr W at the factory to tell him,' she said softly.

But Mrs C lifted her tear-stained face. 'Oh, Meg, please don't go,' she pleaded. 'Not for a minute, anyway.'

Meg nodded at once, and dropped back on her heels. 'All right,' she barely whispered, but watching Mrs C rock Patch's body back and forth, she gave into her instincts and slid her arm about Mrs C's shoulders. Mrs C glanced at her for just a second, a watery ghost of a smile on her lips, before she turned back to Patch, stroking his still head.

*

The following morning, they buried him in the rose garden next to Mercury, and Bob made another small plaque to mark the spot. All the staff and the evacuees came to pay their respects, since the little dog had carved out a place in everyone's heart. The three young girls held hands, crying softly, and Ed felt able to sob into Mary Hillier's skirt, he'd come to love and trust her so much. Meg noticed that even the twins, who always tried to act so grown-up, had unshed tears glistening in their eyes.

Nana May and Meg had stood either side of Clarrie since Wig was going to be detained in London all over the weekend. As they walked slowly back to the house, Clarrie's thoughts weren't so much with the furry body in a little box beneath the earth as with another small coffin in a London cemetery. Nana May had squeezed her hand tightly, the only one who knew and who understood. On her other side was someone else who was more precious to her than gold, someone who couldn't know just how much she meant to her, and just how much comfort her presence had brought her. Her dearest, darling Meg.

*

'Here you are, lad.' Ada's voice cracked as she brusquely thrust something wrapped in greaseproof paper into Bob's hands. 'It's my best Christmas cake recipe. In case they don't give you one. It'll keep till then if you keep it somewhere dry.'

'Thanks, Mrs P. Ada.' Bob nodded, his bottom lip folded over the top one as he pushed the cake into his army-issue haversack. As soon as he'd received his call-up papers, he'd taken the train up to his parents in Norfolk. Saying goodbye to them had been awful, and he hadn't thought this could be as bad. But it was. Especially with Sally standing by his side, trying to be strong. It made him realise just how much she meant to him. They'd known each other barely a year, and yet when he came back – *if* he came back – he thought he might pop the question.

'And here's some paintings of the house and the grounds I did for you.' Meg handed him a tiny bundle of three-by-two-inch pieces of sketch paper tied with a ribbon. 'I made them really small so they wouldn't take up too much room, but I've put a lot of tiny detail in them.'

Bob nodded and grunted what sounded like thanks, clearly too choked to speak. Everyone was gathered in the hall, the people who'd become his second family. Even all the evacuees were there, since in the few short months they'd known him, they'd also become very fond of him. And this parting, not knowing what the future held, affected them all.

Wig coughed delicately beside him. 'And here's a little extra funding. No, no arguing,' he said as Bob went to protest. 'Think of it as a bonus. You never know when you might need it.'

'Well, I've got nuffing ter give yer but me prayers and me best wishes.' As Sally stood aside, Penny enveloped Bob in a bear hug, squashing him against her voluminous bosom. When she finally let him go, his face was red from embarrassment and lack of oxygen.

'If you can survive that, you'll survive anything,' Meg heard Ralph joke in Bob's ear as they all trooped out into the December frost.

'Cheers, mate.' Bob managed a grim chuckle, and then the two young men embraced, patting each other on the back. They'd been friends for years, but Meg imagined that sharing a room for the last few months had brought them even closer.

'In you get, then, or you'll miss the bus,' Wig urged, getting into the Daimler. 'Don't want to be put on a charge for being late reporting for duty on your first day.'

Meg had to hold back the lump in her throat as she saw Bob's chest heave nervously inside his itchy brown uniform. Mrs C stepped forward, hand outstretched. Bob shook it, but after a second or two's hesitation, Clarrie gave him a brief hug, and then they nodded at each other in knowing silence. And then Sally disappeared inside his embrace for one last, brief moment, chin wobbling as she managed to fix a smile on her face.

Meg lightly placed a hand on Sally's shoulder and, concealing a sniff, the girl stepped back. Bob threw his haversack into the back of the car, blew Sally a final kiss and then climbed into the front passenger seat. Moments later, the car purred down the drive and turned out onto the lane. Waving arms dropped, heads shook, and slowly everyone turned back into the house. Meg slipped her arm about Sally's waist and Ralph patted her shoulder. They knew what each other was thinking. It would be their turn soon.

It was all too much for Sally. She hadn't wanted to go and see Bob off at the bus stop. It would be too final. Too heart-breaking. She wanted to have her friends all around her when they said their last farewell. Normally a happy, confident soul, she turned to Meg now and buried her face against her shoulder, sobbing quietly. She was shivering, and hushing her gently, Meg walked her back inside into the warm.

'There are times when I'm glad I've never had a sweetheart,' she heard Louise mutter sadly to Ada. And Meg was grateful that Sally didn't appear to have caught Louise's words as they headed for the kitchen and the ubiquitous cure for all ills: a nice cup of tea.

Outside, Clarrie was left alone. First Vic had been called up, and now Bob. So far, not much had happened in this war. But it would. In the last war, she'd been lucky. Because of his expertise in designing machinery to make bombs – not just the shell cases produced in his own factory – Wig hadn't been called up. He was too useful as a gifted engineer. And this time, he was too old. But he'd been contracted to design a machine to manufacture a small component for something top secret. Even he didn't know what it was for. He'd simply been given the specification of the item that was needed. So, Vic and Bob had gone, and her darling Wig would stay safely at home. There was only one other among the household who was eligible to fight, and that was Ralph.

Clarrie's heart drummed in her chest. It was no secret how Meg and Ralph felt about each other. She'd seen them holding hands, snatching a quick kiss when they thought nobody was looking. It was like a dagger in Clarrie's side. For what if, after all she'd been through already, her Meg were to lose Ralph as well? Oh, the poor child. Clarrie simply couldn't bear to see her suffer like that.

She turned back to the house, her heart dragging with fear.

'Ho, ho, ho!' Father Christmas's voice wobbled with jollity as he walked into the servants' hall, brushing some pretend soot off his shoulder. 'You need to get your chimneys swept for next year, you know! Now I wonder what toys I might have for some good little children,' he said, swinging the old sack he was carrying onto the floor. 'You have all been good, I hope?'

A warm tide of happiness swept through Meg as she saw the wonderment on the little faces of the younger children. Bella stared up at the old man, thumb plugged in her mouth, while Johnny's jaw dangled open in disbelief. Sammy's, and even Ed's, eyes were stretched wide, and the three girls were holding hands and jumping up and down in excitement.

The hours that Meg and Mrs C had spent up in the sewing room after the children had gone to bed, straining their eyes in the poor light to stitch the costume together, had been worth every minute. Nana May had knitted scarves and woolly rag dolls and soft toys, and Meg knew that Gabriel had spent every evening for the past few weeks whittling wood into trains and cars for the boys and animals for the girls.

''Ere, that ain't Father Christmas,' Meg, to her horror, heard Leslie declare to his brother in an amused whisper. 'That's Mr Gabriel!'

'Sh! Don't spoil it for the little ones!' Joyce hissed at him under her breath. 'Anyway, it's not Mr Gabriel. It really is Father Christmas. *I'm* going to believe in the magic anyway. You can do what you want.'

'Yeah, all right,' Leslie grinned back good-naturedly. ''Ere, Father Christmas, shall I go up on the roof and give Rudolph a carrot for yer?'

'Ho, ho, yes please, young man,' Father Christmas answered with a cheery wave, and Leslie grabbed Cyril and dragged him outside.

Meg shook her head with a chuckle, and glanced across at Ralph who was lounging by the door, laughing, as the twins pushed past him. He winked back at her, and a delicious little knot tightened inside her. He was so handsome in her eyes, so kind and strong and understanding. Oh, she was so lucky to have his love. He had even insisted on going with her two days previously on the long, long walk back to her home village to visit her parents' graves, even if it had been bitterly cold.

It had also meant he'd had to work extra hard on their return to bring in all the vegetables that were needed to feed so many mouths with as close to normal seasonal fayre as possible. Everyone, it seemed, had been striving to make Christmas as happy a time as possible for those who were spending it at Robin Hill House, away from their homes and loved ones.

'Somehow it still hasn't been the same this year, though, has it?' Meg said later that evening when all the festivities were over and the children had all gone to bed. 'Even though everyone's worked so hard to make everything jolly and happy. I suppose it's the uncertainty. The worry about what's to come.'

She and Ralph were wandering, arm in arm, around the lake, Ralph shining the slit of light from the masked torch onto the ground so that they could just about see their way. The dogs were racing about, sniffing and generally enjoying their last walk before bedtime.

'Hmm, it hardly would be the same with Penny determined we were all going to have a proper East End party!' Ralph grunted. 'And it doesn't take much to get the twins going, as well.' Ralph's tone nevertheless held much amusement at the fresh memory of all the children playing Blind Man's Buff and Simon Says in the servants' hall. 'What a racket they were all making!'

'It was good, though, to have the house full of fun and laughter. Especially for the children being away from their parents. I know those who could came to visit last weekend instead. And at last, Penny's husband managed to get some time off from his shifts on the railway to come and

visit his family. A nice chap, but as skinny as Penny's fat!'

'Yes,' Ralph chuckled. 'Look a bit like Laurel and Hardy together.'

'Mmm.' Meg couldn't suppress a laugh. 'Everyone had a good time, but it can't have been the same.'

'The twins' mum and dad were noticeable by their absence,' Ralph scoffed. 'Never been back, have they, since that first time?'

'I'm glad they haven't, to be honest. Hard on the boys, though. And who knows what might have happened to their dad by next Christmas. To any of us, for that matter.'

'Hmm.' It seemed to Meg that Ralph paused thoughtfully before he went on, 'We need to concentrate on the good things. The village children's party, for instance. I hear it was absolute bedlam with all the evacuees as well.'

'Yes, it was,' Meg confirmed. 'As patron of the village committee, Mrs C said that next year, they might have to organise two parties. Mind you, I think she should put Penny in charge of all the games. I mean, today she insisted, didn't she, that we were all going to have a proper knees-up once the younger ones were asleep? She's worse than Mrs Sofia would've been! And you know how much she likes a party!'

'Especially when she's had a few too many,' Ralph commented with wry fondness, picturing Mr W's glamorous sister-in-law whisking around the house in her film-star manner. 'So maybe it was a blessing in disguise that Mr Perry cancelled at the last minute. And for the second year running.'

'Well, last year they all went down with 'flu, so you can't blame them for that. And this year, they were invited to some bohemian do somewhere, something to do with art that Mr Perry felt he shouldn't miss. And art is his livelihood, after all. Pity, though. I like them both, and I'd have liked to see the boys again, too, even if they are a bit of a handful.'

'Yes, they're good lads at heart. Just never been disciplined. Expect they've both calmed down since they've been at that boarding school, mind. And they're what? Fourteen and sixteen now?'

'I guess so. And I'm sure they'll all come to visit next year sometime. And at least Ada was pleased that she didn't have to bother with all that blooming vegetarian cooking, as she put it!'

Meg stifled a giggle and then leant into Ralph more closely. It had turned bitterly cold the last day or two, as if winter was about to start with a vengeance. Today had been a lovely interlude, the calm before the storm in more ways than one. And now that dreadful fear nobody dared speak of was niggling at the back of Meg's mind again.

'That wasn't really what I meant, though, about things not being the same. I know we did everything we normally do. Brought the Christmas tree indoors and put the same decorations on it so that it looked just as magical as always. And we brought in heaps of greenery to decorate everywhere and make garlands. We were even able to have more or less the same food—'

'That's going to change, though, with German U-boats already starting to attack our merchant ships. It's no wonder petrol was the first thing to go on ration. I wonder what'll be next,' Ralph put in grimly.

'I know. That's it, isn't it? It's there all the time, no matter what.'

'Yes. And what with Vic having been called up early, and now Bob's gone, as well.' Ralph sucked in his lips. He still hadn't been able to say what had been on his mind during the festivities. But he had to. And this was just the right moment. 'Meg, you know when we all had to fill in those forms,' he said quietly, 'I told you I'd put down to join the RAF? Well, I got a letter yesterday. I didn't tell you because I didn't want to spoil your Christmas. But I've got to go and see them in a couple of weeks.'

Meg felt a cold iciness take hold of her. She knew it had to come. But so soon? Her feet continued to move mechanically, placing themselves in front of one another. She couldn't stop them. But her heart cramped so viciously that it caused her physical pain. She couldn't look at Ralph, couldn't speak, the inevitable ripping at her throat as she remembered another Christmas night when they'd stared up at the moon and Ralph had told her that he'd always dreamt of flying. Back then, it'd seemed a fantasy, but now…

'Anyway, I can't leave you, not knowing… if I don't come back, not having known what it was like to love you. To love you properly, if you know what I mean. So, my darling,' he said, his voice ragged as he dropped down on one knee, 'will you do me the honour of becoming my wife?'

This time, Meg halted in her tracks. In another place, another time, she'd have shrieked with joy. But now a river of sorrow, of fear and sadness, streamed through her. Ralph wanted to marry her because he loved her.

Because once he was called up, he might not come back.

Meg's head spun, her heart torn with indescribable joy and agonising fear. All she knew was that she loved Ralph beyond anything else in her life. And that the thought of losing him was unbearable.

'Yes, I will,' she barely whispered in reply.

It was Ralph who let out a cry of delight, picking Meg up and twirling her round so that she became disorientated in the darkness. His happiness, though, was infectious, and she found herself laughing back.

'We'll go and see the vicar tomorrow,' Ralph announced breathlessly. 'And I suppose I should ask Mr W's permission. That's what you used to do when you were in service, or is that too old-fashioned?'

'Remember I'm not actually *in* service,' Meg reminded him, 'so you don't need to ask anyone.'

'Well, in that case, I might just ravish you on the spot and have done with it!'

He went to pull her to him, but Meg squealed with laughter and slipped away, running up the rough grass to the tended lawn. Ralph nearly caught her, but she dodged around one of the urns by the steps before escaping again. He snatched her arm as they rounded the corner of the house, the dogs barking furiously at this great game. She yielded to him, then, out of breath, laughing, euphoria overtaking her at last as he crushed her in his strong embrace, his lips coming down, soft and sweet, on hers.

'Oh, that's tremendous news!'
They had told Ralph's parents first thing on Boxing Day morning. As expected, Gabriel and Mary had been delighted. Mary had mysteriously disappeared, returning a few minutes later with a tiny box that she held out to them.
'This was your granny's,' she said wistfully. 'I don't know if you remember it, Ralph. You were only a small boy at the time. But when she was dying, she said maybe, one day when you'd found the girl of your dreams, you might like to give it to her. Now, you might not like it, and if you don't, I'll fully understand. But if you'd like it for Meg, it's yours.'
    Meg caught Ralph's gaze. He was clearly as taken aback as she was.
'Go on, open it,' Mary urged. 'We couldn't have been happier with your choice of wife, and I'm sure my mum would've been, too.'
Meg held her breath as Ralph opened the little box, and then snatched in a little gasp. The ring held a tiny, single diamond in a silver setting. It might not quite match up to something Mrs C might have worn, but to Meg it was perfect and more beautiful than anything she could ever have dreamt of.
    Mary saw the awe on both their faces. 'Slip it on and see if it fits.'
Meg could feel Ralph's hand trembling as he took the ring and eased it onto her finger. A shiver tingled through her. *Mum, Dad, I'm engaged to the most wonderful man.*
      'Go on, kiss her, then. Ho, ho, ho!' Gabriel laughed. And Ralph obliged.
Ten minutes later, Ralph and Meg had asked to have a word with Mr W and Mrs C after breakfast. They knew that Mr W would be going back up to the factory that evening ready for the early shift the following morning, so they wanted to make the announcement while he was still there.
Clarrie jumped up out of her chair with pure joy swirling in her breast. It was what she had hoped for. Prayed for. There was nothing she could do to secure their future. To make sure Ralph was still alive at the end of the war, whenever that might be. But she'd known Ralph man and boy, and she felt she knew Meg well enough to know that the two were crazy about each other, despite their rocky introduction. And Clarrie was determined to make sure that whatever time they had together was going to be just perfect.
She simply couldn't contain her excitement. Her Meg getting married. And to Ralph, who was such a good young man. Throwing propriety to the wind, she stepped forward to hug Meg tightly, relishing those few seconds, holding her, loving her as if she were her own flesh and blood. She even gave Ralph a quick hug, since her happiness for them both knew no bounds.
    'Well, congratulations!'
Wig was pumping Ralph's hand, and when he turned to Meg, he also bent to brush a kiss against her cheek. The girl's face was radiant, and he was thrilled for her. She deserved such happiness, and it occurred to him in that moment how cherished she had become to him, too.

'Thank you, Mr W,' she beamed back. 'And we want to get married as soon as possible. Before Ralph gets called up.' A shadow dimmed her expression, but in a trice, she'd driven it aside. 'And so I was wondering if you'd be kind enough to give me away.'

She watched as Mr W looked a trifle taken aback. But then he replied with a broad grin. 'Nothing would give me greater pleasure. I should be honoured. Thank you for asking me.' Honoured? No, it was more than that. He was so proud that she wanted him to perform this act that should have been her father's role. As if she was almost looking upon him as a second father. And the warmth that spread up inside him took him by joyous surprise.

'Oh, this is so exciting!' Clarrie broke out afresh. 'Oh, Nana May!' she cried as the old lady came into the room. 'We've just had some wonderful news! Ralph and Meg… Oh, but I should let them tell you themselves.'

A few seconds later, there followed another round of congratulations, with Nana May grinning from ear to ear, her face creasing into deep lines. As for Meg, she was smiling so much that her facial muscles were beginning to ache.

'Have you told anyone else yet?' Nana May asked when everyone had caught their breath.

'Just Mum and Dad,' Ralph answered.

'Well, I'm sure they're as thrilled as we are,' Clarrie declared. 'Now I expect you want to go and tell everyone else. So, off you go. Oh, there's going to be such a lot to think about! A wedding in the… house!' She'd nearly said family, but stopped herself at the last moment. To cover up, she ushered them out of the door and then turned back to Wig and Nana May, her face on fire with elation. This must be one of the happiest days of her life. For it also meant that Meg, her Meg, was likely to stay at Robin Hill House for ever!

Ten

1940

'Well, a Happy New Year to you both!' Clarrie beamed, inviting the happy couple into her sitting room on Monday 1st January. 'And a very exciting one it'll be for you two, too! Now do sit down,' she said, waving her hand towards the settee. 'Well, we've been thinking,' she went on once they were settled. 'Wig's gone back to work, of course, but we discussed it over the weekend. Now that awful Mrs Durr has gone back to London, you can have the chauffeur's cottage when you're married. Not that I wish the woman and her children any harm, of course, but they made every effort *not to* fit in. I phoned Mrs Jenkins this morning and fortunately she hasn't had any more requests to accommodate evacuee families. It seems that with no bombs falling, many are returning to London rather than the other way round. So, what do you think?'

Meg felt a little tightening in her chest and her heart began to race. Oh. It was so kind of Mrs C, but… She glanced sideways at Ralph, her eyes widening. He'd understand, wouldn't he?

'That's most generous, Mrs C,' he said cautiously, and Meg felt so grateful to him for speaking for her. 'But we rather thought that, with Bob gone, Meg could just share my room in the attic. We don't want to make any fuss. And, well…'

The smile on Clarrie's face changed into one of sympathy. 'Yes, I do understand. It was where that abominable Nathaniel Green lived. But it was over three years ago now, and it is a pretty little cottage. We'd give you complete carte blanche to redecorate it exactly as you wish, and while such things are available, Wig and I will buy you a brand new bed as part of our wedding present. We couldn't expect you to sleep in the same one that creature did. Anyway, think about it. The cottage is there and it's not being used for anything else.'

Meg's pulse had calmed down and now she found her voice again. 'That really is terribly good of you, Mrs C, and I hope you don't think me ungrateful, but I'm really not sure.'

'Well, as I say, you think about it. And you can change your mind at any time. It's just standing there empty. But now I need to speak to you about something privately, Meg. Oh, don't worry. It's just that traditionally it's something the groom shouldn't know about. And we've only got five weeks, so I understand.'

Mrs C beamed at them, and Ralph gave that little laugh Meg loved so much. 'Ah, ha, I know when I'm not wanted!' he joked, and then left the room, throwing a wink at his fiancée as he went.

As soon as he'd closed the door, Clarrie took Meg's hands in hers. 'Oh, I'm so happy for you, my dear! Now, do tell me what plans you have. I understand Jane and our three young guests are going to be your bridesmaids?'

'Yes. You know Jane and I have been particularly close, and we went through so much together. But I thought it would be nice to have the girls as well.'

'Well, I think that's an excellent choice. And have you thought about outfits? And what about a dress for yourself?'

Meg bunched her lips thoughtfully. 'Well, I was just going to run something up on the sewing machine. Something sensible that could be used afterwards. I'd planned on going into Tunbridge Wells to get some material on Wednesday. Needs to be something warm at this time of year, of course.'

'Well, would you allow me to pay my dressmaker to do the bridesmaids' dresses? I'm sure she could do with the business, and you never know how things might go for her as the war progresses. And you could choose whatever you wanted.'

'Oh.' Meg was taken aback. 'I can't accept—'

'Of course you can!' The smile that lit Clarrie's face shone like the sun. 'Oh, my dear Meg, you can't know what joy this is to me. Never having a child of my own to see married, this is the next best thing. And, then, for yourself… Of course, you might not like the idea, or might not like the actual dress, but you would be more than welcome to borrow mine. It might need taking in at the waist a little, but we're of similar height.'

Meg blinked at her. So much to take in at one go. But then if she and Ralph wanted to be married quickly, they would need to get on with things. She had to admit that she had wondered quite where she'd find time to make all the outfits. And she'd seen Mrs C's wedding dress in a photo on the sideboard, and it was beautiful.

'Oh, Mrs C, this really is kind of you.'

'That settles it, then.' Mrs C's face split in a grin. 'I'll telephone my dressmaker and make an appointment for us all to go and see her on Wednesday. We can make a day of it. And if you'd like to have a look at my dress and try it on, and then you can decide whether or not you'd like it. And there's no time like the present. So, shall we?'

Meg felt as if she'd been swept up in a whirlwind as Mrs C linked her arm through hers and walked her along the corridor and up the main stairs. Meg had been in the master bedroom often enough, especially when she'd first come to Robin Hill House and Nana May had been training her up as a lady's maid. The time for such luxuries had long since passed, but Meg was still trusted to enter the room on an errand. She'd never rooted about in the wardrobes and cupboards, mind, and so was surprised when Mrs C asked her to help lift down a large box from the top shelf of one of the wardrobes. Meg held her breath as they put it on the bed and Mrs C opened it with a reverence on her face.

'Now, I won't be offended if you say no,' Mrs C was smiling as she unfolded some sheets of tissue paper and then lifted the dress out by its shoulders. 'There. What do you think?' she asked, shaking it out.

Meg's hands went involuntarily over her mouth. The garment was breathtaking, and hadn't faded in all the years it had been stored. It was perhaps a little old-fashioned now, high-necked and pinched in at the waist, with a slight bustle and a train that would sweep the floor. But that in itself was its charm.

'Oh, Mrs C,' she breathed.

'Well, you can't really tell without seeing it on. Pop into the dressing room. It buttons down the back, though, so I'll have to do those for you.'

'Oh, Mrs C, are you sure?'

'Of course! It would be nice if such a thing got worn twice in its life!'

Meg carried the gown with the utmost care into the dressing room. Even if she decided against it, what a pleasure it would be to try on such a beautiful thing. But as soon as she slipped her arms into it, she knew. It was utterly transforming. She'd never imagined she'd ever wear anything so elegant and expensive in her life!

She went back into the bedroom feeling like a queen.

'Oh, you look perfect!' Mrs C cried. 'But do you like it? Let me do it up so you can see properly.'

Meg watched in the mirror as Mrs C fastened the little pearl buttons at the back for her and the bodice tightened over her slender form, fitting her like a glove. Then Mrs C leant over her shoulder and together they studied her reflection. She saw the anticipation on Mrs C's face, and her own broke into a broad grin.

'Does that mean yes?' Mrs C asked.

'It most certainly does. I can't thank you enough!' Meg turned, and without a thought, laced her arms round Mrs C's neck in a hug. She knew she shouldn't have, but when she pulled back, Mrs C was smiling delightedly.

'No, it really is my pleasure,' the good lady beamed. 'And you know the old saying, something old, something new and so on. Well, this can be the something old *and* the something borrowed. And my, it doesn't need taking in at all. I must have been slimmer than I thought back then. Now, you stay there, and I'll see if I can find the veil. And I'm sure I had a white fur cape I used to wear when we went to society do's when we lived in London. Can't have our beautiful bride catching cold.'

Before Meg could stop her, Clarrie turned away and busied herself rummaging through all the cupboards. Her heart was as light as a butterfly's. She couldn't get any closer to this, her second daughter, than this, could she? Lending Meg her wedding dress? Fate had been so cruel to both of them, but it had also thrown them together to help each other heal, and Clarrie would treasure this moment of pure joy for ever.

*

Ralph turned the key in the lock and, pushing the door open, stood back so that Meg could enter the cottage first. She went in hesitantly. She'd been in there before, of course, particularly when trying to teach Mrs Durr how to use the range. But it was a different matter when she was deciding if she could live in it or not. She stepped over the threshold, and glanced back at Ralph for reassurance as he followed her inside.

As Mrs C had said, it was a delightful little building, similar to the one next door where Ralph's parents lived, but not exactly the same. Unlike Gabriel and Mary's cottage, this one had no hallway, but opened immediately into a front room with a cast-iron fireplace and tiled surround, and the kitchen was at the back with its infamous range. There was even a tiny bathroom leading off from the kitchen, plumbed in and with the hot water supplied by a back boiler in the range.

'I really don't know what that Mrs Durr had to complain about,' Ralph stated, shaking his head. 'She probably had an outside lav and a tin bath in London. And there's electric light,' he added, turning a switch on and off.

Meg's eyes scanned the rooms, sucking in her lips as she took in every detail. Under other circumstances, she would have loved the place. But as she climbed the stairs, her pulse accelerated. She opened the door to the back room first, where the two little beds for Mrs Durr's children were covered with dust sheets. And then, girding up her courage, she pushed the door to the front bedroom. But she had to take a hold on herself to step inside.

It was a lovely room with another pretty fireplace and a sloping roof. But there was the bed where that monster had slept… Meg quickly paced across the room to the leaded window and pretended to gaze across the orchard and up to the big house in an effort to conceal the tears that had suddenly pooled in her eyes. But Ralph knew her too well, and came up behind to wrap his arms about her.

'It was a long time ago now,' he murmured into her hair. 'And that devil and Esme Carter are both behind bars where they belong. But if you let them stop you from having this lovely little cottage as a home, then, don't you see? They've won. You're stronger than that, Meg. Much stronger. And us, you and me, we're far more important. Being together, wherever we can for as long as we can, that's all that counts.'

Meg had found herself drawing on every word that Ralph was uttering. It was hard. But, yes, he was right. She shouldn't let the past spoil whatever time they might have together. Slowly, she turned round in his arms and lifted her face to receive his kiss. When they finally parted, the moisture in her eyes was draining away.

The blackout blind was propped next to the window, and she glanced down at it.

'I could make some green gingham curtains for these windows,' she said quietly, 'and a matching bedspread. And maybe red ones for downstairs.'

'We could paint these walls a pale green, too,' Ralph chipped in. 'You know Mrs C said we could redecorate it if we wanted. I'm not sure about red walls downstairs, though.'

'No,' Meg answered, ready to chuckle now. 'Maybe cream or a light grey.'

'And we'd have to hang some of your own pictures on the walls. Make it really homely.'

As she gazed at this good man she loved so much, Meg's excitement was growing. Their own little home. Better than just an attic room in the male servants' quarters. Their own proper space to live as man and wife.

'Shall we… shall we tell Mrs C yes, then?' she asked, almost afraid of her own words.
'I think so, yes,' Ralph replied, his tone solemn and yet buoyant at the same time. 'Mind you, I'd live in a cave as long as it was with you.'
'A cave, Mr Hillier? Well, I'm not so sure about that!' she teased. 'Compared to a cave, I think this will do very nicely indeed, thank you very much!'

*

'And how are we supposed ter make you two a proper wedding cake with this rationing lark starting today? And having ter register wiv just one grocer *for the duration*?' Penny grumbled a week later. 'A mouthful of bacon, four ounces of butter and twelve of sugar a week. How's a body supposed to survived on that?'
Meg had to stifle a giggle as she passed through the kitchen. There was only one grocer in the village anyway, and Meg was sure she never consumed anything like that amount of sugar, at least! Everyone adored Penny, but losing a bit of weight might not be a bad idea for her, and her chubby offspring. So rationing might have its benefits for some people. And Meg chuckled at the way the woman had said 'we', when it was Ada who'd be baking the cake.
Ada must have heard her thoughts. 'Well, we've still got plenty of butter in the fridge,' she informed Penny, 'so I propose putting the fruit into soak today and making the cake tomorrow. And I could always use a bit of margarine if I had to. Oh, Meg, there you are. I think we'd better only make your wedding cake two tiers, though, if that's all right.'
'Oh, Ada,' Meg beamed back, since under Penny's influence, they were all on first name terms now. 'I'm sure that'd be lovely! But I reckon just one tier will be enough for us all to have a slice.'
'Ain't you got no one else ter invite, then?' Penny asked sympathetically. 'No aunts or uncles or cousins or nuffing?'
Meg shook her head. 'No, I haven't. Ralph has an old uncle in the Midlands, but he can't travel. Mrs C has said I can invite Mr and Mrs Fenshaw, the people who took over my old home, if they can leave the farm for the day. They're really nice. But other than that, *you're* all the friends and family I need.'
'And Gaud bless you, my dear, for making us feel so welcome.'
Meg held her breath as Penny stepped forward. She knew she was in for one of the woman's bear hugs, and to be honest, Penny seemed to fill the whole house with her capacity for expressing her love for everyone.
When she managed to extricate herself, Meg made her way up to the attic and the eaves cupboard where Nana May had helped her store the various items she'd brought from the farm three years earlier. She hadn't been able to transport much, but she hadn't looked at what she had in all that time. She knew by the weight which box contained her mother's best tea service, and also some everyday dinner plates, bowls and cups and saucers which nevertheless still held sentimental value for her. If her memory served her rightly, she'd packed a couple of tablecloths around the china to protect it. They'd need pressing before they could be used, but she wouldn't unpack them until she'd carried the box over to the cottage.

She and Ralph had spent all their spare time the previous week repainting the kitchen and black-leading the range that Mrs Durr had left in a state. Now as Meg carefully unpacked her mother's things, the old ache raked at her throat, but at the same time, she felt a certain pride that they were going to be used again in a happy home. She had to crush all her fears that it might not be for long. Since Ralph had gone off for his interview with the RAF.

Meg stowed the tea service safely in a cupboard, but the ordinary crockery that she'd need to hand, she stored in the dresser that they'd painted red and white to match the curtains she was making. She opened the drop-down door that served as extra work surface, and started to make a mental list of what she'd need to stock up on. The sugar ration might be generous now, but that could change. What would be next? Tea, maybe? Anything that had to be imported. But at least those two items would keep.

Oh, she was so happy! She was getting married in a month's time to a man she loved to distraction, she would be wearing a bridal gown she couldn't have imagined in her wildest dreams, and they would be having their reception at a beautiful country house. If only her parents had been there to witness her special day, but she was sure they'd be there in spirit.

Just then, she heard a little whine. When she looked down, Thimble was gazing up at her with pleading eyes, ball between her jaws. Meg had to laugh. Time for a game. And with a skip in her step, she made for the door.

*

The day they were married dawned crisp and sparkling. The entire household walked through the frost and lingering snow to the village church, but Wig drove Nana May, Ralph and his parents and Jane, and then made a return trip for Meg and Clarrie and the younger bridesmaids. A bit of a squeeze, but the Daimler was a big motorcar.

Wrapped in Mrs C's fur stole, Meg tried to contain her excitement. She couldn't wish to have a nicer person than Mrs C beside her. She knew that her parents would have been more than happy for her. She had a new family now. And a new home.

As she walked down the aisle on Wig's arm, the train of the gown swept the aisle of the church. A radiant smile spread across her face as the guests turned to greet her, among them Mr and Mrs Fenshaw who'd been chuffed to accept her invitation. And then her heart jumped with excitement as she saw Ralph's tall, straight back, his trimmed, wavy hair just touching on his collar. Beside him, his father was just a little stooped, so proud to step in as best man since Bob couldn't get leave. And Meg felt herself fill up with joy.

When Ralph turned to watch his bride come to pledge herself to him, the vision robbed him of his breath. She looked like a princess from a fairytale book, floating in a froth of silk and lace. Her red gold hair fell in a shining curtain about her shoulders, and when she glided to his side and lifted the veil, her face shone with a heavenly radiance that made his heart bounce with pride.

As for Meg, she was determined to block all thoughts of war from her head. This was her and Ralph's special day, and she wasn't going to let anything spoil it. He looked so handsome, a soft, adoring smile parting his lips, and his brown eyes gleaming. She'd never seen him in a suit before, but it did nothing to hide his broad shoulders and slender hips. Her parents would have approved wholeheartedly of her husband-to-be, she knew. If they were looking down, they would bestow their every blessing. And they would also have been pleased that the man giving her away had also won a place in her heart.

Clarrie sat in the front pew on the bride's side of the church, cradled in fathomless contentment. Nana May was seated next to her, their hands resting firmly together, both proudly sharing this day, and knowing but not needing to say what it meant to them. For Clarrie, this was Rosebud's special day, a day she never thought she'd see. As she gazed on the back of the bride, in her mind's eye was another face, rounder, the hair a more fiery red, the face of a child. For who knew how Rosebud would have changed as she grew?

After Wig had performed his duty at the altar steps and came to sit by her side, Clarrie glanced up at him, still so handsome even if his hair was threaded with silver. He was her life, and this was their daughter's wedding day.

Meg passed the day in a haze of euphoria that she would never forget. Back at Robin Hill House, the war was far from everyone's minds as they celebrated in style. They kept the traditional speeches short and sweet. After all, everyone knew what a joyous occasion it was, and with so many little ones struggling to sit still on their chairs, it wouldn't be fair to prolong the formalities.

After clearing away a sit-down dinner in the dining room, the men moved the furniture to one side and rolled back the carpet. Wig carried in his gramophone and played some dance music to get the party going. There was bottled beer for the men. The twins were allowed one bottle between them seeing as they wouldn't take no for an answer and insisted their parents had let them have the odd sip. Wig had provided champagne, sherry and brandy, and Gabriel had donated bottles of his home-made elderflower and gooseberry wine. Ada had made a gallon of lemonade for the children and anyone who didn't want alcohol.

During any lull in the proceedings, Penny stepped in with the *HokeyCokey* or led a conga all round the house, which the children adored. Penny's chins wobbled as she wept with joy and went round hugging everyone. Later on, the twins buzzed about importantly, fetching and carrying Ada's tasty fayre as afternoon tea was served, the three girls were behaving like little ladies, and all the little ones played in complete oblivion to the occasion. All in all, it was such a tremendously happy day and when it was time for the happy couple to retire to the little cottage, everyone wished them well, and Sally was thrilled when she caught Meg's bouquet.

'Come here, Mrs Hillier,' Ralph invited his new wife, his voice thick, after he'd carried her over the threshold.

'I'll have to get used to that *Mrs Hillier*,' Meg chuckled softly.

'And you'll have to get used to obeying me,' Ralph teased, 'as you've vowed before God to do so.'

'Oh, I don't think we'll take that *too* literally!' Meg giggled back, slightly tipsy.

'Well, if you won't come to me, I'll just have to come and get you!'

Ralph sprang across the small room and Meg squealed with nervous delight as he scooped her in his arms and carried her upstairs. He placed her on her feet in the bedroom, both laughing like children, but as Meg caught her breath, she saw Ralph's beloved face become still.

'Much as you look divine in that dress,' he said huskily, 'you'd look even better without it.'

Meg gulped. 'You'll have to help me. It fastens down the back.'

'I'd be delighted.'

Meg had already removed the veil during the glorious reception Wig and Clarrie had provided. Now, as she turned her back, she pulled her hair over one shoulder to make it easier for Ralph. As she felt his fingers fumbling with the buttons, his mouth nibbled at her neck with tiny kisses. Slowly she felt the tight bodice loosen. Ralph's hands slipped unexpectedly under the material, and she gasped with pleasure as he fondled her breasts. She leant back against him, her body tingling as shockwaves plunged down to that secret place between her thighs.

Ralph slipped the garment from her shoulders and it fell to the floor.

'I'd better…' she faltered.

But Ralph anticipated her thoughts and, picking up the dress, laid it carefully over the chair. Someone – Jane probably – had lit the fire, and Ralph removed the spark guard and threw on another log.

'Now then, Mrs Hillier,' he croaked almost inaudibly, and slowly and delectably, began to peel off her underwear.

Eleven

"Oh, my God, what do they expect us to live on?" Penny groaned one March morning after Ada Phillips announced that **another round of rationing** would begin that day. "First it was butter, sugar, and bacon — and now it's flaming meat! My poor Archie's thin as a rake already. He'll waste away on this! I thought it was *Hitler* trying to starve us, not our own government!"

Meg smiled patiently, used to Penny's dramatic outbursts. "The whole idea is to make things last, so everyone gets their fair share — and to keep shopping simpler than it was in the last war."

"I know, I know," Penny sighed. "But we'll all be nothing but skin and bone before this is over."

Meg had to hide her amusement. It was hard to imagine Penny, with her round figure and hearty appetite, ever looking thin — even if she went without food for a year.

"Meat's being rationed by price, not weight," Ada explained matter-of-factly. "You'll get one shilling and tenpence worth a week. If you buy cheaper cuts and cook them properly, they'll go a long way. And since we're pooling our rations here, none of us will go hungry. I'll see to that — I'm in charge of the kitchen."

"Thank heavens for that," Penny said gratefully. "You're a marvel, Ada. I've learned so much from you already. When this war's over, my Archie's going to think he's dining at the Ritz every night!"

Meg smiled again, amused. Before the war, Penny's family meals had consisted mostly of potatoes, sausages, and the occasional pot of jellied eels — typical fare for London's East End. But since moving to the country, she'd discovered vegetables, fresh eggs, and hearty stews, and her whole idea of food had changed. With her husband Archie working steadily on the railways, they weren't badly off — just inexperienced in cooking anything beyond the basics.

Once again, Meg felt grateful for her rural upbringing — growing their own vegetables, milking cows, gathering eggs, and using every part of a pig when one was slaughtered. Country people wasted nothing and knew how to make do.

At that moment, **Clarrie** came bustling into the kitchen with the three girls, laughing and carrying the day's collection of eggs. Meg noticed the lively expression on Mrs. C's face — how she had blossomed since the evacuees arrived. Before the war, Clarrie had never been the type to gather eggs herself, but now she seemed to take real pride in doing her part for the war effort.

Doris, too, had changed so much in the six months since coming to Robin Hill House. She still wouldn't go near the cows or pigs, but she had grown comfortable around the dogs and hens. Though she missed her parents terribly, their monthly visits helped ease her homesickness.

"Meat rationing starts today, Mrs. C," Ada reminded her kindly.

Clarrie nodded, setting the basket of eggs on the table, her voice brisk but cheerful. "Then we'll just have to be cleverer with what we have, won't we? Britain's beaten worse odds before — and we'll do it again."

'Yes, I know, Ada,' Mrs C replied. 'But I'm sure you'll still keep us all adequately fed. And we've plenty of other things to eat. Now then, girls, let's see how many eggs we need today, and whether there'll be any left to preserve.'

'We won't go short of eggs, though, will we, with the hens?' Joyce questioned. 'And they're not on ration.'

'Not yet,' Penny put in glumly. 'But they probably will be before we know it. So, best be prepared, eh, Ada?'

'Yes, but I'll need all of those eggs to make a birthday cake for young Ed. His mum and dad are coming down to celebrate with him at the weekend. Such a happy, chatty little soul. We're having a little party for him, aren't we, Mrs C? Mr Gabriel's making him a toy aeroplane, and I think everyone's making a present of some sort for him. Just like we did for you, Joyce, on your birthday. Mind you, I didn't make a cake for you. Not with your dad being a master baker and bringing one for you, anyway. And the pastry you two girls make is better than mine, too!' Ada grinned, dipping her head at the sisters who both blushed with pride.

All the while as she listened to the conversation, Meg had been thinking about how the new rationing would affect her and Ralph. In the month since they'd been married, she'd been cooking their own meals on the range in the cottage and so had taken charge of both their ration books. It had really made her feel as if they were man and wife, living an idyllic existence in the countryside. She looked after the animals, with Cyril's help now, and Ralph tended the vegetables in the kitchen garden and greenhouses, with the assistance of his father, Leslie and even the girls. Ralph was gradually digging up the lawned terrace as well, in response to the Dig for Victory campaign, and would soon be planting it up with vegetable seedlings. But in the evenings, he and Meg retreated into their own little home, settling down after their meal in front of the open firebox of the range with Thimble curled up at their feet, and finishing the day with a cup of Ovaltine or Cadbury's Bourn-Vita served in Meg's mother's best tea service.

Oh, if only it could go on like that forever. But it wouldn't. Ralph had learnt that he'd been accepted into the RAF. He'd passed his assessment with flying colours, and was going to train as a pilot.

When he'd told Meg, a rock had solidified in her chest where her heart should have been, and she'd had to fight against the pain. It was the knowing and the waiting that was killing her. Trying to force it to the back of her mind. But it was there, niggling all the time. Every minute of every day. The moment when she would have to say goodbye to him, possibly forever, was coming as surely as night followed day.

*

They stood by the bus stop in a cold April drizzle, Thimble sitting patiently beside them. It was as if they were strangers, not knowing what to say to each other, and yet exploding with a million things they wanted to say, a million words of love, but couldn't. Meg's brain was numbed, unable to put her torment into words.

'I-I just wish…' she tried to croak, but her throat closed up in agony.

'I know, my darling.' Ralph took her hands, his chestnut eyes boring into her own sapphire blue orbs. 'But I am only going on training. I probably won't even get off the ground before I come home again on leave.'

'Maybe. But it's going to come,' Meg forced her voice to utter in a whisper. 'The war's not going away. I'd hoped and prayed it would, but now Hitler's invaded Norway and Denmark, it's confirmed his intentions. This is just the beginning.'

She saw Ralph give a sharp, almost imperceptible nod of agreement. He was her rock, her one and only. She mustn't let herself even think about losing him.

A distant rumble made her heart clench. The bus. That would take Ralph away. Coming nearer. They only had a minute.

'Be careful, my love,' she murmured, her hands patting his chest, wanting to hold him, keep him safe.

'I will,' he promised, and taking her in his arms, enclosed her in his strength.

The engine became louder, she could sense the bus come to a halt beside them, and Ralph's embrace slackened so that he could deliver one last kiss.

'Be strong, my darling,' he whispered as he picked up his case and climbed aboard. And then he turned to wink at her over his shoulder. ''Bye, Mrs Hillier. I love you beyond the stars.'

Meg watched, her heart bleeding, as the bus's wheels began to turn. Ralph waved at her from his seat by the window, smiling, and then she couldn't see him anymore as the bus chugged around the bend at the far end of the village green, and was gone.

Meg stood for a moment, her soul empty, tears trickling down her cheeks. She brushed them away. Didn't want anyone she knew in the village to see her cry. And what Ralph had said was right. It would be some time before he was actually flying. But it would come. Hadn't that Winston Churchill said that the war would be fought in the skies? Something inside Meg froze solid.

'Come on, Thimble.'

Struggling to pull herself together, she tugged on the lead and the dog stood up and shook herself before they turned back down the lane. Meg was so glad she'd brought the collie with her. She was company on the lonely walk home. But when they were only partway along, Meg felt moisture misting her vision again, and she was suddenly helpless against the tears that welled in her eyes.

Dropping onto her haunches, she buried her face in the animal's thick fur and wept until her heart would break.

*

The gradual lifting of darkness crept beneath Meg's closed eyelids and she began to stir. Dawn was breaking, the birds starting their early morning chorus as if greeting the new day with joyous, tuneful song. It was early May, possibly Meg's favourite month of the year when the world was full of hope and renewed life.

The bed was warm and comfortable, and she stretched out a sleepy arm to touch Ralph's strong, toned body next to her. The space was cold and empty. He wasn't there. The familiar churning took hold of her yet again, that horrible sinking feeling settling deep down in her stomach as reality lurched back into place.

It was no good lying there, wishing it away, because she knew it wouldn't go. The best thing was to rise from the bed and get on with the day. The cows wouldn't mind being milked a little early if she got there before Cyril, and she could enjoy nature's tranquil peace before the rest of Robin Hill House awoke. She cared deeply for each and every one of the people with whom she shared her life, but sometimes she felt the need to be alone, and this was one of them.

As ever, Thimble was ready for her early morning adventure. As they headed outside, a bank of mist was rising over the lake, but the sky was a pale, clear canopy that promised a warm spring day. The dew was thick on the luscious blades of grass in the field the cows were currently grazing, and the animals plodded over at the sound of the clanking buckets, ready for their heavy udders to be emptied. Meg nevertheless tethered them to the fence as it meant they were less likely to knock over the bucket beneath them.

By the time she'd finished and carried the pails of milk up to the house, the servants' door had been unlocked and Meg was able to let herself inside. In the kitchen, Jane, Sally and Louise were already at work, the electric kettle starting to boil and the girls carrying through to the servants' hall everything that would be needed for breakfast: marmalade and the jams they'd made the previous autumn, packets of Cornflakes and Shredded Wheat, and everyone's morning ration of butter, cut into a tiny square by Ada the previous evening before she left for her little house in the village. Since Ralph had been called up for training, Meg had gone back to eating with the rest of the household, and so had handed her ration book back to Ada to be pooled with everyone else's.

'You must've been up early,' Jane greeted her, observing the buckets full of milk. 'Cyril won't be pleased. He likes helping with the milking.'

'I know. But it's a school day for him,' Meg reminded her, 'so there really isn't time anyway. But he can help me tonight instead. Can you give me a hand straining the milk?'

'In a minute. I can hear the baker's boy coming up the drive on his bicycle. I'll just get the bread from him, and then I'll give you a hand.'

Meg set everything up while she waited. She'd learnt it was best to get things done before Penny appeared with her brood. They were usually the first down, and Bella, who'd just mastered the new and exciting skill of walking, was apt to get under everyone's feet.

'There.' Jane came back in and dumped an armful of loaves on the kitchen table, her face set in a scowl.

'You don't seem your usual self this morning,' Meg quizzed her. 'Anything the matter?'

'Yes.' Jane's elfin face pouted. 'Eric's got his interview with the panel today.'

'Ah, yes, of course.' Meg cursed herself for forgetting. Despite being in a reserved occupation, Jane's policeman sweetheart wanted to join up and was going before the board. Meg knew exactly how the scullery maid felt. Now twenty-four, as a full-time gardener capable of producing a good crop of food, Ralph would have been exempt from being called up had he been but a year older. But Meg was sure that he, too, would have tried to enlist anyway.

'I just don't understand him,' Jane protested, starting to saw doorsteps from the first loaf.

'I'm sure he feels he wants to do his bit,' Meg tried to pacify her. 'But try and cheer up. It's a special day today, and you don't want to spoil it by being grumpy.'

Jane's eyes slowly opened wide as she remembered. 'Oh, golly, yes. Nana May's birthday. Crikey, can you imagine being eighty?'

'Not really, no. But if I ever live to be that age, I hope I'm as sprightly as she is!' Meg grinned, glad to have changed the subject. 'We have got the cake hidden, haven't we, in case she comes in here?'

'Morning all!' At that moment, Penny breezed in, carrying a protesting Bella while her two small sons raced through the kitchen towards the servants' hall to see what was on offer for breakfast. 'Did I 'ear you mention the birthday cake? Well, a darned funny thing it looks with cardboard instead of icing,' she grumbled.

'Need to save our sugar rations for other things,' Ada reminded her, arriving through the servants' entrance. 'Cake's sweet enough without proper icing. Well, what a lovely morning! It's on days like this that I really enjoy my walk into work. Hard to believe...' She broke off, shaking her head. She didn't need to finish the sentence. They all knew how it ended. *That we're at war.*

Meg, though, was determined to make the day special for dear Nana May. She'd bought her half a pound of her favourite pear drops in the tiny sweetshop-cum-newsagents in the village, since although sugar was rationed, as yet sweets weren't. Meg had also painted a beautiful, ethereal watercolour of the irises by the lake, one of Nana May's favourite spots. Mrs C had planned a birthday picnic down there for later in the afternoon, weather permitting, and it looked as if they were going to be in luck on that front.

Nana May thoroughly enjoyed her birthday, and when it was time for the picnic, Sally carried an upright kitchen chair down to the lake for her, since she found getting in and out of a deckchair too difficult these days. Meg had brought down a cushion to make it more comfortable for her. Clarrie had transported her own deckchair, as she saw no reason why she should be waited on now there was a war on. Everyone else had sat around either on one of the picnic rugs or on the grass that had dried out in the sunshine. They'd feasted on sandwiches filled with their own eggs and watercress, and the delicious fruit cake that had been made possible by pooling their butter and sugar rations, and adding in a little margarine to make up the fat weight. It didn't seem to matter that it was hidden beneath a hat of white cardboard as it was such a delicious treat. And all was washed down with copious cups of tea which wasn't yet on ration, and milk from the cows for the younger children. Little Bella was so exhausted, her little tummy bulging, that she'd fallen asleep on one of the rugs, and everybody was trying to keep their voices down so as not to disturb her. They all knew how she could bawl if she didn't have her afternoon nap!

'Why don't we all go and play a game of hide-and-seek,' Mrs C suggested in an animated whisper, 'then we won't wake her up.'

Within a trice, everyone had leapt up, even Penny moving more quickly than she would have done six months previously, Meg noted, since she had actually lost a little weight and was consequently far more active.

'I'll stay with you, Nana May,' Meg offered. 'We can't all desert you on your birthday!'

'Are you sure, my dear? I don't want to spoil your fun.'

'Oh, I think I've played enough games of hide-and-seek and tag and what have you recently to last me a lifetime!' Meg grinned, collapsing into the deckchair next to the old lady that Mrs C had just vacated. 'Besides, Mrs C looks as if she's having a whale of a time. I think she's really enjoying having so many children to take care of, don't you? She seems in her element.' She paused to watch Mrs C happily directing everyone towards the woods where they'd find plenty of hiding places, and was surprised when Nana May answered her so candidly.

'Poor Clarrie, she'd have loved to have had a family, so I suppose this has been the next best thing for her.'

'Yes, I suppose so.' Meg released a thoughtful sigh. 'She is so very good with children. I've thought that before, when I've watched her running the village children's party at Christmas. She doesn't just organise it, she really takes part.'

'She certainly does. And… and what about you, Meg dear?'

'Me?'

'Yes. Will you be wanting a family?'

Meg blinked at her, taken aback by the forthright question. But then, Nana May was probably the most directly spoken person she'd ever met, with the possible exception of Penny. 'I… well… I suppose so,' she murmured. 'Eventually. But all I really care about is that Ralph is still alive at the end of this war. And just now that seems a dreadfully long way off. I mean, things are going to get an awful lot worse. Hitler's going to try to invade us, too, isn't he?' She glanced sideways at the octogenarian who pursed her wrinkled lips in defiance.

'He's got to get to the coast at the other side of the Channel first. And he'll have the British Bulldog spirit to contend with. We'll fight him off, mark my words.'

'I hope so.' Meg's voice was suddenly tiny. 'But many will die doing so.
I-I just hope Ralph isn't one of them.'

She almost squealed the last few words, and had to brace herself against the tightening in her throat. The tears that stabbed the back of her eyes. It didn't seem right, sitting there in the sunshine, watching the still, calm waters of the lake when it could all dissipate into dust.

Dear Nana May, though, didn't offer her any ridiculous platitudes. Instead, she said in a quiet, steady tone that quivered with sincerity, 'You know, when I was young, I was always jealous of my friends who'd found someone to love. Were getting married. I never did, and I thought they were so lucky. But when the last war came along, I realised that I was the one who was lucky. Because I didn't have anyone like that to lose. Love is the greatest gift life has to offer. But it can also be the most cruel.'

Meg lowered her eyes, and clasping her hands against her chin, let her tears drip silently over them. How wise the old lady was. Oh, Ralph. Ralph. She felt a light pressure on her arm. And when she looked across, a knotted old hand was touching her sleeve.

Twelve

'Are you all right, Mrs C?' Meg frowned as she passed across the back of the hall. 'You look as if you've seen a ghost.'

Five minutes earlier, Meg had answered the telephone to Mr W who had asked to speak to his wife. Meg had found Mrs C and had left her to it, not imagining there was anything out of the ordinary. But now the good lady, having returned the receiver to its cradle, was standing rigid by the side table, her face as white as a sheet.

She stared at Meg for several seconds, and then her brow slowly wrinkled. 'Come into the drawing room, and we'll turn on the wireless,' she articulated in a small voice, and turned the corner into the wide corridor that led to the drawing room.

As Meg followed her, she could see that she was shaking, and Meg's heart began to pound. Mrs C, she had learnt over the years, could be very strong if she could see a practical way to face a problem, but she was also extremely sensitive to other people's suffering. Meg realised this must be one of those moments, and she wondered what on earth had happened.

Meg saw that Nana May, who was already sitting in the drawing room enjoying the May sunshine streaming through the open French doors, had also recognised that expression.

'Clarrie, dear, is anything the matter?'

Mrs C paused as she stepped towards the radio on the sideboard, and supported herself by leaning her hands on the back of one of the armchairs. 'Wig just rang,' she answered in little more than a whisper. 'It's all over London. Germany swooped into Holland and Belgium and Luxembourg overnight, and they're attacking French towns on the border. And the government's in uproar. They're calling for Chamberlain to resign. The Labour Party are refusing point blank to serve in a national government under him.'

'Oh, Lord.' Meg watched the old lady's face blanch. 'And who's going to take his place? We need someone really strong if things are going to get worse.'

'It'll be between Lord Halifax and Winston Churchill, won't it?' Meg put in, emerging from her own shock.

'Yes,' Mrs C gulped, regaining her own composure. 'Who knows how long France will hold out, and then it'll be Britain. We need someone with the mental strength of an ox to fight back, and Churchill's the only one who fits the bill. That's what Wig thinks, anyway, and he's had dealings with Churchill, as you know. So, let me turn on the wireless and see if there's any more news.'

Meg stood where she was, lips bunched, and glanced across at Nana May. The look on her face was unfathomable as she threw Meg a wan smile. Germany was on the move. Something was happening at last, all the months of agonised waiting at an end. But it was hardly a relief, for God knew what horrors would be in store for them all. And now the country appeared to be without a government or a leader.

A familiar numbness, one she'd felt too often, cramped Meg's muscles. Her thoughts flew across the miles to where Ralph had been training with the RAF. He'd promised to ring whenever he could, but ever since he'd left the previous month, Meg's soul had been in tatters. At long last, she'd found some true happiness again, only for it to be snatched away almost immediately. Her heart yearned for him, for his physical presence. She kept trying to tell herself that while he was in training, he was safe. But how safe was the future going to be for any of them? Reluctantly, mechanically, she forced herself to perch on a chair while Mrs C was clumsily tuning in the radio.

*

It wasn't until just before the nine o'clock news that evening that Neville Chamberlain broadcast to the nation. With the younger children and the three girls already in bed, the adults and the twins had been sitting on the terrace outside the open French doors to the drawing room, drinking in the warm still evening, and relishing the peace – while it lasted. Clarrie and Nana May had remained inside, glued to the wireless, and called everyone in when the speech was announced.
Mr Chamberlain said that he had resigned, and that Churchill was forming a new government. The hour had come when the country was to be put to the test. They were all to rally behind their new leader and, with unshakeable courage, work and fight until the wild beast that had sprung out of his lair was finally disarmed and overthrown.
It was the speech of a patriot. Afterwards, the residents of Robin Hill House sat in stunned silence, each lost in his or her own thoughts. It was beginning.

*

Clarrie was sitting in a deckchair on the terrace, enjoying the last peaceful moments of the June afternoon before she went inside to change for dinner. Just because there was a war on, she wasn't going to let her standards drop, even if she had to dress herself nowadays. She wasn't going to disturb Nana May who'd dozed off in the comfortable armchair that had been carried out from the drawing room for her. All was quiet for a few minutes as Penny had gone upstairs to change Bella's nappy, taking Johnny with her, while Joyce and Maureen were keeping an eye on Sammy and Ed while they played on the rough grass down towards the lake. With school over for the day, the twins were busy tending the lower terrace, three quarters of which they'd worked hard to turn into another huge vegetable plot. But for that, it was still impossible to believe that anything was any different. That the country was at war.
Clarrie released a deep, wistful sigh. Across the Channel, both the Dutch and Belgium armies had quickly fallen after the German invasion, leaving the British and French troops fatally exposed. The most extraordinary event had then taken place when flotillas of small boats manned by civilians of all ages had risked their lives to join the Royal Navy in rescuing the hundreds of thousands of soldiers trapped on beaches under constant bombardment from the Germans around a place called Dunkirk. Never had the British spirit been so united. On the final day of the evacuation, Churchill had made such a rousing speech that Clarrie had choked on her tears. *We shall never surrender* still echoed in everyone's head. And now, with Italy, too, having declared war on Britain and France, Churchill was apparently trying to prop France up, even though the Germans had already reached Paris. But it seemed to Clarrie a lost cause. And then what? Glancing at the four

dogs, Clarrie's heart saddened. She did still miss Patch, but that was nothing to what might be in store.

Just a few feet away, Meg was taking a well-earned break from her chores. Her closeness brought a contentment to Clarrie's soul. She could not have loved her more if she really had been her own daughter, although she would never let on to the young woman. It might be nearly four years since Meg's parents had died in that tragic accident, but Clarrie understood that she should never presume to take her mother's place in Meg's heart.

It hadn't been a school day for the junior children, but Doris was sitting in the deckchair next to Meg, her fiery red curls bent over a letter that hadn't arrived for her until the second post. It was from London, so was probably from one of her parents. The child reminded Clarrie more physically of little Rosebud, but it was still Meg who felt like her daughter come back to her.

Suddenly, Doris gave a sharp gasp, and her hand went over her mouth, eyes wide and staring at the thin paper that had fallen into her lap. Clarrie at once sat up straight, but Meg was nearer and put a hand on the younger girl's shoulder.

'Anything the matter?' Meg asked gently.

'It's from Daddy,' Doris hiccupped, and when she turned to Meg, her chin was wobbling. 'He's been called up. Into the navy like he wanted. But it's immediate and he won't have time to come here to say goodbye. And he and Mummy were going to come for my birthday next week.'

'Oh, Doris.' Meg breathed a sigh of sympathy, and kneeling down in front of the chair, wrapped the child in her embrace. 'I'm so sorry. But…

it's going to come to us all with the way things are going.'

'I know,' Doris sniffed. 'And now poor Mummy's all on her own.'

'Well, it could be like Ralph,' Meg tried to encourage her. 'That your dad'll have a long period of training and he'll be able to see you before he goes, well, wherever they send him. And maybe your mummy could come here? What d'you think, Mrs C? We could find a bed of sorts to squeeze into Doris's room, couldn't we? Or Joyce and Maureen could have the spare room in the cottage with me.'

But before Clarrie had a chance to answer, Doris shook her head. 'That'd be very kind, but Daddy's put in his letter that he's suggested that – well, not to come here, of course, but that she moves to the country. But she won't. She says she's not giving up our little house. And she's got herself a part-time job as a nippy in a Lyons Corner House. You know, one of those waitresses. She says she wants to be there for when Daddy comes home on leave. I'd rather she stays on here when she comes for my birthday. But she won't.'

'Well, you just enjoy having her here next week,' Meg encouraged her. 'And we'll be starting hay-making before too long. We might not be able to borrow the tractor this year, so we'll all have to pitch in to do it by hand. That can be lots of fun. I'm sure you'll love it, especially if the weather's good.'

Out of the corner of her eye, Clarrie watched as Doris's face brightened. Clarrie couldn't have cheered the child up any better herself. Just as she was thinking how proud she was of Meg, Penny came hurrying along the terrace, puffing and panting and her face red as she blundered up to them as fast as her fat legs would carry her.

'It's just been on the wireless!' she wheezed. 'France are signing a blooming armistice with Germany. And Gaud knows what'll happen next!'

Clarrie snatched in her breath, and gazed across at Meg and Doris whose faces also reflected their shock. They'd known it was coming, hadn't they? And yet there always had to be that hope. But now it had happened. France had fallen. And France was only just across the Channel.

Clarrie's heart began to thunder so violently in her chest that for a moment, she thought it might give out, and her vision wavered. She had to fight to pull herself together. She was mistress of the house, and must show leadership. Even now, Penny was looking at her as if demanding answers.

'Poor France,' she muttered, and then her voice lifted. 'But we have Churchill. Now let's go and see what Ada has cooked for us tonight. Nana May, time to wake up, dear,' she said, gently shaking the old lady's shoulder.

Meg rose to her feet, but lingered a moment on the terrace after the others had gone inside. She gazed up at the clear, cloudless sky. And said a little prayer.

For Ralph.

Thirteen

'Cor, what d'yer fink that's all about?'

Leslie and Cyril stopped in their tracks and their eager young faces turned towards the late July sky. They were supposed to be mowing what remained of the lawn, taking turns to push the mower and empty the grass cuttings into the wheelbarrow before trundling it down to the compost heap. But among the distant, wispy clouds, groups of small aircraft were gathering from all directions, and that was infinitely more interesting than lawn-mowing! The planes appeared to be aiming to converge over the south coast, resembling swarming gnats against the azure canopy of the sky.

'Them's been scrambled from all the airfields, I s'pect,' Cyril answered with a knowledgeable shrug. 'The Luftwaffe's probably started attacking again, and we've got ter fight 'em off. Don't yer pay any attention ter what's in the news?'

'Course I do. Calling 'em dog fights, ain't they?' Leslie retorted indignantly. 'Trying ter stop the Krauts bombing our airfields. Cor, d'yer fink we might be able to see 'em from here?'

'Dunno. Probably a bit too far away. Maybe we could ask if there's a pair of them bino-what-d'yer-call-'em thingies somewhere in the house.'

'Well, if there is, bags first go.'

'It was my idea.' 'Fight yer for it.'

The next instant, they were chasing each other around the lawn, arms outstretched like wings, making engine and machine-gun noises.

Meg came to a halt as she reached the top of the steps leading down from the terrace. She closed her eyes, taking a deep breath. In the last few days, so many young airmen on both sides had been shot down over the Channel or just inland. Ralph was still in training, but one day, it could be him up there. She shuddered as she looked down on the twins' game. Boys would be boys. But one day, they became men.

'Look who I've got here!' she called, forcing her thoughts to the back of her mind. And she stepped aside to let them see the young soldier balancing on crutches beside her.

'Bob!' the twins cried in unison and, forgetting all about asking for binoculars and pretending to be aeroplanes, they raced up to their old friend.

'Hey, you two! Don't knock me over! I'm only learning on these things.'

'Yes, you boys be careful!' Sally warned, though as she came up behind Bob, her ruddy face was split in a huge grin.

'We heard yer got hit. Cor, can we see the scar?'

'Still hidden under a dressing, I'm afraid. But when it's better, you can.'

'So when yer going back then?'

Meg saw that Bob shot Sally a wry glance. 'I'm not. My ankle was smashed up pretty bad. They say I'll probably be given a desk job instead.'

'Oh, right.' Leslie's exuberance wavered for just an instant before he piped up brightly with, 'Did it hurt lots?'

'Now you two get back to doing the lawn.' Meg took charge of the situation. 'Bob's tired after his journey, and needs some rest. He's staying for a couple of days so you'll have plenty of time to talk to him.'

'Spoilsport,' Leslie pouted, and then his face brightened as he pointed skyward. 'Looks like there's gonna be a huge dog fight over there.'

Bob shrugged his eyebrows warily. 'Let's hope we win, then.'

'Come back inside,' Meg urged, desperately trying to put aside all thoughts of the war. It seemed to be the only way she could cope, burying herself in what remained of her parlourmaid duties, together with caring for the animals and growing and storing their fodder. 'Mr W's going to open a bottle of something. While there's some left,' she finished with a grimace.

'It was good of him to drive me down from London,' Bob said as all three of them went in through the open French doors to the drawing room.

'Well, you couldn't have managed by train, and how would you have got here from the station? Lucky, though, that he had enough petrol ration left.'

Inside, all the adults had been invited to take a glass to celebrate Bob's return, even if he wasn't quite in one piece. But at least he wouldn't be going back, which delighted Sally, of course. She clearly couldn't bear to leave his side, fluttering around him and anticipating his every need.

'Sally's thrilled to bits you're back for good,' Meg mused when Sally eventually peeled herself away from Bob's side to start collecting up empty glasses.

'Yes, I know, even if I am going to be a bit of an old peg-leg for the rest of my life.' Bob smiled at Sally's back across the room. 'I'd been thinking that I might pop the question next time I came back on leave. And there on the beach, when I was trying to drag myself towards the water and praying I'd get picked up, all I could think of was Sally. So, I've made up my mind. I'm going to ask her later. When we get a private moment. You won't let on, will you?'

Meg felt a burst of happiness in her heart. It was always uplifting to have good news among so much gloom. 'No, of course not. Mum's the word,' she winked. 'But Sally's not the only one who's glad you're home safe and sound. Well, almost sound. We all are.'

'Not everyone was so lucky.' Bob's voice suddenly dropped to an agonised whisper, and Meg squeezed his hand.

'It must've been awful, trapped there on the beach,' she said with deep feeling. 'Of course, we didn't know you'd been involved or that you'd been injured until Sally got your letter from the hospital.'

'It was utter hell, Meg.' Bob's face had moved into solemn lines. 'Dunkirk. I'll die with that name on my lips. But I tell you, the bravery of all those men in their little boats who came to help. Just shows what people can do when they all pull together. But God knows how we're going to fight off this Hitler. He's got too far. Got almost the whole of Europe now. How's little us supposed to stand up to him?'

'I don't think he'd bargained on Churchill, mind. Rumour has it he's in negotiations with America for their support. And getting some. I reckon he could be pretty persuasive.'

'Huh, words don't win wars. And ask the people of the Channel Islands what they think of him.'

Meg nodded grimly. On the last day of June, the Nazis had invaded the Channel Islands and Churchill had decided not to take any action. 'Yes, that was a huge blow,' Meg sighed. 'But they say Churchill was devastated, only there was little he could do about it and his hands were tied. But people are really getting inspired by his speeches. *We shall fight them on the beaches, we shall fight them in the hills*, remember?'

'We might have to—'

'I don't think Churchill's giving up yet,' Wig assured him, catching the end of their conversation as he came over to join them. 'Not by a long chalk. As far as he's concerned, it's just the beginning, even if he has nothing to offer but blood, toil, tears and sweat. You know what he said in the same speech. *Victory at all costs*. I for one have confidence in him.'

'Well, I hope you're right,' Bob said glumly. 'You've met him in person, so you should be a better judge than us.'

'I have indeed,' Mr W agreed. 'He's the sort of man whose strength rubs off on others. If anyone can hold the country together, it's him. But changing the subject, can I have a word with you, Meg?' Mr W went on, taking Meg gently by the elbow. 'In private? Don't worry, it's not bad news.

Just something I need to tell you.'

'Oh. OK,' Meg frowned, allowing him to steer her out onto the terrace. 'What is it?'

Mr W looked uncharacteristically uncomfortable. 'I had a visitor at the factory last week.'

'A visitor?'

'Yes.' Wig studied her face before he continued, 'It was Esme Carter.'

Meg was at once shot through with the old hatred. The very thought of her made Meg explode. 'Esme! But I thought—'

'On remand for good behaviour.' Mr W's tone matched her own bitterness. 'But, with her criminal record, she hadn't been able to get work.

So she came to me, full of remorse and asking for a job.'

'What a cheek! Well, I hope you didn't give her one.'

'That's not like you, Meg. But I understand how you feel because I feel the same. So, I told her she could never be forgiven, but I'm afraid I did give her a job,' he concluded, somewhat abashed.

'What!' Meg's eyes flashed, but she saw Mr W's lips twitch at the corners.

'The worst one I could think of, and the least well paid. She now has the unenviable task of cleaning the toilets for nearly a thousand people, and working twelve hours a day for peanuts. She's going to wish she was back in prison.'

Meg put her hand over her mouth to stifle a giggle. 'There is justice in the world, then. Thank you, Mr W. But what about Green?'

'Still inside, as far as I know. He'll probably be released early as well, but I expect they'll put him straight in the army. So, if you're not too cross with me, shall we go back to this little celebration?'

Meg nodded briefly. She couldn't say anything, of course, but hopefully there'd be an engagement to celebrate as well later on. It did you good to have normal, happy events to enjoy when there was so much gloom in the world.

She followed Mr W back into the drawing room. And then she stood still with shock. Whilst they'd been outside, another visitor had arrived, a grin creeping across his face as he stretched out his arms. Meg hadn't recognised him for a second in his smart, grey-blue uniform, but now her heart soared as she flew across the room and into his arms. He lifted her off her feet and she clung to him, drawing everything about him, the feel of him, the smell of him, into her very soul.

'Oh, my darling,' Ralph murmured into her ear as he set her on her feet. But she was having none of it, and wrapped herself around him again, too emotional to speak.

'Ralph, my boy.' Wig and Clarrie coming over to welcome him meant that Meg had to let him go. 'It's good to see you. We had no idea—'

'Nor did I until last night, so I thought I'd surprise you.' He smiled down at Meg again and she exploded with joy. 'Where are Mum and Dad?'

'I've just sent Cyril over to fetch them. We've got Bob here for a few days as well, so we were just having a little drink. Now we can have a double celebration!'

Meg was swept up in euphoria as she hugged Ralph again, and then everyone was welcoming him home.

'I said to Meg earlier,' Bob grinned, balancing his crutches so that he could clap his friend on the shoulder. 'Congratulations on becoming an old married man! I was gutted I couldn't get home to be best man.'

'Oi, not so much of the *old*, if you don't mind!' Ralph laughed back. 'And you're here now. So maybe we can enjoy the next day or two together instead.'

'Tell you what,' Jane piped up, catching their conversation as she passed by with a tray of teacups. 'There's a hop on at the village hall tomorrow night. Just someone with a gramophone and some records. Not the band we have for the dance after the summer fête. That's not till next month. Eric and me are going, so why don't we all go?'

Ralph saw the look on Bob's face. Jane was always so well-meaning, but she didn't always think. 'I'm not sure that'd be such a good idea,' he muttered, using his eyes to indicate Bob's leg.

'Oh, that's all right,' Jane shrugged in her inimitable way. 'If we can't get a lift for Bob, Eric'll wheel him on his bicycle. And I know you can't dance, Bob, but wouldn't it be fun just to be there?'

There was a moment's silence as everyone exchanged glances. But then Bob declared with a broadening grin, 'D'you know, she's right! After weeks of hospital wards and what have you, it'd be great to let my hair down.'

'That's settled, then!'

'Ralph, son!' Gabriel and Mary hurried in through the French doors, and Ralph stepped across to greet his mum and dad with long hugs. Meg knew she shouldn't, but she felt jealous of every second Ralph spent speaking to his parents or anyone else, but she jumped across to his side and clung to his hand all the while as if they were glued together. And to think that morning, she'd had no idea what an amazing day it was going to turn out to be! And although it wasn't a surprise, she was utterly thrilled when some time later, hobbling back from a few minutes alone with Sally at the far end of the terrace, Bob announced their engagement, his face shining with pride.

'Any idea when the big day will be?' Meg asked, sharing Sally's excitement, when the rounds of congratulations had died down.

'Well, as soon as possible,' Bob answered, still grinning. 'They're sending me on to a convalescence home for a few weeks, and then we'll arrange the wedding. Mrs C has offered for us to have it here, which is so kind of her.'

'Oh, that'll be lovely!'

'Well, my family's in Tunbridge Wells,' Sally put in, 'so it makes sense. Only Bob's parents will need to travel down from Norfolk.'

'And by then, I should know where they'll be posting me.'

They chatted on about the plans for some time, and it wasn't until later that Meg and Ralph were able to extricate themselves from everyone else, and go for a stroll in the woods, with Thimble, as usual, prancing about their ankles. They didn't know, but when Wig had noticed them setting off, he'd given the twins, who were likely to be the main culprits, instructions not to follow them.

'I can't believe everything that's been done outside,' Ralph mused. 'I know you said in your letters, but it's different seeing it for myself. The kitchen garden and greenhouses are fuller than I've ever seen them, and I see someone's dug up most of the lawn and turned it into a vegetable patch as well.'

'Yes, we've done such a lot for the war effort since you've been away. The twins have been terrific, and they've been helping your dad, especially with the heavy work. And everyone helped me get in the hay from the front fields. We did it all by hand, and it was great fun. It's been such a good summer that I think we'll get a second cut later, too. And we're going to get a couple of extra pigs soon, now meat's on ration. Oh, but never mind all that. It's so good to have you back! I just hope I've got enough tea, with it being on ration now.'

Ralph gave a soft laugh, but then the glow faded from his face. 'I've only got a forty-eight-hour pass, so I'm only here until the morning after tomorrow, I'm afraid. And I've got something to tell you.' 'Oh.' Meg felt panic grip her chest.

'Don't worry, it's not bad. It's just that you know I was accepted to train as air crew rather than ground crew. Well, they've decided I don't have what it takes to be a fighter pilot. Too steady, whatever that means. But my strength seems to be in navigation, so my training from now on's going to be as navigator-cum-co-pilot. Probably as bomber crew on meticulously planned missions. It's a totally different ball game. But it means my training has to be extended for a while yet, and I'm going to be sent further away. So a forty-eight-hour leave won't be long enough to come and see you.'

'Oh, is that all?' Meg couldn't contain her relief. It was a temporary reprieve, at least. 'And if you know in advance, surely I can travel up to you.'

Ralph's forehead pleated. 'I'm not sure I fancy you travelling alone nowadays, Mrs Hillier. The trains are crammed full of soldiers, and they're not all true English gentlemen. And the railways are sitting targets for German bombers. They're the country's lifeblood, which is why people like Penny's husband are so important and almost in as much danger as people in the forces.'

'Yes, I realise that,' Meg sighed. 'But even if I can't see you, at least it means you'll be safe for a while longer, and by then, well, who knows?'

'The war won't be over,' Ralph told her gravely. 'But at least I'll be a lot better trained than some of the poor devils in these dog fights that are starting over the Channel. Some of them have only had about sixteen weeks' training, and last hardly any time before they're shot down. But our air power and our training are rapidly improving, and if we don't stop Hitler now, the next thing we know, he'll be invading us.'

'I don't think Mr Churchill's going to let that happen,' Meg smiled wryly. 'And we're all trying to carry on as much as possible as if everything's the same. You know, the village committee wondered about having the annual summer fête next month, but Mrs C insisted that it goes ahead. And all the profits raised are going to the Spitfire Fund, so she wants to make it even bigger and better. I've been doing some smaller paintings for the raffle, and a couple of bigger ones for an auction. People are giving all sorts of things.'

'Really? Well, that's good. Pulling together, just like Churchill wants. But I don't want to spend all my leave hearing about the village fête.' Ralph pulled up the cuff of his uniform jacket to consult his watch. 'I don't suppose you fancy an afternoon nap, do you?'

His grin was half bashful, half teasing. Meg pretended to slip from his grasp, but danced about him until she let him catch her hand again.

'Let's not run,' she gasped. 'If anyone sees us, they'll realise straight away what we're—'

'I don't care if they do. The sooner I get those clothes off you, the happier I'll be!'

He slapped her behind and she squealed with laughter as they ran towards the cottage. Thimble had just slipped inside with them before Ralph shut the door and snapped the Yale lock closed.

'Now, you, dog, can stay down here,' he said sternly, 'while your mistress and I go for a snooze.'

And then, eyes shining, he swept Meg into his arms and carried her, breathless with desire, up the stairs.

Fourteen

'Can anyone else hear that?'

It was late afternoon on Saturday 7th September. It had been such a lovely day that Clarrie and Nana May had decided they ought to make the most of the good weather while it lasted. Instead of tea, there was going to be a picnic outside. The summer had been glorious, and it seemed incongruous that the country was at war. But it most definitely was.

The six weeks or so since Ralph and Bob's visit had been fraught with activity in the skies over the Kent coast. Only a few days after Ralph's return to his training, on the night of the twenty-eighth of July, the distant, deep-throated rumble of heavy aircraft had woken

Meg from her sleep. She'd scarcely fought her way to consciousness when a couple of crashes way off shook the cottage, making the glass rattle in the windows.

Her heart jerked painfully, snapping her fully awake. She could instantly feel the pent-up energy coiled inside her and she leapt from the bed and drew back the curtains. A half-moon shone brightly, and searchlights probed the night sky while aircraft droned overhead. Shutting the curtains again, she grabbed her dressing gown and ran outside, pulling it on as she went. Thimble gambolled around her, eager for this unexpected adventure, tongue lolling out in anticipation.

In the darkness, Meg almost collided with Gabriel.

'You all right, girl?' he asked his daughter-in-law anxiously.

'Yes, but… the planes. And those explosions. But I didn't hear the air raid siren.'

'I did, but I was already awake,' Gabriel told her in his slow drawl. 'Don't sleep so well when you get to my age. But it wasn't our village siren I heard. It was in the distance.'

'You don't think we need to wake everyone and get down the shelters, do you?'

'No, not at the moment. I'm sure our own sirens will go off if need be. But maybe we should wait a while before we go back to bed, just in case.

D'you fancy a cuppa?'

'Oh, yes, please,' Meg answered gratefully. 'I don't think I'd go back to sleep just yet anyway.'

'Come on, then. The range is still quite warm, so if I open it up, it won't take long to make some Ovaltine. Young Ed's an avid Ovaltiney,' Gabriel

chuckled, 'so if Mary spots any, she has to buy it!'

'Thanks, that'd be lovely.'

Meg nodded. It wasn't always easy to get what you wanted in the shops, even if it was something that wasn't on ration. Thank goodness they produced so much of their own food at Robin Hill House. And Gabriel grew a wide range of herbs to make simple meals really tasty. Yet again, Meg reflected how lucky she was to be living where she was.

*

A thin slither of light was already peeping underneath the bedroom curtains before Meg finally drifted back to sleep. She didn't usually bother with the blackout blinds, because at that time of year, it was only dusk when she went to bed so she didn't need a light, and dawn had already broken by the time she got up again. Downstairs was a different matter, though, as she sometimes needed to turn on the light before she retired for the night, and the glowing coals from the range firebox as she banked it up could also pose a danger.

Her sleep for what remained of the night was uneasy and disturbed. She dreamt that a bomb had fallen on the main house, and that she was trying to rescue all her friends but her own legs refused to work. And then she had become Ralph, her head whirring as the plane she was piloting spun earthwards, out of control, smoke heavy with the stench of oil seeping into the cockpit, flames licking around the instrument panel…

She awoke with a start, pulse hammering. As she realised it was just a dream, she waited for her heart rhythm to return to normal before she dragged herself out of bed to start the day. But a tiny tremble persisted inside her.

Later that day, they learnt that a couple of bombs had fallen by the railway line near Edenbridge. It was the start of the war arriving right on their doorstep, making Meg wonder quite why Kent had been deemed a safe place to evacuate children to.

After that night, she decided to move back into the main house, feeling happier to share her old room with Jane rather than be alone in the cottage, even if her in-laws were right next door.

The dog fights became so widespread and intense that on several occasions, the village siren was sounded and they all had to dive down the shelters. They could hear the whining of the engines as the light fighter planes chased each other overhead, the rat-tat-tat of the guns. Thimble pushed herself against Meg in fear, and Meg took comfort in stroking her silky head. Thank God Ralph wasn't up there. Was still training. But he would be in just as much danger when his missions began.

The fight in the skies was being called the Battle of Britain. In midAugust, three separate days of attack had seen particularly bitter dog fights over all the south-east coast when, though many British planes were downed, enemy losses far outstripped those of the RAF. Churchill made a rousing speech in the House of Commons of which one line was widely reported: *Never in the field of human conflict was so much owed by so many to so few.* Over five hundred young British airmen had given their lives in June and July alone, but Fighter Command was beating back Hitler's attempts to destroy Britain's airfields in preparation for an invasion. But the German Fuhrer refused to accept defeat and the battle for the skies raged on. Churchill had nothing but admiration, gratitude and empathy for both Fighter and Bomber Command. But all Meg could think of was burning planes falling from the sky, engulfed in greedy, scarlet flames while smoke streaked out behind in black demonic ribbons.

Because of the threat of downed aircraft falling on their heads, Sofia Stratfield-Whyte refused to bring her family to her brother-in-law's house for their usual summer visit.

'Perry and the boys think it'd be so exciting,' she moaned to Meg down the telephone line. 'But just think if a Jerry plane came down in the grounds. It'd be hideous. I had enough to worry about in the last war with Perry making his sketches for the government at the Front. Oh, no, we're staying put. It's so much safer here in Cornwall! I don't know why darling Clarrie and Nana don't come down to live with us. They'd be more than welcome.'

'Well, I'll go and get Mrs C so that you can speak to her yourself,' Meg answered. 'But I don't think she'll want to be so far away from Mr W. And she takes her responsibilities for looking after all our evacuees very seriously.'

Meg had been right, of course. But she was as disappointed as Wig and Clarrie that Perry, Sofia and the boys wouldn't be coming. Mrs Sofia, with her extravagant, film-star gestures and sometimes outrageous behaviour, was always fun, and Meg would miss her boisterous sons and Mr Perry, too, in his loose-fitting, bohemian garb. She found it hard to imagine him out in France in the previous war, dodging enemy fire as he drew hasty sketches to turn into official war paintings on his return to Blighty. But then she could only ever see him as an artist, and never a soldier. Mind you, apart from those already in the regular army, none of the men out there were really soldiers. Even most of the enemy were just ordinary men who'd been ordered to go and fight. Oh, what a terrible thing war was.

Two events during that August lifted everyone's spirits, however. The first was the village fête which fortunately wasn't interrupted by any nearby dog fight.

'Cor, this is great!' the twins declared, scampering about the stalls like two puppies on their first walk and launching themselves into throwing balls at the coconut shy and plunging their hands deep into the tombola drum. Cyril won a large fluffy rabbit which he shyly gave to Doris who happened to be near him. Meg smiled wryly to herself. Although Doris still expressed her worries over both her parents, being among so many friends of her own age did seem to be helping her.

With bunting fluttering in the breeze, a small cordoned-off ring for the dog show, cutest baby competition and crowning of the village princess and a little brass band playing out of time as it attempted to march around the green, the London children had never seen anything like it. As organiser-inchief, Clarrie was delighted by its success – and the substantial sum that was raised for the Spitfire Fund, especially by the auction which was a new event and all her idea.

The other uplifting happening was Bob and Sally's wedding on the last day of the month. More than anything, Meg's soul flew to the moon when Ralph managed to wangle some extra leave so that he could take up the role of best man that Bob had been unable to perform for him. It was a wonderful day, a beacon of light in those dark times – even if it was now actually *illegal* to put icing on the outside of a cake. But deep inside everyone lingered that numbing, crushing fear that they all tried so hard not to let foam up to the surface.

'We're going to miss you,' Meg told Sally, giving her friend a meaningful hug. 'Are you sure you want to live in London? We're not that far so you'd still be able to see Bob, and after that air raid last week—'

'No, my place is by my husband's side,' Sally said wistfully, glancing across with adoring eyes at Bob who was smart in his uniform and off crutches now. 'Bob was really chuffed when he was posted to the War Office. Made him feel really useful again, and he'll have to do defensive training and exercises all the time, too. I'll take my chances with the bombs, and if that raid was anything to go by, it wasn't that bad. Besides, I've got my new job on the buses. I'm looking forward to that!' she grinned.

Now, a week later, as Meg was supervising the three older girls in spreading out some rugs on the grass for the picnic tea, she wondered how Sally was getting on. She was so willing and hardworking, a breath of fresh air after Esme Carter whom she'd replaced. With her outgoing nature, everyone had taken to Sally at once, and Meg couldn't imagine a jollier clippie on the London buses. But Meg couldn't help worrying about both Sally and Bob, as well as Mr W, of course, and at Leslie's words as they prepared for the picnic, their eyes all swivelled towards the sky. Meg titled her head to concentrate her hearing.

'Sounds like an air-raid siren, only really in the distance,' she frowned.

'Yeah, yer right, Meggy.' Leslie almost dropped the folding chair he was carrying. 'Must be a raid somewhere. But far enough away so they ain't set off the sirens here.'

'Well, we'd better be ready to go down the shelters if they do,' Nana May announced in an authoritative tone as she arrived beside them, going slowly with her walking stick. 'Are we all accounted for, and has everyone got their gas mask?'

'Bleeding hell!' Everyone gasped at Leslie's sudden cry. The boy knew such language wasn't tolerated at Robin Hill House. But as all eyes turned on him, they saw his jaw drop down below the binoculars he wore permanently round his neck and which he'd trained on the skies. 'There's bloody dozens of 'em!'

'Let me see.' Cyril snatched the binoculars from his brother's hands, nearly choking him. 'Blimey, yer right. Bombers. And they're… blooming heck, they're *German*.'

'What!'

A chorus of alarm ricocheted around the little group as Meg hurried to round everyone up, and every adult and child, including Gabriel, Mary and young Ed, gathered on the lawn. The picnic was forgotten as all eyes squinted in the direction Leslie had pointed in, and the binoculars were passed round in a frenzy.

'They must be coming straight up the Thames Estuary,' Nana May said, her wrinkled face pale. 'They're launching another direct attack on London!'

'Oh, my God, Wig's up there!' Clarrie all but squealed.

'Don't worry, Clarrie dear. He'll have gone down a shelter somewhere.'

''S'all right! Here come our fighter boys to chase 'em off.'

'And the barrage balloons are coming up.'

'But look, they're still coming. This ain't gonna be like the one the other week, and that was bad enough. This is gonna be a full-scale attack.'

'Shut yer gob,' Penny hissed behind him. 'Can't yer see Mrs C's upset?'

Leslie's face dropped, but not for long. He didn't say a word, though, as through the binoculars they could see wave after wave of giant, threatening vultures droning towards London. White vapour trails criss-crossed the sky around them as Spitfires and Hurricanes engaged with the fighter planes escorting the bombers. The boom as the first bombs exploded was like a dull, distant thud, followed by another and another and another, endless, relentless.

'I don't fink we'd better have this picnic after all.' Unexpectedly it was
Penny who took charge. 'Just in case we have ter make a dash for it.' 'Ah-oh,' Leslie protested in disappointment.

'She's right,' Meg agreed, admiring Penny who was obviously keeping her fears for her own husband hidden. 'Bring everything back in. Just you boys can take your tea outside if you want. But you stay right here on the lawn, and if anything changes, you come straight in to tell us. OK?'

Leslie and Cyril nodded in unison while everyone else retreated indoors. Meg could tell that Penny was trying to keep up a constant conversation – not difficult for her – in order to distract everyone, and anyway the distant, thunderous explosions were less audible from inside. But Meg noticed that scarcely a morsel of food passed Mrs C's white, silent lips.

As darkness fell, the glare over London grew brighter as the East End dockland burned and a black pall of smoke drifted down over the Thames. And still they came, bright flashes cutting through the night sky like fireworks, the muted echo of bombs exploding every few seconds, the staccato rattle of the ack-ack guns. On such a still evening, the sounds travelled miles.

The atmosphere in the house was tense and eerily quiet as everyone tried to put a brave face on it. The twins, whose father they'd learnt in the rare scribbled note they received had not yet been called up, were quite exhilarated by the attack; in their youthful exuberance, not able to grasp the horror of its reality. Meg dispatched them up to their rooms to watch the horrifying spectacle from the windows. Doris huddled in a chair, arms laced about Topaz's neck for comfort as she prayed for her mum's safety, and Joyce and Maureen, doubtless thinking of their parents above their bakery, were trying to distract each other with a game of Snap, but breaking off each time there was an extra-loud explosion.

Penny's young children, oblivious to what was going on, were already asleep, but everyone else felt too unnerved to go to bed. However, it was decided everyone should try to get whatever shut-eye they could, while the adults would take turns to keep watch. *Just in case*, as Penny put it, but they all knew what she meant.

It was some hours later when Meg felt someone gently shaking her out of a restless twilight doze. 'Meg dear, it's your turn.'

It only took her a moment to scrape herself from the drifting haze that was the best she'd managed in the way of sleep. Her mother-in-law's familiar voice was strangely calming as she slid out of bed and put on her shoes. She hadn't bothered to undress. Indeed, it had been agreed that if they had to make a dash for the shelters, it would be better to remain fully clothed.

'Thanks, Mary. Is it still going on?' she whispered, trying not to wake Jane in the other bed.

'Two o'clock, and yes, it is.'

'Good God. All those poor people. Oh, well, I'll take over. You try and get some sleep now.'

'I will. And Gabriel's going to do the shift after you. You know we've kipped down in Bob and Ralph's old room?'

Meg nodded. Just as she had decided she felt safer in the main house after the bombs at Edenbridge, Gabriel and Mary had decided it was better to sleep there as well for that night, at least. Young Ed was tucked up in a makeshift bed on the floor, while the older couple had taken a proper bed each.

Meg tiptoed down the stairs with her mother-in-law to the middle floor. While Mary hurried along the connecting corridor to rejoin Gabriel and Ed up the other stairs on the far side, Meg followed more slowly past Nana May's room and then along the corner to the larger guest room where Penny was snoring loudly. The sound brought a smile to Meg's face. She wondered how it didn't wake the comely woman's children, but she supposed little ones would sleep through anything, which was a blessing nowadays. Then she put her head around the door to the other guest room where Doris had squeezed in with Joyce and Maureen as she didn't want to be alone. But thankfully all three girls appeared to be sleeping soundly.

It felt strange to Meg, wandering about the spacious house alone at night, with just a torch to see her way. Was the bombing raid to cover up the expected invasion? Was there a German soldier lurking in every shadow? Meg had to steel her nerves. It didn't help that Thimble was pressing against her legs, trembling. No doubt the young dog's hearing was ultrasensitive to the distant bangs.

Meg eventually followed up the stairs to the male servants' quarters. Once it had been forbidden territory, but with the twins sleeping up there alone now without Bob and Ralph, it had become more familiar. Mary had doubtless checked on the two boys as she went to try to get some sleep herself, but Meg thought she'd look in on them anyway. They must have been watching together from Leslie's room until they couldn't stay awake any longer, and she smiled as she found the brothers slumped down on the one bed, gangling arms and legs all over the place.

Meg knew the best view over London in the entire house was from the three male servants' bedrooms, and so she went into Cyril's room and walked over to the window. It wasn't necessary to strain her eyes. The livid orange glow in the far distance was like a shimmering golden curtain. It reminded Meg of the night they'd watched Crystal Palace burn to the ground nearly four years ago now, except that this was further east and a hundred times bigger. The whole of the East End of London must be on fire, all the dockyards and warehouses that helped feed the nation, the houses where the dockers and their families lived, the factories, the shops, the schools. Meg's blood ran cold. It must be a raging inferno. Collapsed, burning buildings. How could anything – or anyone survive? No wonder Mrs C had turned white, clamped up like a shell. There'd been no word from Mr W, no reassuring telephone call. But then, the telephone system would have been destroyed, too, wouldn't it? Meg wondered if poor Mrs C was getting any sleep at all.

The room was warm and stuffy, and Meg opened the window as she continued to stare towards the capital. She could still hear distant explosions. There must have been hundreds of bombers, unless the same ones were returning to their bases in occupied territory just across the Channel, reloading and then flying back with another deadly cargo. The monsters, they deserved…

Meg pulled herself up short. In that instant, she knew what Mr W had meant when she'd argued with him over the ethics of his factory. War was a terrible machine. You got sucked up into it whether you liked it or not. Mr W making bombs, Bob having fought in the army, Doris's dad in the navy now, and Ralph… destined to fly in lethal bombers himself.

Meg's vision blurred as she stared blindly at the flaring dazzle on the distant horizon. She had the most appalling sensation that this was just the beginning.

Fifteen

Meg's fears were proved right.

Wave after wave of German bombers roared up the Thames every night, week after week. Every evening, Meg prayed for rain or cloud cover to make an attack less likely. She scoffed whenever the moon shone brightly, her mind jumping back to the evening of Christmas Day a few years back when she and Ralph had stood in the snow down by the lake, gazing up at a waning moon. She had explained to him how her mother always used to say it was good luck to watch the moon when it was on the wane because it meant it had been sprinkling its lucky dust on the earth below. But now it hurt Meg so deeply to think that her dearest mother had been so utterly wrong.

The newspapers published photographs of each night's destruction, interiors now open to the elements, suspended staircases, doorways leading into nothingness. Tall, tottering walls that had once been the fronts of department stores, flats or warehouses, now with a vast emptiness behind them. Burnt-out buildings, their hearts exploded away, their metal girders a tangle of twisted limbs. People standing in stunned shock among the pile of rubble that had once been their home. Bloodied and crushed survivors being pulled miraculously from beneath tons of brick and masonry. Raging infernos being tackled by brave firemen directing pathetic-looking hoses onto towers of flame. And then, in the morning, the ghostly remnants of an alien planet.

Meg forced herself to blank out the agony of the civilians, innocent women and children, crushed, burnt alive, and wondered how there could possibly be anything left of London to bomb. And yet still the dragons came, breathing their clouds of flame and dropping their cargo of death. And as the weeks went by, the evil began spreading to other towns and cities, bringing terror to everyone in the land. And in return, the RAF had started bombing first military targets in Berlin and Essen, and then Cologne.

Where would it all end?

By some miracle, Wig's factory had escaped any damage, but unsurprisingly, fear had turned poor Clarrie into a fragile ghost. Meg, too, was worried about Mr W, although she tried to keep her concerns hidden for Mrs C's sake. Despite the reassurances she had heard Nana May giving Mrs

C on the evening of the first attack, Meg knew very well that Mr W was an ARP warden for his own factory. If an incendiary landed on the roof, he and his team had to put it out using a stirrup pump, before it could do any damage. So far, it had worked.

On the rare occasion Mr W managed to come home for a few hours, Meg couldn't help but see how strained he looked, his hair turning rapidly to grey. Mrs C, so thin she resembled a stick insect, would cling to him when it was time for him to leave, and Nana May had to drag her away. Meg appreciated how Mrs C felt. But at least the older woman saw her husband more often than Meg saw Ralph. For weeks, all she'd had were his letters to console her.

At Robin Hill House, they kept to the same routine as that first night, although they created a rota so that each adult was on duty every other night. Sometimes the attacks seemed worse or longer than others, sometimes the children slept, while at other times they lay awake, torn with concern over members of their families left in the capital. And now there was the added worry of Bob and Sally. Oh, how Meg wished the happy-golucky girl would come back, but she refused to abandon her new husband. 'You sort of get used to the raids. Hitler and his bombs won't scare me!' she'd laughed down the phone, but Meg was convinced it was all bravado. People were calling it the Blitz spirit, claiming defiantly that they'd show Hitler. But how could you do that if you were dead?

It was while she was roaming the house during one of her night-time vigils that Meg caught the sound of stifled sobbing coming from the main suite. Meg tiptoed up, holding her breath. The door was open just a crack. It had a habit of doing that. And because, on the other side, there was a short corridor passing the bathroom and dressing room, the occupants of the bedroom itself wouldn't realise the latch had slipped.

Meg pushed the door further open. Mrs C was weeping exhausted tears that cut Meg to the quick. So often had she done the same thing after her parents had died. Should she try to offer some comfort? She knew she wanted to. Mrs C had been so strong for her in the past, and for the evacuees in her charge, but lately she seemed to have crumbled. Not surprisingly, Meg considered, given the circumstances.

Meg padded silently along the passageway and popped her head around the corner. Mrs C was curled up on the bed in her dressing gown, crying like a baby. Meg felt her chest squeeze with compassion. She had to help. It was the only thing to do.

    'Mrs C, are you all right?' she whispered.

She crossed the carpet to the bed while Mrs C attempted to gather herself together. By the time Meg reached her, she'd sat up, but Meg could still hear her sniffing. She set the torch on the bedside table, but didn't want to blind Mrs C by turning on the light. Besides, even though they checked the blackout blinds nightly, there was always that fear. Who knew if a stray bomber returning from London might drop anything it had left on a glimmer in the blackened countryside? After all, those bombs had fallen on Edenbridge back in the summer, and that wasn't far away.

Mrs C turned her ghostly face to Meg, her eyes red-rimmed. 'Oh, Meg,' she croaked. She reached out, her features a macabre study of fear and misery. Meg responded as only one woman can to another, a moment when the joining of two souls in torment is the only way forward. Meg rocked Mrs C in her arms, tears trickling down her own cheeks.

The older woman's heaving shoulders gradually stilled and she drew back, gulping hard. She attempted a watery smile, and a trembling hand reached out to hook a stray strand of hair behind Meg's ear.

'Oh, my dear little Meggy,' she sighed distractedly. 'What a comfort you've always been to me. I'm just so afraid. I can't lose Wig as well.'

'I know, I know.' Meg rubbed Mrs C's arm, something she'd never have thought appropriate before. Being called little Meggy made a smile tug at her lips. She had recently turned twenty, was a married woman, and an inch taller than Mrs C. Hardly little any more. But what did Mrs C mean, she couldn't lose Wig *as well*?

Meg didn't have the chance to ponder further as Mrs C pulled herself together and said, 'I shouldn't be behaving like this when we've all got someone to worry about.'

'But sometimes it just gets too much, doesn't it? I know. That's why we women all have to stick together. And we should never be afraid to show how much we need each other.'

'Oh, how very wise you are, Meg.' Mrs C used the heel of her thumb to wipe away her tears. 'And here I am, when you've got Ralph to worry about.'

Meg's thoughts clouded. 'Yes. His training's over. That's why they've given him an extra-long leave so he can come home for a few days before he starts on missions.'

'It's Tuesday he's coming, isn't it?'

'Yes.'

'Well, we'll pool our rations and make a cake. Everyone'll have some, anyway.'

'Thank you, Mrs C.'

'And let's forget the formalities, shall we?' Mrs C took Meg's hands and smiled. 'If Mrs Phillips can become Ada, then I can be plain Clarrie. It's about time. We're a sisterhood now.'

Meg lifted her eyebrows. A sisterhood. Yes, she supposed they were. A sisterhood at war.

*

'Telephone for you, Meg!' Nana May winked, hurrying into the kitchen as quickly as she could since she used her stick all the time these days. 'Seems he can't wait until tomorrow.'

'Ralph?' Meg skated down the corridor with a whoop of joy and snatched up the receiver. 'Ralph! Oh, how wonderful! I can't wait until tomorrow, either!'

'Meg? Oh, my darling!' He sounded so far away. 'It's fantastic to hear your voice!'

'And you, too! What time d'you think you'll get here tomorrow?'

'Oh, Meg, I'm so very sorry. That's why I'm ringing. They've cancelled my leave. It seems my night navigational skills are exceptional and I've been drafted into something special. It's highly secret. I don't know any details yet, and I couldn't tell you if I did. But we're being taken off for briefing tonight.'

Meg felt her insides rupture. 'Oh, but—'

'I'm so sorry, Meg, darling, really I am. But there's one good thing. I won't be flying bombers. I won't be killing hundreds of innocent people.
My conscience will be clear.'

A spear twisted in Meg's side. She wondered if conscience mattered any more. She reared away from the terrible, shameful thought. 'Does... that mean it won't be dangerous?' she faltered, for perhaps there was some other good in it, too.

'Nothing's without its dangers, love. Let's just say, pray for some of that moon dust, eh? They've told us this is really important stuff.' 'Ralph—'

'What? Oh, I'm sorry, sweetheart. They say I've got to get off the line. I'll ring again the minute I can. I love you, my darling!'

'Ralph? Ralph!' Meg screamed down the phone as there was a dull click and the line went dead.

Slowly, her hand went down to replace the receiver, and then she stood stock-still, unable to move a muscle as her mind trawled back through the conversation. Ralph was going to be flying secret missions at night. That's what he'd meant, wasn't it? Not bombers or fighters, but something else. Something special. Was that why his training had seemed to go on for so long? He'd said before that he and a couple of others in his class had been creamed off for special instruction. Was that why?

She walked back to the kitchen as if in a dream, suddenly recalling the amazingly accurate map Ralph had drawn from memory when he'd been explaining the situation in Europe to Jane. Like Meg herself, in his youth Ralph had won a scholarship to attend grammar school. But whereas she had declined the opportunity as all she wanted to do was farm, Ralph had welcomed it. But he wasn't just more educated than some; he had a gift for interpreting maps. Had that natural talent been spotted during his RAF training? Was it good news? Bad news? She had no idea. All she knew was that the old emptiness had screwed down in her stomach again.

'So what time's he coming?' Jane beamed innocently.

Meg blinked at her friend, utterly dazed. 'He can't come,' her bloodless lips articulated, and then she burst into tears.

Sixteen

'Well, Merry Christmas, everyone!'

Wig raised his glass to all those who'd squeezed around the dining table. Large as it was, it had been difficult to accommodate everyone present in the house, even with the servants' hall overflowing as well. Wig's brother, Peregrine, had managed to persuade Sofia that life was safe at Robin Hill House now that the Battle of Britain had been won. He kept quiet about the fact that Sevenoaks had been targeted by bombers on numerous occasions on the way to or from London because of its proximity to several airfields. So much so that local children had been offered evacuation to Devon, although at just ten miles away, Robin Hill House was deemed out of the danger area. Fortunately Sofia hadn't discovered that her husband had been a little economical with the truth, and she had agreed to travel up for Christmas.

They'd arrived a couple of days earlier, having set out the day after Boris and Max had come home from their boarding school for the holidays. Not having seen them for so long, the boys seemed to have grown up so much. The elder one, Boris, seemed almost like a young man now.

Peregrine, unusually for him so Wig claimed, had possessed the foresight to organise his petrol ration so that he'd been able to motor up with his family. Perhaps the last time he could do so *for the duration.*

'God knows how difficult it might've been by train, and it would have been ghastly!' Sofia had pronounced dramatically on their arrival. Now she waved the flimsy, diaphanous scarf about her bare shoulders. 'Wiggy, darling, it's freezing in here. Is the heating broken?'

'Haven't been able to get any more oil for the boiler, I'm afraid,' Wig answered cheerfully, 'and we can only get enough coal to keep the range going. So we have to rely on log fires for our heating. Fortunately we had several dead trees in the woods that we cut down back in the summer, and they should see us through this winter. And we've started felling others to season for future years. But you must have the same problem.'

'Yes, but at least we only have small rooms, so an open fire's sufficient. I suppose there are compensations for being poor.'

Peregrine gave a wry smile. They were hardly poor, but the rooms in their thatched cottage were small compared to those in Robin Hill House. 'Couldn't you put on a jumper, my angel?' he suggested mildly. 'Like the rest of us?'

'A jumper? For Christmas dinner? Well, I suppose I do have that pretty pink cardigan with the Peter Pan collar. Meg, dear, you wouldn't like to fetch it for me, would you? It's hanging over the back of the chair in the bedroom.'

'Meg's not a servant anymore,' Clarrie put in gently. 'No one is. Not while the war's on. You can see how we live here now. We all have our household duties, even yours truly, especially since we lost Sally. We just all pitch in together.'

'Yes, and I think it's delightful. We can have a proper knees-up later. Show old Hitler he can't keep us down. Perry, would you mind—?'

'No, it's OK, Sofia. I don't mind going. Won't be a jiffy, only don't start without me.' Meg slipped on her duffel coat before traipsing through the deep snow to what was still considered as her and Ralph's cottage. Peregrine and Sofia were sleeping there since their two boys had bagged the empty room in the attic. Meg suspected that being tucked away up in the male servants' quarters with the twins, they were all having a whale of a time! And Sofia for her part had declared that the little cottage was quite romantic.

Meg didn't mind Peregrine and Sofia taking temporary possession of her home. Ralph couldn't get leave over Christmas anyway. In fact, Meg hadn't seen him since he'd been flying these secret missions. She still didn't know what they were. In his letters, he simply put things like *had a bit of bother, but back safely.*

It was a relief for Meg to have a few moments to herself, to send a mental message to Ralph winging across the miles that separated them. But it was equally good to return to the dining room where the lively chatter was a distraction for her heavy heart.

'To absent friends and families,' Wig went on, resuming his toast. 'And to those who've perished or been injured, or lost loved ones or their homes in London and all the other cities Jerry has seen fit to bomb. And above all, to victory!'

'To victory!'

Unbidden, everyone stood up, scraping their chairs on the floor and solemnly clinking their glasses. As well as London, so many other cities had taken a devastating pounding: Southampton, Merseyside, Bristol, Sheffield, Manchester. Coventry seemed to have been almost flattened, losing its beautiful cathedral, the scant remains of which had become a symbol of Germany's treachery. It was thought that about forty thousand civilians had lost their lives, and the figure was rising.

After Wig's toast, everyone was lost in thought for a few moments before sitting down again, and as they did so, Meg heard him mutter under his breath to his wife, 'I just hope Hitler knows it's Christmas Day.'

'You should've said *Death to Hitler*, Uncle Wig,' Boris declared adamantly. 'I can't wait to get my hands on Jerry the minute I'm old enough.'

'Let's hope it'll all be over by the time you are, Boris, lad.'

'Come off it, Uncle Wig. I'm nearly seventeen and a half, so I can sign up soon. Then I could be called up any time after I finish school in the summer. It's hardly going to be over by then. Haven't made much progress so far, have we? A few raids on Italy, and tickling the German underbelly in North Africa. We'll be lucky to keep old Adolf off our own shores, let alone drive him out of all the other countries he's occupied.'

'Oh, don't, Boris, darling!' Sofia waved a hand over her forehead. 'I can't bear the thought of little men with funny haircuts and silly moustaches marching up and down our high streets.'

'Don't worry, Sofia,' Wig reassured her. 'It won't come to that. Churchill won't let it.'

'Let's just hope he persuades America to stop sitting on the fence, and come and join us,' Peregrine put in. 'It's just like the other war all over again, only much bigger with all the trouble brewing in the Far East as well.'

'Well, I think we should stop talking about it and get on with this lovely meal,' Sofia declared. 'Gabriel's done you proud, Clarrie, with this huge spread of vegetables. It's more than we've seen since before the war began!'

'The twins work really hard in the garden, too,' Meg told her. 'And the girls. And they help ever such a lot in the kitchen. We all get on so well. And Penny, that's Mrs Higginbottom, she's a marvel at bolstering everyone up. She and Ada, that's Mrs Phillips as was, they get on like a house on fire.'

'I certainly don't know how they manage to stretch the meat rations the way they do. But if this keeps up, we'll *all* have to become vegetarians before too long.'

Everyone knew Peregrine and his family were of that persuasion, so at the mild joke, a titter of laughter wafted about the crowded room. Soon the clink of china and cutlery fragmented the conversation, each person talking only to his or her neighbours. The clatter around the table allowed Meg to retreat into her private thoughts for a while. Where exactly was Ralph today, and what was he doing? She only prayed that he was safe. But even if he was, would he be the next day, and the next? What would the New Year hold for them all? Victory? Peace? It didn't seem likely. But only time would tell.

*

They didn't have to wait long to find out. Not even into the New Year.

'Sweet Jesus!' Peregrine, who hadn't seen anything like it in his safe home down in Cornwall, cried out in shock as what only an hour previously had been ink-black darkness over London exploded into an incandescent, blazing aurora.

Despite the bitter weather, everyone spilled out onto the terrace – apart from the boys who rushed up the stairs to their rooms to get the best views. The dazzling light grew and grew until it resembled a mountain of fire, flames leaping a hundred feet into the sky. Even from that distance, they could see the banks of grey smoke lit up with a strange, eerie glow.

'My God, it's worse than ever.' Wig was so astounded, his voice was a mere tremble.

'They're trying to burn London to the ground.'

'Yes. Yes, they are. They must be dropping incendiaries rather than explosives. There's an exceptionally low tide tonight. It'll be difficult to get water out of the Thames. My God, no wonder there was a lull over Christmas. They were waiting for this!' Wig's words had risen to a crescendo as realisation dawned.

'Oh, Wig, what about the factory?' Clarrie squealed.

Meg narrowed her eyes as she calculated the angle. 'I think this is further west than when they bomb the docks,' she told Wig. 'We've sort of got used to judging where it is.'

'Good God, it must be the City, then. They want to destroy the very heart of the country! They haven't managed to bomb us into submission yet, so they think this'll do the trick.'

'Well, I'm going to get it on canvas the minute I get back to the studio,' Peregrine announced bitterly. 'People everywhere need to see what a bastard Hitler is.'

'And I'm going to try ringing my manager on duty at the factory, if I can get through. I was going to stay here a few more days, but I'd better get back tomorrow.'

'Oh, Wig, d'you have to?'

Meg noted the controlled hysteria in Clarrie's voice. Poor woman. But it was the same for everyone. She prayed nightly for Ralph's safety. Was it better or worse never knowing where he was or what he was doing? She really didn't know. All she did know was that the aching emptiness never let up. They might have been able to bring in the Christmas tree and decorate it as usual, fill the house with greenery and garlands and exchange small presents. But they were just fooling themselves. Christmas simply couldn't be the same.

And perhaps it never would again.

Seventeen

1941

The photograph was everywhere. The majestic dome of St Paul's Cathedral rising proudly above the blazing maelstrom that raged through the streets of the City in an ocean of flame. But for all his efforts, Hitler couldn't destroy the soul of London, and on the first day of the new year, RAF Bomber Command emptied its lethal cargo on Bremen in reply, showing that Britain could give as good as it got.

God was on Britain's side, and the spirit of the British people was, if anything, strengthened by the Luftwaffe attacks. Hitler went on trying, though, continuing to bomb the capital and spreading his campaign of terror to even more cities than before – Cardiff, Portsmouth and Plymouth. But the British people had faith, and reports of some successful campaigns in North Africa early in January gave them hope.

'Can I help you?' Meg asked, opening the front door to a middle-aged woman in a WVS uniform one bitingly cold Saturday morning towards the end of January. She seemed oddly familiar, but Meg couldn't think why.

'Mrs Jenkins. Billeting officer,' the woman smiled.

Ah, yes. Meg remembered now. Mrs Jenkins had been to check on their charges a couple of times during the first few months, but had been so satisfied with conditions for the evacuees that she hadn't needed to return.

But perhaps it was time for a routine visit.

'Do come in,' Meg invited her. 'What can I do for you?'

'Sad news, I'm afraid.' The woman glanced about her as if satisfying herself everything was still in order. 'Is Mrs Stratfield-Whyte at home?'

Meg knew she shivered. God knew how Clarrie would take it if anything had happened to Wig. 'It's not her husband, is it?' she forced herself to ask.

'Oh, Lord.'

'No. It concerns one of your evacuees. Doris Sergeant.'

'Doris? Oh, no—'

Meg felt her stomach flip over. Doris, who'd been the most sensitive of the evacuees, whose confidence had taken such strides. This could destroy her, and Meg could only pray that the news wasn't *too* bad.

'Perhaps if I could speak to Mrs Stratfield-Whyte first?' Mrs Jenkins enquired gently but firmly. 'And then if you could fetch Doris? And anyone else you think should be there. But not any other children. It isn't always helpful.'

'Yes, of course. Mrs Stratfield-Whyte's in the sitting room. Please follow me.'

Meg could feel her heart beating hard. Oh, Lord, what was she to say to poor Doris? The three girl evacuees had become as thick as thieves, the friendship between them a delight to witness. At least Doris would have that to help her through whatever the bad news was.

Meg went into the kitchen. It was a hive of activity, Louise and Penny mixing up some water glass for preserving surplus eggs, while Ada was overseeing the three girls as they prepared vegetables for a giant pot of soup. Nana May was doing her best to keep an eye on Bella who was not far off two now and quite a handful. Fortunately her two elder brothers were busy playing with their toy cars on a race track Meg had drawn out for them on the flattened remains of a cardboard box.

Meg quietly told Nana May of their visitor. The old lady was like a grandmother to them all, and Meg felt she should be there for Doris as well as Clarrie. Clarrie, she knew, would be ultra sympathetic to anyone else's misfortune, but Nana May was always the solid rock.

'This little lady had better go back in her playpen, then,' Nana May said sombrely, dipping her head at Bella.

'I'll do it,' Meg offered, since she knew Nana May would struggle. And then, as she popped the protesting toddler in the playpen and got her interested in some of her toys, she had to grit her teeth as she turned to the young girl working at the table. 'Doris, there's someone to see you,' she said steadily.

Her heart broke as Doris's face lit up and she jumped to Meg's side. 'Oh, is it Mummy?' she cried with joy as they followed Nana May along the corridor.

Oh, dear God, what could Meg say to her? She stopped, taking the girl's small hand. 'No, it's not your mummy. It's someone… I'm not sure it's going to be good news.'

Doris's face blanched. 'Oh, Meg…'

She gripped Meg's hand tightly as they continued on to the sitting room. Meg could feel her shaking. As they went in, Nana May was lowering herself onto a seat, and all three older women's faces turned to them in a wall of compassion.

Meg gulped. 'This is Doris,' she whispered lamely.

'Yes, I remember Doris. I picked you up from the station in my car the day you were evacuated. Do you remember, dear?' Mrs Jenkins asked gently. And then turning to Meg, she went on, 'Thank you, but this is… a private matter.'

'No, I want Meg to stay.' Doris astounded them all by the conviction in her voice. Perhaps she'd grown up even more than anyone realised. 'If it's bad news, I want her to be here.'

Mrs Jenkins glanced at Clarrie, but she nodded back. Clarrie knew that a strong bond had developed between Meg and Doris, and understood the younger girl's feelings.

And so, accepting Clarrie's opinion, the billeting officer went on gently, 'All right. But you'd better sit down.'

They did so, sitting side by side on the small settee. Doris hadn't let go of Meg's hand, and Meg felt her fingers tighten like a vice.

'I'm afraid I come with bad news,' Mrs Jenkins continued gravely. 'I don't need to tell you about the raids on London. I'm afraid… your mother wasn't feeling well and couldn't face going down the shelter. Her neighbour tried to persuade her, but she wouldn't get out of bed. And… your house took a direct hit. If it's any comfort, your mother wouldn't have known anything about it. I'm… so deeply sorry.'

Meg felt the cold horror of it open up her own wounds. Poor Doris. She knew exactly what the child would be going through. She felt her stiffen beside her, and then remain perfectly still for some moments.

'Will there be a funeral?' were the first words Doris spoke.

'I expect so. I'll find out for you.'

'I see. Thank you.'

A frown creased Mrs Jenkins's brow, and she glanced at the other women in the room. 'Well, I'll leave you with your friends, now,' she said, her voice soft. 'Unless there's anything I can do for you, dear? Any questions you want to ask?' And when Doris silently shook her head, she concluded, 'I'll be in touch. You have an auntie in London, I understand. Your mother's sister. She'll be making all the arrangements. I've given her the telephone number here. I expect she'll ring, if that's all right?'

Clarrie hadn't uttered a word. Her face was grey, shocked as they all were. Now she nodded in reply.

'If you'll excuse me, then, Doris, dear. Mrs Stratfield-Whyte has my number if you need me.'

'I'll show you out.' Nana May heaved herself to her feet and the two women respectfully left the room.

Meg swivelled round to face Doris who was staring down at their hands that were still clamped together. 'Oh, Doris, I'm so very sorry,' she croaked.

'Thanks, Meg. I'd like to go back to the kitchen now, please. I'd like… can we do some painting together?'

'Of course. Anything you want.'

Doris raised her eyes, bright with sorrow, to Meg's face, but her grip on Meg's hand didn't slacken. Meg exchanged glances with Clarrie. Each was so lost in a whirlpool of emotion that there was no room for words. Poor Doris. She was obviously deep in shock. How would she cope when the news sank in? Would a funeral help? Would it be wise for the girl to go to London? It had been a direct hit, so would there be anything to have a funeral *with*?

Meg's feet dragged as they walked slowly, numbed, back to the kitchen. How could they tell the others, knowing their parents were in as much danger? Was this the beginning? First it had been Bob, injured and invalided out of active service, although now working in the War Office; now Doris's mother. What, or who, next?

Suddenly Robin Hill House didn't feel safe anymore. But where was?

*

'No, I'm going.'

That night, Doris had sobbed her little heart out. Meg had stayed with her, both Thimble and Topaz curled up on the rug, until the poor child had finally drifted into an exhausted sleep in the early hours. For two days, she hadn't eaten a thing and had barely spoken a word. But now, her elfin face was set like granite as she stood squarely in the sitting room, her chin jutting stubbornly.

Horror tore through Clarrie's soul as she watched the young girl with the bright red curls gaze steadily at her, eyes blazing with defiance. She understood her pain, but she couldn't let her take the risk, not for someone who was already dead. She hadn't been up to London herself to visit Rosebud's grave since the bombing had started. Hadn't been for years, in fact. It wouldn't bring her little darling back. It was part of the healing, accepting that she was gone. Since Meg had come into her life, Clarrie had no longer felt the need. And so she couldn't let Doris risk getting caught in an air raid herself, just to say goodbye, because you never really did.

Fear for the girl scorched inside her head, but she had to keep calm. 'No, I'm sorry,' she said levelly, though her pulse was racing. 'Your parents wanted you to be safe. So as I'm *in loco parentis* I'm afraid I can't allow it.'

Doris didn't know what *in loco parentis* meant, but she could guess. 'I don't care,' she protested. 'I know you want to protect me, Mrs C. Clarrie. But Daddy's somewhere out in the Med and they can't repatriate him just because his wife's been killed. There's a war on, you know,' she added bitterly. 'So if Daddy can't go, one of us needs to be there, so it'll have to be me.'

Clarrie inwardly gulped. She couldn't believe this was the same shy, nervous little waif who'd come to Robin Hill House eighteen months earlier. She wouldn't say boo to a goose then, and now she was standing up for something she believed in so strongly that she was willing to put her life in danger. But Clarrie couldn't allow it, even if every bone in her body sympathised with how Doris felt.

'I'll take her,' Meg said quietly.

Clarrie stifled a gasp and every bone, every muscle in her body groaned. Oh, no. They couldn't both go! Not the two girls who had come to mean so much to her. Great whirlwinds of terror whizzed about in Clarrie's head like red tornadoes.

'B-but you don't know London,' she stammered. 'And even if you did, it'll be much more difficult getting around than normal.'

'I'm sure I can find my way. And I've got a tongue in my head to ask people. And Doris will know, anyway.' And then, coming over to Clarrie and lowering her voice, Meg ended with quiet determination, 'I know exactly how she feels, remember. She *needs* to do this.'

Clarrie drew her forehead in tightly as she waited for the scarlet arrows to clear. Of course, she understood, but she had to protect these two surrogate daughters of hers as she hadn't been able to protect her own child. There was only one way she could do that. And though she scarcely knew the East End of the capital, she was a Londoner by birth.

Her lips felt like rubber as she said, 'Then I'll come, too.'

Eighteen

Doris sat in the crowded train, staring out at the late morning drizzle, part of her still numb with shock at her mother's death, part of her scared. Not of any bombs that might fall on London that day, but of quite how she would say goodbye to her mummy. And yet overall, the whole situation felt unreal. This wasn't the journey home that she'd planned. Dreamt of. She'd imagined going home after the war full of joy. Not like this. Although it wasn't a troop train, they were nevertheless squeezed into the compartment among a group of soldiers coming home on leave from God knew where. Weary, drained, but in good spirits. If their eyes had been drawn by the beautiful young woman sitting between a girl with red hair and an older, elegant woman, they'd soon noticed the wedding ring on her finger. The little girl wore a black armband and was carrying a small posy of snowdrops as if going to visit a grave or attend a funeral. The soldiers understood death and wouldn't intrude on the little one's grief. Besides, they were soon being bombarded with relentless questions by two young lads who were so identical they had to be twins.
'We'll come with yer, too,' Leslie had announced when they'd learnt that Clarrie and Meg were taking Doris up to London for her mum's hastily arranged funeral. 'We ain't heard nuffing from our mum and dad since way before Christmas.'
    'Nothing,' Cyril corrected him absently.
A frown twitched on Leslie's forehead, but he ignored his brother's comment. 'They ain't written ter us or answered our letters for months, so I wanna know what's going on.'
'Oh, no, I can't possibly let you go off on your own,' Clarrie protested. 'I'm responsible for you, remember?'
'But we're fourteen, Clarrie,' Leslie argued. 'We know the area like the back of our hands. Far better than you. Yer far more likely ter get lost than we are. We're not stupid, yer know.'
'We won't take any chances, I promise,' Cyril, the steadier of the two, insisted. 'If we run inter any problems, we'll find a phone box and ring back here, so yer'll know we're OK.'
    'Well, I suppose if Meg came with you—'
'Nah. Meg'll be no good. She don't know London. She'd be more of a hindrance. And Doris needs her at the funeral. We'll be OK on our own, honest we will.'
Clarrie chewed on her lip. Everything the twins had said was true. They were young men nearly, born Londoners and far more street-savvy than she was herself. So most reluctantly, she gave in. But she'd be glad when the day was over and they were all safely back home.
When the train pulled into London Bridge among a cloud of hissing steam at noon on the day of the funeral, miraculously without any hold-ups en route, they went some way before parting company with the boys, but arranged to meet back up for the return journey at the same spot at six o'clock sharp. *No matter what*, Clarrie warned then sternly.
As they made their way through the streets, the horror of what the capital had suffered ripped silently into their hearts. They'd seen plenty of photographs of the destruction in the newspapers, which was bad enough, but to see it in reality struck deep. Huge gaps where mountains of rubble and charred remains made it impossible to guess what sort of building had stood there before it had been blasted to smithereens.

Meg shuddered, for perhaps bodies still lay trapped and rotting beneath. Some bombsites had been cleared, leaving an eerie nothingness where people had once lived and played and worked. Other damaged ruins, a tottering facade on the brink of collapse with perhaps a staircase or a suspended floor hanging as if in mid-air, had been hastily shorn up with props and heavy beams whilst they awaited demolition. A twisted bedstead open to view where a wall had collapsed, a bathroom, intimate snatches of someone's broken life, tattered curtains waving macabrely through frames whose glass was shattered. Windows that looked through to emptiness, heavy wooden joists and rafters splintered like matchwood and lying in chaotic piles.

It was all so horribly real and hostile, and yet it almost seemed *un*real. Alien. People were carrying on as normal, walking through the streets as if nothing had happened and stepping over debris that had yet to be cleared. Women with scarves on their heads and baskets on their arms on their way to queue for hours to glean whatever they could in the half-empty shops. People greeting each other cheerfully. Becoming immune.

With Doris between them, Clarrie and Meg glanced at each other over her head. Meg for one felt sickened at the wanton devastation. So this was what Hitler was doing. No wonder they needed to retaliate. She understood now what Wig had said to her all that time ago. You got sucked into war and there was nothing you could do about it.

They didn't exchange a word, except to find the bus Doris knew they needed to catch from her outings to the seaside in happier times. Its route was diverted because of repairs to a gas main fractured by a bomb. The last part they had to walk as the bus couldn't get through there, either. They followed Doris, whose step became more certain as she reached familiar territory.

It was fortunate that they'd allowed plenty of time. They called in at a tea room they passed for a quick cuppa – none of them felt like eating anything – before setting off for the funeral which was due to start at two o'clock. They went straight to the church. Except that it had been flattened the same night as Doris's house, but had been quickly replaced by a Nissan hut with a makeshift altar. An auburn-haired woman stepped forward and at once encircled Doris in her arms.

'Oh, Auntie,' the girl mumbled, the first time she'd spoken except to give directions.

'Thank you for bringing her,' the aunt greeted Clarrie and Meg solemnly.

'You must be Doris,' a compassionate voice belonging to a man in long robes and a dog collar said softly as he came up to join them. 'I'm so very sorry, my child. Would you like a few moments with the coffin before the service? It'll be arriving very soon.'

'Yes, please,' Doris answered in a tiny voice, since she'd already been told she wouldn't be able to see her mum, and that it wouldn't be wise, anyway. Young as she was, she could imagine what that meant.

The vicar took Doris and her aunt aside, and Clarrie and Meg knew they weren't needed for a while. So they took their places among the congregation seated on a hotchpotch of chairs gathered from who knew where. About twenty people had come to mourn Mrs Sergeant, mainly women – some neighbours and others fellow nippies from the Lyons Corner House where she'd worked – and a few older men. There were no other children. If Doris wept during the service, she did so silently. Meg's own throat ached, and she bit hard on the inside of her bottom lip to stop herself crying. For Doris. For Mrs Sergeant. For her own mother and father killed some years before, and for everyone who'd died because of Hitler. When she looked at Clarrie, she saw unshed tears glistening in her eyes as if she, too, was remembering someone she'd lost. Her own parents, perhaps.

'I've arranged a little tea at my house,' Aunt Mildred invited them when it was all over. 'You will come back?'

'Yes, thank you,' Clarrie accepted. 'We'll need to leave by five at the latest, though. Two of my other evacuees, twin boys of fourteen, wanted to check on their own family,' she explained. 'We're meeting up later to get the train back together.' At least, she prayed they would. She wouldn't be happy until she had the twins safely back under her wing.

Aunt Mildred nodded. 'I understand. Now, I must ask you, Doris dear. D'you want to see the house? Or what's left of it? The site hasn't been cleared yet. Some people find it helpful. Some don't. Constable Ainsworth – you remember him? – he helped me salvage one or two things that I've kept for you. It was too dangerous to get much, I'm afraid.'

Meg's stomach tightened. Poor Doris. She knew exactly how that felt. The few items she'd been able to bring with her from the farmhouse had helped her cling onto the memories. It had been painful at the time, but now when she used her mum's best tea service and tablecloth in the little cottage that was her and Ralph's home, it brought her comfort. As if it was keeping her parents near.

'No, I'd rather not see the house.' Doris's words had begun calmly but ended in a squeak as she fought back tears. 'But thank you for rescuing the things.'

'That's all right, my love.' Aunt Mildred's face was taut with compassion. 'You can take back whatever you can now, and I'll keep the rest until, well, until this business is all over. And I'll make sure I'm there when they clear the site in case anything else comes to light.'

The good woman had used her own rations to produce jam tarts with bread and butter or margarine, and Clarrie was glad she'd thought to bring a couple of jars of Ada's jam and a bag of carefully stored apples, for which Mildred was most appreciative. Clarrie noticed, though, that Doris didn't touch a morsel of the food.

'Time to go now, I'm afraid, Doris,' she said gently. But she had the feeling the child was glad to get away, as if leaving her memories and her pain behind.

The house hadn't caught fire, so when it was destroyed, Aunt Mildred had succeeded in rescuing a couple of photographs from their smashed frames. Mrs Sergeant's locked jewellery box had somehow survived, too, only cheap costume pieces, but they meant a lot to Doris. A soft toy rabbit from her own childhood – to go with the one Cyril had won for her on the coconut shy, she smiled with a tear. Clarrie carried them for her in the bag in which she'd brought the provisions. A few larger items Aunt Mildred was storing for her.

A biting, icy wind licked cruelly about them as they waited for the bus. It blew its freezing breath up Meg's skirt, attacking the gap between the tops of her stockings – her very last pair – and her knickers. How much warmer she always was in trousers or dungarees as she worked outside in all weathers, but you couldn't go to a funeral in slacks. She felt so sorry for Doris in her long, buff socks and bare knees. The poor child looked more miserable now than she had all day.

'Where's a taxi when you want one?' Clarrie complained under her breath. She'd had enough of the city that she used to love, especially with its gashes and scars, and the heart ripped out of it. She just wanted to be back home in the peaceful Kent countryside.

At last the bus trundled towards them. It was getting quite dark, and it felt so strange in the blackout with no streetlights, and yet with so many people around them, making their way by dimmed torchlight and sometimes bumping into each other as a result. Even the bus was barely visible, driving just on its sidelights and with the inside unlit. Meg couldn't help thinking of Sally working as a clippie. She'd have liked to take the opportunity to meet up with her, but Sally was on shift, and besides, there wouldn't really have been time.

They eventually got back to the appointed meeting place five minutes early. Doris had barely uttered a word, though she smiled and nodded whenever Clarrie or Meg spoke to her. As they waited in virtually pitch darkness, an almost palpable tension tightened its hold on them. To top it all, the people about them were hurrying as best they could, glancing up into the black dome of the sky.

'Oh, where are those boys?' Clarrie cried almost hysterically when they'd been waiting for half an hour.

Meg, too, was starting to feel nervous, her stomach fluttering. Had they been right to trust the twins on their own? They seemed street-savvy, but what if something had happened to them? Should they abandon them? Go to their aid? Clarrie had their home address, but would they still be there? Or maybe they should try to find a phone box and ring Robin Hill House to find out if the boys had left a message there as they'd said they would if they'd run into difficulty.

Meg was still pondering, about to ask Clarrie what she thought, when an unearthly whine stabbed into her hearing, growing in strength until it blared out in a deafening wail, dropping and then howling again, over and over. Oh, good God. The air-raid siren.

A darkness as black as the sky above opened inside her. This was so different from what they'd experienced at home. You could almost taste the panic in the air, feel people brush past them as they hurried instinctively in the blackout along familiar paths to safety.

A light way above her head caught Meg's eye and she glanced upwards. Brilliant shafts of gleaming silver sliced through the blackness as searchlights scanned the now indigo sky, and then the looming shadow of a nearby barrage balloon floated skywards like a great, grey whale. Within seconds, she saw that others were joining it, a shoal of giant, fat fish in the sky.

Meg's heart was smashing so hard and fast against her ribs that there was scarcely a break between each beat. Both Clarrie and Doris seemed rooted to the spot with terror. It was going to be up to her to get them to safety.

She was about to grab them and pull them in the same direction as everyone else was moving, when a familiar voice swamped her with relief.

'Here, mate, where's the nearest shelter?' Leslie called out.

And then Cyril explained briefly, 'Sorry we're late. The blooming bus never came so we had ter leg it instead. Come on!'

In an instant, Meg saw that one of the twins – in the dark, she couldn't tell which – had taken hold of Clarrie's arm and was dragging her along behind the footfall of the strangers all around them – which was about all they had to go by in the pitch black. And then the other twin was doing the same with Doris. Meg snapped herself out of her shock and scurried along behind, hearing the distant thrum of aircraft getting louder as they drew nearer. *Theirs? Or ours going to intercept them?* At least Ralph wouldn't be among them. But what irony if she was to die here, and he was the one who survived? *Oh, dear God, please keep him safe if I am to perish.*

They found themselves going down steps, lots of them, the crowd around them silent as they concentrated on where they were putting their feet. If one fell, it would bring others down, too. They seemed to be going down for ages before reaching a flat surface that opened into a dimly lit tunnel, and Meg realised it was an underground station. She'd never been to London before, let alone on the tube, as she'd heard people call it. A strange smell she couldn't identify filled her nostrils as they came out through a labyrinth of passageways to what appeared to be a platform.

There were people strewn everywhere, some appearing to make themselves comfortable, sitting on cushions they'd brought with them. The lucky ones had got places by the wall so they had it to lean against. Some were even producing provisions from their gas-mask boxes or hastily packed baskets.

Meg gazed about her in bewilderment, pulse drumming in her ears. Then she realised that Leslie was shouldering his way through to a gap he'd spotted, pulling Clarrie along with him, Cyril in his wake with Doris, so Meg forced herself along behind them.

'Plonk yerselves down there,' Leslie ordered. 'Sorry ter be so rough, Clarrie, but best ter be as far away from the entrance as possible in case there's any blast waves. Blow you down or suck you out, they can.'

Meg blinked at him as she joined them on the hard and none-too-clean platform floor. How did Leslie know what to do? But then she remembered how he seemed to have devoured newspaper reports of the bombings, waiting for the paperboy to cycle up the drive every day. Leslie's interest might have seemed a bit morbid previously, but now she thanked God for his knowledge.

'So, did you find your parents?' Clarrie asked once they were settled. It was something to keep their minds occupied, at least.

'Nah.' Leslie's tone was scornful. 'Our tenement block was damaged back in November, and they scarpered. No one's seen hide nor hair of 'em since.'

Clarrie shifted uncomfortably. 'Oh, I'm so sorry.'

'Don't be,' Cyril shrugged. 'Never cared for us much, so why should we worry? Wouldn't surprise me if our dad thinks he'll get out of being called up by disappearing. Anyway, how was things for you, Doris?' he asked softly.

The girl didn't get a chance to reply. From so deep underground, they could no longer hear the thrum of aircraft engines, but just then, the ground shook as there was a sound like the crack of lightning and an explosion roared and echoed down the platform, making the lights sway and blink on their wires.

'Blimey, that was close,' someone said, just before another tremendous, thundering crash reverberated about them even more powerful than the one before. And then the faint, distinctive rattle of the ack-ack guns pounding skywards.

People tried not to, but at each earth-shattering blast, eyes swivelled to the roof of the tunnel. The noise bombarded Meg's ears again and again, and she shuddered and ducked each time it came. She glanced across at Clarrie whose face was so pale, her skin was like a bleached sheet, despite Leslie's attempts to give her a lively account of their day. Meg knew she'd be worried sick about Wig as well as her own safety and that of her charges. And poor Doris was visibly shaking, her eyes wide and staring in fear. Cyril had his arm protectively around her, and Meg saw with a little smile that their fingers were tightly interlaced.

'We're going to hang out the washing on the Siegfried line,' someone started to sing, and almost immediately a chorus of voices joined in, getting louder as almost everyone was soon belting out the words. Someone handed Doris a piece of chocolate. A woman sitting

next to Meg passed them round a cup of tea from a flask. They each took a grateful sip. It tasted foul, but it was something, and above all, it was generous.

'Not come prepared?' the woman asked in a kindly voice.

'No. We'd only come up from the country for the day,' Meg explained. 'Expected to be on our way back home on the train by now, but we got delayed.'

'Bad luck, then.'

'Yes, I guess so. Is it always like this?'

'Yes. But Hitler's got to run out of bombs *some* time at this rate, hasn't he, ducks?' the woman smiled.

Meg was quivering inside, and it was as if she could feel the blood trundling through her veins. After all, bombs had been known to penetrate as far down as the underground. She'd seen photos of a bus that had collapsed down into a tube station where people had been sheltering. Balham, wasn't it? She tried to drive all such thoughts from her brain and concentrate instead on the atmosphere around her. Every now and then, the singing would start up again, and Meg couldn't help admire the courage of those around her, especially knowing that when they finally emerged – and they *would* emerge, she was determined – they could find their houses, their lives, obliterated from the face of the earth. The Blitz spirit, they were calling it. Meg found the strength of these people, these strangers who shared one common cause, truly inspiring.

'Oh, this is all my fault,' Doris suddenly started sobbing when another particularly loud explosion became too much for her. 'If I hadn't insisted—'

'No, it wasn't,' Cyril interrupted. 'Me and Leslie should've set out sooner ter come back, instead of wasting time trying ter find them no-good parents of ours. If you want ter blame anyone, blame us.'

Meg put her arm around Doris from the other side. 'There's only one person to blame here and that's Hitler,' she told the girl firmly. 'Isn't that right, Clarrie?'

She could tell that Clarrie was blaming herself, while Meg felt guilt pressing down on her own shoulders. But they would get out of this, she knew. They had to. And there was certainly no room for recriminations.

They waited, sometimes singing along, sometimes chatting to strangers and finding a strong bond that was almost palpable. Were they to be there all night? But just as they were beginning to think they might, they realised there hadn't been a resounding crash for some time, and then someone yelled along the platform that the all-clear had been sounded.

People started moving stiffly from the floor and packing up their belongings.

'Well, at least that wasn't too long,' the woman with the flask informed Meg. 'Sometimes they go on all night. Been nice to meet you. Good luck.

Hopefully you'll get home tonight.'

'Thank you. And good luck yourself.'

'Yes, well, if my home's gone, I'll find somewhere to rest my old bones, I'm sure.'

It was all pretty chaotic as everyone spilled up the stairs and out into the freezing night air. Meg and her companions reached the pavement just as the final tones of the all-clear faded away. It was like walking into a wall of dust and choking smoke. A burning ruin was casting enough light for them to see their way, its windows and doors like empty eyes, while great jagged piles of what had been other buildings before were outlined grotesquely in the darkness. The fire brigade were already there, hoses run out like snakes across the road.

'Come on. Let's get to the station as quickly as we can and see if there's a train still running. It's only nine o'clock so hopefully there will be.'

Like Meg, the others couldn't get away from the horror quickly enough, even the twins whose boyish fascination had seen sufficient. All was in uproar, but when they finally found their way, the station was in even greater chaos. But the boys were masters at pushing themselves forward, and Clarrie's natural bearing also seemed to impress, and at long last they found themselves crammed into a railway carriage. When they chugged away from the platform, Meg had never felt so relieved in her life. At that moment, she was aware with tearing shame that she cared only that they had made it, and was putting the sufferings of the Londoners firmly to the back of her mind. But never again would she take her simple life for granted now that she'd seen what others had to endure.

The journey took forever. Disrupted by the raid, trains were in the wrong places. Engines had to creep along to make sure they didn't miss any signals; they kept having to wait for points to be changed and lines cleared. Sometimes the hold-ups lasted twenty minutes. Doris fell asleep, her head resting on Cyril's shoulder, while the rest of them were too tired and traumatised to speak.

Eventually at one o'clock in the morning, the train pulled into Tunbridge Wells Station. Meg felt unsteady as they stood on the platform in the dark, watching the huge bulk of the railway engine rumbling off into the darkness. Amazingly, Clarrie seemed to come to her senses again.

'Telephone box,' she announced. 'I just hope someone hears it. I don't like waking Gabriel, but he'll have to bring the Daimler to meet us. Thank God we have it here. And we have some petrol. And as soon as we get in,

I'll try ringing Wig, as well. I pray to God he's all right.'

They trooped outside and as they waited in the darkness while Clarrie made the call, Meg came over so weary, every joint seemed to ache. She couldn't wait to get back to her own bed, although she doubted she would sleep. Her head was reeling with what had happened, her ears ringing with the silence after the terrifying din of the air raid, and she yearned for the peace of the countryside to wash her soul clean. That night would remain imprinted on her memory forever.

Nineteen

'Right, Green.'

Assistant Prison Governor Howard lifted his eyes from the papers on his desk and looked up darkly at the prisoner standing in front of him. He had all types come through his corrective custody: first-time offenders who'd made a stupid mistake they never would again, persistent petty criminals who never seemed to learn, and some guilty of more serious crimes. But kidnapping and terrifying a young woman who he understood was a little on the simple side was outrageous.

He'd never liked Nathaniel Green much. Some of the inmates were repentant, some of the frequent 'guests' were affable, almost like old friends they returned so often, and a few were downright belligerent. But Green, well, he was devious. Kept himself to himself, which was probably just as well for his own protection. There was indeed honour among thieves, and kidnapping a vulnerable young girl would be frowned upon by many echelons of criminal society. And Green was an arrogant blackguard. He'd been caught red-handed so he couldn't deny his guilt. But he claimed he only did it to get what he saw as compensation for his loss of earnings from being wrongfully imprisoned the first time round. He still protested that the horse had caused the fatal accident that had taken the lives of Mr and Mrs Chandler, and not his driving, despite his conviction. But that was no excuse for his second despicable criminal act as far as Howard was concerned. No. There was something really nasty about Green that the assistant governor disliked intensely, and he was pleased he was about to see the back of him.

'You'll be glad to know the board have decided to release you early,' he announced, resting his chin on his steepled fingers and shrewdly observing the prisoner's reaction.

Green slowly raised a sarcastic eyebrow and his lips twisted into a sly, lopsided sneer. 'Someone's seen sense at last, have they?' he drawled, but then anger flashed across his eyes. 'About time, too. I can get back to my rightful life again and make up for all the time I shouldn't have been banged up in here. So when do I leave?' he demanded.

Bloody hell, he couldn't wait to get out of this place. He'd not heard a word from Esme. He'd been allowed to write to her at the women's prison where she was serving her sentence for her part in the kidnapping, but she'd never replied. And then the previous year, he'd been told she'd been released early, and yet still he'd not heard from her. Could she still be of any use to him? She must have a job by now, a little money, a home of some sort, even if it was just a rented room somewhere. If he could track her down, he could at least stay with her until he got himself sorted. And then he could see if he could find another way to make Meg Chandler pay for ruining his life. Only this time, he'd make sure he didn't get caught.

'Not so fast,' Howard warned with metered deliberation. 'You're not being released into civilised society just yet. I have your call-up papers here in front of me. You will be escorted directly from here to the army. So from then on, they'll be in charge of you. You'll be under close scrutiny. And you'll find the military police are pretty unforgiving as well as efficient, so I'd forget any ideas about deserting if I were you.'

It was with grim satisfaction that Howard watched the smirk slip from Green's face. The devil's jaw dangled open for a second or two before he snapped it shut again, and his eyes bulged in fury.

He'd been duped once again, hadn't he? Stitched up. And there was only one person to blame. The person who began it all in the first place.

Meg Chandler.

He might have to bide his time, but Green swore to himself in that instant that, come what may, one day he'd get even with her if it was the last thing he ever did!

*

'Who am I speaking to? It's not Mrs Stratfield-Whyte, is it? I'd have recognised her voice. It's Gerald Soames here. General manager at the factory.'

Alarm bells started ringing sickeningly in Meg's head. Why was Mr Soames telephoning, and not Mr Wig himself? 'Er, oh,' she stammered. 'It's Meg Hillier. Chandler as was.'

'Ah, good. Wigmore said either you or Miss Whitehead would probably answer the phone. He hoped you would. He wanted me to speak to one of you first rather than his wife.'

'So why can't he speak himself?' Meg faltered. 'Is anything wrong?'

'Don't panic, Mrs Hillier. Wigmore's all right. He *is* in hospital, but his injuries aren't too serious. He'll be allowed home to convalesce in a few days' time.'

Don't panic? Meg was jumping up and down with anxiety. She'd long ago come to realise how much Mr W meant to her. 'What on earth's happened?' she almost screeched down the line.

'The factory was hit last night, I'm afraid. During the late shift. The sirens had only just gone and there wasn't time to evacuate. Not the entire factory was affected, though. Just the one work shed.' Mr Soames paused, and his voice dropped in a deep sigh. 'I'm sorry to report that almost everyone in that part of the factory was killed. We pulled a few out alive, but two of them died on their way to hospital.'

Meg felt herself go cold. First Doris's mum, and now this. The war really was closing in. She knew she was in shock. It seemed unreal. Too much to take in. 'And Mr Wigmore?' she forced herself to ask.

'He was helping with the rescue. But a wall collapsed and he got trapped. Got a few cracked ribs, but nothing serious. They want to keep him in for a few days just to be certain there aren't any internal injuries, but it doesn't seem likely.'

'Oh, thank God for that.' Meg felt a tiny piece of her relax. That was some good news, at least. But what about all the employees who'd lost their lives? 'So what'll happen next?' she made herself ask.

'Well, first of all, Wigmore doesn't want his wife coming up to visit him, not with the air raids continuing. And especially after her last experience of visiting London, he says. He'll be coming home soon enough. I'll see him again tomorrow and give you an update. And as soon as he's released, I'll drive him down to you myself.'

'That's very kind of you.'

'The least I can do.'

'But what about all those poor people? And the factory?'

'The rest of the workers will carry on as normal. They have to. As for the… deceased, we're carrying out all the formalities with the authorities. Fortunately we know exactly who was on shift.'

Meg had to bite her lip. She couldn't see anything fortunate about it. But she supposed it was just a bad choice of words for which Mr Soames must be forgiven. He must, after all, be in shock himself. It was probably why he was being so calm and efficient about it all. And if he was in charge of everything, he'd need to keep a cool head.

Meg couldn't be so collected herself. 'B-but what about their families?' she stuttered. 'Mr Wigmore had taken on a lot of women, hadn't he? What about their children, those that weren't evacuated?'

'The WVS are taking care of most of that. And I'm sure Wigmore will see they're all right once he's recovered himself.'

'Yes, I'm sure he will.'

'Well, I've got a lot to take care of this end. So, can I leave it to you to tell Mrs Stratfield-Whyte? And as I say, I'll ring again tomorrow.'

'Yes, thank you, Mr Soames. And good luck.'

'Thanks. You, too.'

There was a click at the other end as he rang off and the line went silent. Meg drew in an enormous breath. Good luck. She was going to need it. She was shaking herself, but how on earth was she going to break it to Clarrie? Since being caught in the air raid, the poor woman appeared to have totally lost her nerve. Meg couldn't imagine how this latest piece of news was going to affect her, even if Mr W was only slightly hurt. Meg would have to be ready to prop her up, just as Clarrie had done for her all those years previously. Girding up her courage, Meg went to find her.

*

Clarrie stared at her unblinking, her heart turning painful somersaults. But the words kept flashing through her brain, *Wig's all right*. It was the only thing that mattered. May God forgive her, but her mind simply couldn't absorb the horror of what everyone else had suffered. That would come later. For now, her fragile emotions were saturated with the fact that Wig had survived.

She felt… yes, ashamed of her weakness. It had always been Wig who'd given her strength. He'd been her rock when they'd lost their darling little Rosebud. It was only because of him that she'd eventually found some peace, and through him she had been able to be strong for Meg when they'd been involved in the terrible tragedy that had left the poor child alone in the world. And the thought that she'd come within a hair's breadth of losing him, the very substance of her life, robbed her of the ability to feel anything for anyone else.

And she rejoiced in Wig's forbidding her to brave the bombings to visit him in hospital. She felt guilty about that as well, but she simply couldn't risk enduring another air raid. How the people of London stood it and yet remained cheerful, she didn't know. She wanted to fly to Wig's side, but she was too frightened. He'd always protected her. Shielded her. And she'd always appreciated it. Come to expect it, perhaps. She yearned to have the strength to defy him for once, but when she searched inside herself, it simply wasn't there.

Instead, she busied herself making everything ready for his return. They'd only be apart for a few days, after all.

She was like an excited child on the day Mr Soames brought him home. The manager didn't even come in for a cup of tea, and Clarrie was secretly pleased. She wanted Wig all to herself.

It wasn't until the third day that Meg found herself alone with Wig in the study. She knew he was drawing up plans to set up the destroyed part of the factory again in a Nissan hut, and restart production as soon as possible. Mr Soames had reported that some of the machinery had been salvageable, so that not all of it needed to be replaced.

Meg knocked firmly on the door.

'Come in,' she heard Wig answer, and turned the doorknob while balancing a small tray in her other hand.

Wig was sitting stiffly in the upright chair at the desk, but managed to turn his head to look over his shoulder without twisting his torso.

'Oh, good, it's you, Meg,' he sighed wistfully. 'I knew it wasn't Clarrie. She wouldn't have knocked. Poor soul's been fussing over me like a mother hen.'

'That's only to be expected, Mr W.' Meg gave a sympathetic smile.

'I know. But I'd rather just get on with it. And please, with everyone else on Christian name terms nowadays, I'd like to be just plain Wig, too. Ah, a cup of tea,' he said, spying the tray. 'You must've read my mind.'

'Well, I thought you'd like one in peace before the children get home from school.'

'Hmm, yes.' Wig gave a half wry, half amused grimace. 'It's not the ones who are at school that disturb me. It's Penny's youngest two. But at least it's quiet now while she's taken them with her to collect everyone from school.'

'Yes, I know,' Meg chuckled. 'But we wouldn't be without our dear Penny now. She keeps all our spirits up, and she took over all of Sally's work without batting an eyelid when Sally left.'

'Yes, she's the salt of the earth is our Penny,' Wig agreed. He paused a moment before going on thoughtfully, 'In fact, overall, it's all worked out rather well, hasn't it? Clarrie's been in her element having the house full of children. You see, she always wanted… but it never happened.' Meg noticed him colour, as if he'd said too much, but then he went on, 'I just wonder, though, how she'll be when they all go home.'

'Well, it doesn't look as if any of them'll be leaving before the war's over, and it's unlikely to end for ages,' Meg said regretfully. 'In fact, it feels as if it's hardly begun. So let's wait and see. And the twins both want to stay here indefinitely, anyway.'

'Tell me, they'll leave school in the summer, won't they?'

'Yes. But we can't send them back to London, especially now their parents have disappeared off the face of the earth. And I know Leslie's still keen to train properly under Gabriel as a gardener, and Cyril's keen to work with livestock. He's a natural with the animals.'

'I just hope the war's over before they're old enough to be called up.'

Meg snatched in her breath. 'Surely… You don't think it'll go on that long, do you?'

Wig's eyebrows arched. 'What've we achieved yet, eh? We've just about managed to keep Hitler off our own shores – so far – and had a few successes in North Africa. And we might've started raiding Berlin and other German cities, but Hitler's bombing the hell out of us. He's so powerful, he's overrun most of Europe. Nobody was prepared for him. Churchill was one of the few who saw it coming, and now Britain will never be safe until Hitler's completely crushed and preferably rotting in his grave. But we will win.' Wig's expression hardened. 'Eventually. We have to. And I have no doubt that Churchill will persuade America to join us in the end, but even so, in my opinion, victory could take years.'

Meg shivered. Imagine all the children in their charge growing into adults and still being at war. The twins even reaching the age when they had to go and fight. And… and Ralph. Oh, dear God…

Her head spun in terror so that she was barely aware of Wig speaking again.

'I'm glad I've got you alone for a minute, Meg,' he was saying. 'Take a seat. I've got something to tell you. Don't worry, it's nothing to do with Ralph.'

Shakily, Meg reached for a chair. It must be something of some importance, and she mentally braced herself.

'It's about Esme,' Wig began softly. 'She was among those killed. Each block has its own lavatories, you see. And she had the bad luck to be cleaning those particular ones when the bombs fell. I just thought you should know.'

'Oh.' Meg drew in a deep, pensive breath as she tried to absorb the information. For a moment, she wasn't sure how she felt, but then an overwhelming sadness filled her heart. Esme might have been her enemy, but having experienced an air raid herself, it just seemed so cruel that anyone should spend their last moments shot through with such fear. 'Poor Esme,' she said quietly. 'She never really had a happy life, did she?'

'She had a chip on her shoulder that she allowed to eat into her. She could've been happy and well cared for here in this house for as long as she wanted. But she felt that life owed her something. Something big and special. But it never happened. Perhaps that's why she took up with Green. She thought he'd give her that something life never had. Anyway, I thought you should know.'

'Yes. Thank you, Mr W. I mean, Wig. I'll… leave you to get on. And I'll tell the others. They ought to know, too.'

Wig nodded, and Meg quietly left the room, lost in thought. That made two people, two civilians, she'd known personally, Doris's mum and Esme, who'd been killed in the war. It was a terrible shock when it was brought to your own doorstep, so to speak. It just went to show. Fate, war, you never knew what was in store…

Twenty

She didn't recognise him for an instant when she first opened the front door. Beyond the shadow cast by the house, the daffodils along the driveway were bathed in dazzling April sunshine that turned the figure before her into a mere silhouette. It wasn't until her eyes adjusted to the contrast that she realised the fellow was attired in a smart RAF uniform, and when he removed his forage cap, her heart took wing.

'Ralph!' she cried in ecstasy, and launched herself into his arms, the glorious feel of him against her like life itself.

'It's so good to see you,' she heard him murmur.

She stood back, allowing her gaze to wander over him. His eyes looked tired, his face drawn, but he was alive. And he was there.

'You didn't say you were coming,' she breathed, as, shocked with joy, they somehow lingered on the doorstep.

'I wanted to surprise you. And I was worried if I told you and then my leave was cancelled at the last minute, you'd be really upset.' 'Well, you're here now!' Meg crowed in delight.

'I should've been here last night,' Ralph almost apologised. 'The bombings might seem to be easing up a bit, but the trains are still all over the place, and you're packed in like sardines. I spent half the night standing in a train, and the other half waiting on a platform.'

'You must be exhausted,' Meg sympathised. But he was *here*, and that was all that mattered. 'Come on in, and have a cuppa and something to eat, and then you'd better get some sleep.'

Ralph rubbed his hand wearily over his forehead. 'I'd rather just go over to Mum and Dad's rather than facing everyone in the house. And then you're right. I need to get some shut-eye.'

'Yes, I understand. I'll come over in a few minutes.'

Ralph nodded, and picking up his duffel bag, walked off towards the side of the house. Meg turned back inside, wondering in her excitement what she should do next. She didn't know what Ralph had in his kitbag, but wouldn't it be comforting for him to have a pair of his old, familiar pyjamas to sleep in? But they'd been in the unheated cottage all winter and wouldn't be aired. Although Meg had been sleeping back there since the air raids had lessened, she hadn't lit the range. There was no need as she still ate in the big house or with her in-laws. If she wanted to spoil her husband – which she wanted so desperately to do – she'd have to collect some of his pyjamas and take them across to the kitchen in the big house to warm through. She could make him a hot-water bottle while she was at it. She was sure he never had that luxury wherever it was he normally slept.

'Ralph's just turned up!' she announced gleefully as she reached the kitchen.

'Oh, what fantastic news!' Jane exclaimed. 'So where is he? We all want to say hello!'

'Gone over to his parents,' Meg replied, draping her husband's nightclothes in front of the massive range. 'But he looks exhausted and needs to have forty winks, so you'll all have to wait a bit.'

'Yeah, we understand, ducks,' Penny said with a knowing wink, which made Meg blush.

'No, *really*,' she laughed nervously. 'He's been up travelling all night.' 'Well, we'll believe you, luvvie,' Penny chuckled back.

Meg shook her head in amused exasperation before pouring the hotwater bottle. She took it over to the cottage with the warmed pyjamas and then having got their own small range lit and warming up, she hurried into Ralph's parents' next door. Ralph got up from the kitchen table at once, leaving a half-eaten sandwich. He must be utterly exhausted, Meg considered, if he couldn't finish the snack.

Back in their own cottage, Ralph was undressed and into bed and asleep in minutes. Meg watched his deep, steady breathing, the familiar line of his jaw, his cheeks even leaner than before, creases forming around his eyes where the skin used to be smooth. Meg played her own part in this war, helping to look after their evacuees and to keep them supplied with milk, eggs, ham and bacon, but it was nothing compared to the men who risked their lives on a daily basis. It set her mind thinking. Perhaps there was some way she should be doing more?

*

'There you are! Come here!'

Ralph's beloved voice startled her as she supervised Cyril milking the cows that evening. His hand on her arm swung her round to face him. She scarcely had time to notice that he'd changed into some old civvies before he pulled her towards him, crushing her against him, his mouth covering hers in a long, slow, lingering kiss that sent shivers down her spine. Her body melted into his, her arms going around his neck, fingers in his hair. It felt so good as she drew strength from him, and gave back all the love and comfort she could.

'Co-oor,' they heard a young voice sighing not so far away. 'Like the bloody movies.'

Meg drew back, aware of the deepening beetroot in her face. But Ralph tossed his head with that unique laugh she knew so well, and whipped her back into his embrace. This time, his kiss was more passionate, urgent, and Meg's lips parted in delicious response.

'You all right to finish the milking on your own?' she realised Ralph was asking over her head.

''Course,' Cyril's proud voice came back. 'Been doing it long enough, ain't I?'

'Then we'll leave you to it.'

The next thing Meg knew, Ralph had taken her hand and was leading her back towards the cottage. She knew what was to come, and suddenly felt awkward. It had been so long…

'Cyril's really quite competent with the animals,' she found herself saying. 'When he and Leslie leave school in the summer, they're going to stay on here, Leslie helping your dad full-time, and Cyril's perfectly capable of looking after the cows and the pigs and growing the fodder. So they really won't need me here,' she joked, although something at the back of her mind was telling her there was more to her thoughts than that.

'Well, I shall always need you,' Ralph said thickly as he swung her into his arms and led her across the threshold and up the stairs.

They made love slowly, unhurriedly. Delectably. Ralph excited every inch of her skin to fever pitch, and when the moment finally came, Meg felt she'd never reached such dizzy heights before. For that brief, delicious while, she was totally enraptured in her love for Ralph and the rest of the world dimmed away.

Afterwards, she lay curled up against him, head on his shoulder and her arm draped across his chest.

'I wish it could be like this forever,' she murmured as reality crept back into her mind.

'It will. One day,' Ralph assured her, twisting his neck to drop a kiss on her head. 'We just need to be patient.'

'But we don't know that for sure.' Meg propped herself up on one elbow to gaze into his steady, warm caramel eyes. 'We're not getting quite so many raids, but when they come, they're still pretty bad. And nobody knows who's going to get it next. They say Plymouth was even more

heavily bombed than London when it was hit last month.'

'Yes, going for the Royal Navy Dockyard obviously.'

'But the entire city was flattened, and so many people killed. It said in the paper people are going up onto Dartmoor every night to keep safe. I know I would. I tried not to show it for everyone else's sake, but I was terrified when we got caught up in that raid in London. But the Londoners, well, their courage is unbelievable.'

'Hmm, so they say. But I suppose if you've no other choice, you have to find some way to cope with it. But I do worry about Bob and Sally. You just have to hope and pray. Which is why, my darling, I want you to stay here in relative safety, and not venture up to London again.'

'Oh, don't worry, I won't! But Doris wanted so much to go to her mum's funeral.'

'Poor kid. She seems to be coping OK, though, doesn't she?'

'With everyone's support, yes. Though who knows what she's thinking deep down.'

'Yes, I know.' Ralph's expression was grave, but then it deepened into a look of intense longing. 'But I don't want to spend all my leave talking about other people. I want to enjoy being with my wife. And kissing her like this,' he teased, lifting his head from the pillow so that his lips brushed fleetingly against hers. 'And like this,' he repeated, gently pushing her onto her back and rolling on his side to lean down and kiss her deeply this time.

And she sank into the vast realms of his love once again.

Later, they made their way over to the big house.

'So anything new I ought to know before I see everybody?' Ralph asked as they climbed the steps up to what remained of the lawn. 'Don't want to put my foot in anything.'

'Oh, nothing really, I don't think. Louise still hasn't got a young man, but then she probably won't with them all being called up.'

Ralph sucked breath in through his teeth. 'That's a pity. I mean, she's reasonable looking, and she's such a sweet girl.'

'Yes, I know,' Meg sighed. 'But hopefully she'll meet someone one day. As for everyone else, Penny's Archie rings her occasionally, but he doesn't get much chance to visit. Joyce and Maureen's mum and dad survived all the raids unscathed. Ed had his birthday the week before last. Can't believe he's nine now. His mum came down for the day, but his dad's been called up now. I just hope he'll be OK. But mainly we keep an eye on Doris, with her dad somewhere or other on the high seas.'

'Yes, poor kid. But I know you'll all be looking after her. And have you heard from Sally at all? I've not heard from Bob, but he always was a diabolic letter-writer.'

'Actually, Sally rang the other day. From a call box so we only had a few minutes. She's fine. Happier now the raids seem to be petering out, and the evenings are getting lighter. Makes it better for her when she's on a late shift. She says Bob's ankle's getting stronger all the time. But then the pips went.'

'Ah, the dreaded pips,' Ralph attempted to joke. But they both knew how everyone hated being cut off. You never knew if or when you might speak to the person again.

But when they went inside the house, it was like a huge celebration. It was only during Ralph's conversations with the others that Meg learnt that as he hadn't had any leave for so long, Ralph had been given two weeks of freedom. Two whole weeks!

*

It all went far too quickly. Meg was relieved of all her duties, the spring weather giving them plenty of opportunity for long walks in the countryside. And when it rained, the marital bed was always waiting, a disgruntled Thimble lying outside the closed door.

Meg glanced up at Ralph one afternoon as they sauntered through the woods. He looked so much better, far less haggard, than when he'd arrived a week ago. But the next week, she knew, would slip away before they knew it. And the terrifying thought that always niggled at the back of her mind would begin to eat away at her again.

'I wish you didn't have to go back,' she murmured, helpless against the overwhelming fear.

'I know. But I must.' Ralph's voice was ragged. 'It's the same for everyone.'

'Yes. But it *feels* as if it's only us.'

Ralph nodded. 'Would it help if I explain what I actually do? Not that I can tell you that much. Each mission is so different.'

Meg considered a moment before she answered. 'Yes. I think I'd like to know. Then I can think of you more. Imagine it in my head. So that I can feel I'm watching over you.'

'Like my guardian angel,' Ralph chuckled, and then he went on more seriously, 'Well, it's no secret that there are highly organised resistance groups setting up in the occupied countries. France, Denmark, Norway and so forth. They blow up munitions dumps, railways, bridges – anything that disrupts German military movements. And they radio back information. Intelligence. It's highly dangerous. If they're caught, well, don't think about it. Suffice it to say, they're issued with cyanide pills.'

'Cyanide?' Meg's heart froze into a lump of ice. 'You mean…?'

'Yes. Men, women, some still children almost. The SOE support them. Special Operations Executive. And we support the SOE. They're calling us 138 Squadron. We mainly fly a plane called a Lysander. Only small. And painted a dull black so it's less visible in the dark. My pilot, Neville, is in the front cockpit, and I'm in the rear. I'm called the observer. I help with navigation, the drop, anything really. Sometimes I'm armed with a machine gun. And if anything happened to Nev, I could take over flying the plane. We fly in equipment and operatives in the dead of night. Often it's just a parachute drop, but sometimes we might have to land on a makeshift strip. If we're bringing an agent out, for instance. The rear cockpit's really small, so it's a real squeeze if we're transporting someone. The rendezvous could be just a clearing in a wood, something like that. The co-ordinates are sent to us by coded radio message. That's why navigation is so important. And we have to find a route in and out that's less likely to be detected. That relies a lot on intelligence, too. We're flying over enemy territory, but it's stealth rather than the massive force of a bombing raid, for instance. We plan each mission in meticulous detail, and timing's really important. We tend to fly several days either side of a full moon, but the weather, everything, plays a huge part. And luck.'

Meg had been listening carefully without interrupting him. Her heart stood still as she imagined Ralph flying in to a secret meeting place in the middle of the night, eyes straining to pick out the landing strip from the surrounding darkness. It sounded terrifying, but she attempted a wry chuckle. 'Cloak and dagger stuff, then?'

'You could say that. Except that it's deadly serious. But I don't want you to worry.' Ralph suddenly swung her towards him, taking her face in his hands. 'I'm damned good at what I do. I don't know if it's being a gardener, but I have a *feel* for the land. And Nev, he's the best. I'd like you to meet him one day.'

'Oh, I'd like that—'

'But I want you to know,' Ralph interrupted her, his voice vibrating with earnest, 'that if anything happens to me, no one could ever have made me happier than you, my darling Meg. And no matter what, my love for you will never be any more than a whisper away.'

Meg stared up at him, tears welling in her eyes as his mouth covered her lips with a tender passion that silenced her soul. She really didn't want to think about what the future might hold for them. All she wanted was to lose herself forever in the ocean of love that flooded through her as she drowned in his embrace once more.

Twenty-One

Meg had begun counting the days. She missed Ralph so much, somehow almost more now that she'd tasted his love once again. It had become a permanent ache in her heart, a constant pain that never let up, even when she was with her friends, or walking Thimble and the other dogs, or tending the animals. Where was Ralph at that moment? Would he be flying a mission that night from which he might not return? The fear was a threatening, black cloud that pressed down on her with relentless force.

But as each day passed, there was something else gathering strength in her mind. It was seven weeks since Ralph had returned to his base, and she was late. Could it be that he'd left her a parting gift? Oh, what joy it would be to have a child of her own. Ralph's child. Her heart was overflowing with elation, and yet on the other hand, could it be that this was fate warning her that he wasn't coming back from his next mission because now she would have his child instead, since her luck wouldn't stretch to the joy of having them both? She prayed to God not. But if she was pregnant, would she want to bring a child into such a world? A world fragmented with strife?

Meg's emotions were tangled up in a twisted knot, and yet she hadn't shared her troubles with anyone else. She wouldn't until she was sure. It was true that she and Ralph had been so swept in the euphoria of being together again that they hadn't thought to use anything to stop her conceiving. But with all the stresses and strains of the war, her cycle was all over the place. She'd been this late before when there'd been no possibility of her being pregnant, and she didn't feel nauseous at all, but then not everybody did.

It was so hard keeping it to herself, and yet she felt it was the right thing to do. She hadn't even mentioned it to Ralph the few times he had managed to ring her. She didn't want anything to distract him from concentrating on his missions. Until she was absolutely sure, she would have to bottle it up.

And if it was true, she wouldn't know whether to rejoice or be worried sick. *'I may be right, I may be wrong, but I'm perfectly willing to swear,'* Jane was singing along to Vera Lynn on the radio as she helped Louise clear the table in the servants' hall after lunch.

And then everyone else joined in with, *'That when you turned and smiled at me, a nightingale sang in Berkeley Square.'*

Everyone else except Meg. She just couldn't bring herself to sing just now, and she gave a wan smile instead. Clarrie and Nana May shared the servants' table nowadays. It hardly seemed right for just the two of them to be waited on in the spacious dining room anymore. They had managed to purchase another wireless set to place on the sideboard in the servants' hall. The talking, singing machine had become so important in everybody's lives, listening to the BBC news and speeches by Winston Churchill, and the programmes of music and comedy helped to keep people's spirits up. But not Meg's. Not today, anyway. She didn't notice Clarrie throw a frown in her direction as everybody dispersed. It was a school day for the younger children, so the twins had shot off back to helping Gabriel outside, and Joyce, who had gone up to the senior classes, had taken it upon herself to go and clean some of the bedrooms. Ada had taken Johnny out to the kitchen while Penny went upstairs to change Bella's nappy, leaving Clarrie, Nana May, Jane and Louise.

'I've got some mending to do,' Meg told them, 'so I'll be up in the sewing room if anybody wants me. I know the twins work really hard, but they're forever tearing their clothes or wearing out their cuffs.' 'Boys will be boys,' Nana May grimaced happily.

Meg took herself up the servants' stairs, but as she got to the sewing room, she decided to nip up to the female servants' toilet before she started her mending session. As always during the past few weeks she held her breath. She felt a little damp down below, but it was probably nothing. But when she took down her knickers, a red stain stared back up at her.

She gazed down on it, disbelieving. She knew you could still have a show, but there was more in the pan. Oh. She wasn't pregnant after all, and she hiccupped back a tear as her heart crumpled. She didn't want a baby, did she? Because she didn't want to have to fear for its future. A river of relief swept through her, but that in itself made her feel guilty. And if Ralph didn't return from one of his missions, she wouldn't have the comfort of his child. Oh, dear God, what did she think? Feel? She just didn't know.

Bury herself in mending the twins' clothes. That was the answer. She went back downstairs and hurried across to the cottage to sort herself out, and then went back to the sewing room. She hoped no one would see her. She really didn't want to talk to anyone until it sank in. Unnerved, sad, confused. She just wanted to sit quietly on her own.

The room faced north, but the casement window still admitted plenty of light, and she got to work, plying her needle in and out, sewing on a patch here, darning a hole there. Kept her head down. Let normality wash away the turmoil of emotions that spiralled inside her until she felt she could face the world again.

A light tap on the door lifted her head. Oh, no. She didn't want to have to put on a smiling face. She just wanted to be alone.

Clarrie put her head around the door before stepping inside and closing it softly behind her. She came across to Meg and sat down in the chair opposite her, her face so intense with compassion that Meg felt she couldn't ignore her.

'Meg, my dear girl, something's been bothering you,' she said, her voice like silk. 'I can tell. I know you're worried about Ralph. We all are. And all the menfolk. But you've been different recently. Tell me to mind my own business, and I'll go away. But if there's anything I can do to help, you know I will.'

Her eyebrows were knitted in earnest, her gaze so warm and steady that despite herself, Meg felt drawn down into its depths. She fought against it, but though every bone of her body wanted to resist, she felt herself falling into Clarrie's kindness.

She lowered her eyes to her trembling hands and put the sewing down in her lap.

'It's just… I thought I was pregnant', she mumbled, 'and now I know I'm not. And I don't know whether I'm relieved or broken-hearted.'

It was suddenly all too much and, though she tried to hold back, tears began to roll down her cheeks. Unable to look at Clarrie, she tried angrily to wipe them away, but they kept on coming. The next thing she knew, Clarrie had sat down beside her, and had gathered her in her arms, and she was sobbing against the other woman's shoulder.

Clarrie held her tightly. Oh, how she'd longed during all those years to hold Meg against her as if she were her daughter. But not like this. Not when Meg's soul was in agony. All she could do was rock her gently, let her know that she understood her pain.

Quite suddenly, she felt so calm. As if she was ready to face all the suffering and yearning of her adult life. She stroked Meg's hair as she said softly, 'I know. More than you think. Wig and I wanted so much to have children, but it never happened. This…'

She broke off. She still couldn't bring herself to tell Meg everything. That would be too much. It was still so painful that she never wanted to talk about it with anyone but Wig and Nana May. Didn't want anyone else to know. But… maybe all those years of wanting to keep it a secret, to bury her pain, were gone. Perhaps it would be better to share something of her grief now. But not all of it. She wasn't quite ready for that.

She took a deep breath. 'This room was to have been the nursery,' she barely whispered. 'That's why we painted it lemon and it's stayed that colour ever since. Because lemon would do for a boy or a girl.'

Her voice had drifted off as she imagined the cot, the nursing chair, the curtains printed with little animals that she'd planned. It would have been such a happy room. The sound of children's laughter…

'Oh, I'm so sorry, Clarrie.' Meg pulled back as her tears subsided, leaving Clarrie feeling a little empty. 'I should've thought. When I first came here, I asked Nana May if you had any family, and she just said that sadly you didn't. So it was thoughtless of me.'

Clarrie shook her head. 'No, my dear. Don't think that. Just because I know how you feel doesn't mean your pain is any less than mine. And you're young—'

'I just need Ralph to stay alive,' Meg blurted out, in a flash seeing clearly through the tunnel of her anguish. 'It's all the fault of this damned war. And I wouldn't really have wanted a child until it was over. To bring a child into such a world would be wrong. B-but what if—?'

'Let's try not to think the worst, eh?'

Meg met Clarrie's gaze. Of course, that's what they all had to do. If they wanted to keep their sanity. 'Thank you, Clarrie,' she managed to gulp. 'You've always been so kind.'

'I'll always be here for you, Meg, you know that. To talk things through. And I won't say anything about this, I promise.'

'And I won't say anything about what you just told me, either.'

'Thank you. It'll be our secret. Our pact.'

Clarrie watched as Meg nodded with an understanding if watery smile. And something inside her rejoiced. She'd only told Meg part of the story. Perhaps she'd never tell her the whole truth. But for now, their hearts shared one pain, and what could bring them closer than that?

*

'Blooming 'eck, I don't believe it!' Penny cried, picking Bella up and squeezing her to her breast as if to take comfort from her. 'I fought Hitler and Russia was supposed ter be friends!'

'Huh, you can't trust anything that Hitler says!' Ada scoffed, rolling out pastry with far more vigour than she should. 'Russia's got oil, and now he wants it for himself. Isn't that right,

Meg?' she asked, since she knew Meg would know more about it than anyone in the kitchen just then.

Meg nodded. 'Yes. And it's rich in other minerals as well. Things that'll help him make weapons. But at least it means that now he's attacking Russia, the pressure's off us. That must be why the Blitz has more or less stopped.'

'I wouldn't be so sure about that. Wouldn't trust 'im as far as I could throw 'im.'

'I'm sure he'll remind us every now and then,' Meg agreed, 'but hopefully the worst is over. And it'll give us time to build up our armaments to fight back. The factory's working flat out again, and Wig's been designing new machinery for the government to make bigger and better weapons in bigger factories, as well. The world's gone mad, and all because of one crazy little man.'

'I doesn't know how he came ter power in the first place.'

'Well, he has. But all this chatter isn't going to get dinner prepared for all of you lot tonight,' Ada declared forcibly, and Penny winked at Meg behind her friend's back.

'Yes, I'll go and find Gabriel, and see what vegetables he has ready for us,' Meg offered. 'We're so lucky to have all this at our fingertips. It must be awful to be living in cities and queuing for hours just to get whatever you can.'

She turned towards the back door, but just at that moment, she heard the tinkling of the front door bell.

'Oh, goodness, I'd forgotten,' she said, clamping her hand over her mouth. 'That'll be the vicar. Clarrie and Nana May are waiting for him in the drawing room. I'd better go and let him in. I'm still supposed to be parlourmaid, after all!' she laughed, changing direction and then hurrying along the corridor to the hall.

'Good afternoon, Vicar!' she beamed at the elderly gentleman waiting on the doorstep. 'Do come in.'

'Thank you, Meg my dear. What a beautiful afternoon for walking out here.' He smiled wryly. 'Hard to imagine we're at war when the weather's so nice.'

'But you must have heard about Germany starting to attack Russia yesterday?'

'Yes.' The smile slid from Father James's face. 'While I was giving my sermon, Hitler was doing his worst again. Terrible business. But at least it might give us a breather, though it grieves my Christian soul to say such a thing.'

'I know. It's terrible. But you've come to discuss the summer fête. Are we still going to have one this year?'

'But, of course,' the vicar confirmed as Meg showed him along the corridor to the drawing room. 'We've got to keep things up. And I hope you'll do us some more of your lovely paintings to auction again.' 'Yes, I will, if you'd like some,' Meg agreed.

She opened the door to the drawing room and led him across the room to where the French doors stood wide open to the June afternoon. Sunshine was streaming in, casting large, bright rectangles on the carpet and onto the armchairs where Clarrie and Nana May were waiting to greet him.

'I'll just go and get you all some tea. Have to be a bit weak, I'm afraid,' she grimaced.

'Not at all,' Father James smiled again. 'Now then, Mrs StratfieldWhyte, Miss Whitehead, how are we this fine afternoon?' he asked.

*

'D'you think mine will be good enough to auction, as well?' Doris asked.

'Or maybe just put in the raffle.'

She and Meg were sitting in the rose garden together, painting. The August morning was overcast, but the light was better for observing the precious blooms and it would have been too hot to sit out in the full sun. With most of the terraced lawn now dug up for vegetable growing, Clarrie refused to give up the rose garden as well, although the feathery leaves of carrots flourished rather prettily in the spaces between.

Meg lowered her own paintbrush and tipped her head to one side as she studied Doris's picture. 'Yes, I think so. You've come on in leaps and bounds. But wouldn't you like to keep it for your dad when he comes home?'

'Yes, I suppose so.'

Doris's tone was unusually flat, and Meg sucked in her cheeks. Doris was eleven years old, no longer a child. And she was mourning her mother, probably would all her life. But Meg wasn't prepared for what came next.

'D'you think Mummy suffered when she died?' Doris asked, her voice detached and almost scoured of emotion. 'That she was badly damaged? D'you think that's why they wouldn't let me see her?'

Meg felt as if her blood had frozen in her veins. Poor Doris. It had been some months since her mother had been killed. Had she kept that horrible thought bottled up inside all that time? Meg's heart began to race. Whatever she said next could affect Doris for the rest of her life. At least she'd been able to sit with her parents' bodies to say goodbye, to kiss their marble cold foreheads.

'I… I don't know,' she answered, her voice little more than a whisper. 'And that's the truth. All I can say is that she wouldn't have known anything about it, it would've been that quick.' Meg put down her brush, and turning to Doris, took her hands. 'What you must remember is that she loved you very, very much, and try and think of all the good times you had.'

Doris had been looking steadily at her, and now she lowered her eyes with a little nod and a wan smile lifting the corners of her mouth. Meg's heart lurched as her thoughts flew back through the years to when Clarrie had said virtually the same thing to her. Dear God, she'd never thought to be offering the same advice and comfort to someone else.

Neither of them had heard Cyril come up behind them.

'Cor, that's good, Doris,' he praised, looking over her shoulder. 'We were going ter walk inter the village ter see if we can get any sweets or chocolate. D'you want ter come?'

To Meg's relief, Doris seemed to perk up at once. 'Better than potato and cocoa truffles.' The girl managed a full smile. 'But I need to put my painting things away first.'

'No, that's all right. I'll do it,' Meg offered. She didn't want Doris's brightened mood to be spoilt. Poor girl needed cheering up. Hopefully now she'd spoken to Meg, she might feel a tiny bit better and the horrific image she had in her head would gradually fade.

Meg noticed with a little smile that as the two young people went down the garden path, Cyril took Doris's hand. It was a natural, childlike gesture, but somehow it spoke volumes. Meg was so pleased the twins were to stay on at Robin Hill House now that they'd left school. They were part of the family and she couldn't imagine life without them. And after the war… But that was a long way off, and how far off, nobody knew.

Meg couldn't blame poor Doris, but their conversation had unnerved her. And though she took up her brush again, for some minutes, all she could do was stare at the petals of the delicate rose she was painting.

Twenty-Two

It came to her in a flash.

It was the very end of August, and one of those rare sultry summer nights, too close to sleep. Meg had tossed and turned, finally deciding that the only thing for it was to get up. She swung her legs over the side of the bed and sat, wondering what to do next. A glass of water, and then try again to get to sleep? Somehow she didn't think it would work.

She'd left the dress she'd been wearing the day before over the back of the chair. It would be a beautiful night for a wander around the grounds, mystical and exciting. Everything looked different in the dark, although tonight a bright half-moon was shedding a silvery, liquid glow on the earth beneath. Meg wouldn't need a torch, not that the slit in the cardboard they were obliged to tape over the beam afforded much light anyway. She'd be able to see by the moonlight, and she knew the grounds like the back of her hand, so she'd be perfectly safe.

She dressed quickly and went downstairs, Thimble frolicking about her ankles in excitement at this adventure as Meg opened the front door of the cottage. She ambled towards the lake, Thimble snuffling hither and thither in this magical world. The moonlight shimmered on the silken sheen of water, velvet-smooth in the stillness. Not a breath stirred, heavy with the scents of late summer, calm and peaceful.

Meg allowed her thoughts to wander at will as she lowered herself onto the bench. She loved Robin Hill House and all the people there. Her own parents would always be special and nowadays her memories of them were happy, not sad, ones. But she'd found a new family, a different sort of happiness. And she had Ralph.

Oh, dear God, *please* let him survive this war. She truly wouldn't want to go on if anything happened to him. *Couldn't* go on. After those two glorious weeks back in the spring, and then the anguish when she'd thought she was carrying his child, and the even greater turmoil when she discovered she'd merely been late, it was all just too much. The only thing that mattered was that he returned home safely after every one of his secret missions.

As if to drive the knife further into the wound, her ear latched onto the distant drone of aircraft. She looked up. Two small planes were making their way across the sky, tiny silhouettes as they headed home. They must have turned slightly, since the moonlight glinted on them for just a second, and then they disappeared into the night.

Meg sighed deeply. One of them could have been Ralph, although she knew it wasn't. If only there was something she could do to keep him safe. She was happy here, and yet she felt as if she should be doing more, almost as if that would help Ralph stay alive.

Now that the twins had left school, Meg was scarcely needed. Cyril was more than competent with the animals now, and he and Leslie were hard workers outside. With Gabriel overseeing everything, they could easily provide the manpower needed, and the girls helped to some extent as well. And inside the house, well, there was an army of females to take care of everything, with Clarrie firmly at the helm. They could manage perfectly well without Meg. But what could she do?

Wig had mentioned that women were likely to be conscripted into war work by the end of the year. She'd probably be drafted into a munitions factory of some sort, and she'd hate that. Being inside all day, doing the same monotonous task over and over again. But what if she joined the Women's Land Army first? And what if...?

Her heart took a bound. This had never exactly been part of her plan. She would reach the magic age of twenty-one at the end of the following month, and her *plan* had always been to take on her own farm tenancy when she was legally old enough. But because of the war, she'd had to put that idea on the back-burner. She'd never even told Ralph of her aim, since her love for him was more important to her than anything in the universe, and she was prepared to give up her dream for him. But if anything could help keep her mind from worrying about Ralph, it was this.

She sat back, letting the serenity of the warm night air waft over her. It wouldn't exactly be helping Ralph, but at least she'd have something to distract her from her constant fears for him. And with that thought to calm her mind, she went back to contemplating the moonlit waters of the lake.

*

The next morning, she was up with the lark despite her disturbed night. Ada hadn't yet arrived, and only Penny was in the kitchen with her young brood. With it being the end of the summer holidays, the older children had no need to be up in time for school. Only Cyril had been up shortly after dawn. Meg had heard him whistling tunelessly as he passed the cottage on his way to milk the cows.

Meg grabbed a mug of tea and some toast while telling Penny she was going out for a few hours. The homely woman didn't question her, and ten minutes later, she set off on her bicycle.

It took her over an hour to get there. She shuddered as she passed the spot where her mum and dad had died. It was nearly five years ago, and she *must* put it behind her.

Everything was just the same as she arrived at Home Farm. As it always did on the rare occasions she'd been back to visit the Fenshaws, the tenants who'd taken over after her parents had died, excitement foamed up inside her. For she really did feel as if she was coming home.

There was no sign of life as she entered the farmyard, but then there wouldn't be at that time of day. The cows would have been milked at the crack of dawn, and being summer, would be back out in the fields, as would the flock of sheep. Meg knew she would get a warm welcome, but nonetheless, her heart pattered nervously as she knocked on the back door.

'Oh, hello, Meg!' the farmer's wife greeted her with a beaming smile. 'What a nice surprise! We've not seen you much since your wedding. Come on in, my dear.'

'Up till now, I've been kept pretty busy,' Meg explained, going inside. Once again, it felt so strange entering her old home. Part of her, part of her parents, still lingered in the very walls of the old farmhouse, and yet she felt a stranger, empty and full at the same time.

'Are you on your own?' kindly Maggie Fenshaw enquired as she stood back for Meg to go inside. 'Ralph not on leave or anything? He is... all right?' she dared to ask, gesturing for Meg to sit down at the kitchen table.

'Oh, yes. He had a fortnight's leave in April which was wonderful, but I've not seen him since,' Meg explained. 'He manages to ring me about once a week, but he's only allowed a few minutes on the phone.'

'Well, at least that's a few minutes men don't get if they're serving abroad,' Maggie said sadly. 'Did you know our son, Paul, got married recently? And he's just got his call-up papers, and all. Chose the army.

Wanted his feet firmly on the ground as God meant us to be, he says. Loves the land, and can't wait to get back here and he hasn't even gone yet. Mind you, we're not sure this farm's big enough to support two families, assuming Paul, well, survives the war,' Maggie went on with a catch in her voice, 'and has a family of his own one day. Cuppa, dearie?'

'Yes, please.'

'But in the meantime,' Mrs Fenshaw continued, busying herself with the teapot, 'once Paul's gone, I'm not sure my Alan can manage on his own, not with the quotas the man from the ministry's set us. We're no spring chickens. Had Paul late in life, you see,' she added confidentially, pushing a mug of tea in Meg's direction.

'Thank you, Mrs Fenshaw.'

'I should be thanking you. Given me a good excuse to sit down myself. I think we'll have to ask the Land Army for help. Though I'm not sure I fancy a stranger living in our house and sleeping in Paul's old room. Living with his new in-laws, he is at present, and coming over here each day. Though what we'll do without him, I don't know.'

Meg's heart was banging against her ribcage. She couldn't believe her luck – if the Fenshaws agreed, of course. 'You might not have to,' she ventured, her eyebrows arched in anticipation. 'Have a complete stranger in the house, I mean. I know we don't know each other *that* well, but we seem to get on. The thing is… Now that our twin evacuees have left school, and they do so much at Robin Hill House, I'm not really needed anymore. So I've decided the best way I can help the war effort is to join the Land Army.

And I can't think of a better place to work than here.'

She watched as Mrs Fenshaw's jaw dropped before a huge smile spread over the woman's face. 'Well, I'm sure Alan will agree,' she grinned. 'So when can you start?'

Joy seemed to fill up the empty place Ralph's absence had left in Meg's soul. 'As soon as you'd like me to,' she answered, spilling over with delight. 'I'd like to make it official, though, and join the Land Army first. That way, they won't try to call me up to munitions work or anything at a later date. And I'll have to change my rationing registrations and so forth.'

'As a Land Army Girl, you'll qualify for extra cheese ration, or so I believe,' Maggie Fenshaw laughed, 'although what difference an ounce or two a week is supposed to make, I really don't know! But you really are the answer to our prayers, young Meg. I'm sure Alan will be as delighted as I am.'

Meg was beaming back at her. She knew Clarrie and Doris and Nana May would be upset at her leaving, although she also knew they'd support her in her decision. But it was the right thing for her to do, and it was as if the words were shining above her head in sparkling gold letters. *She was coming home!*

*

'Oh, Meggy, we're going to miss you so much!' Doris clung about her neck longer than most on the morning she was leaving. She was crushing Meg to her almost as much as Penny had!

'No, you won't,' Meg tried to laugh, though she felt a lump rising in her own throat. 'And it's not as if I'm going far. I promise I'll come back every fortnight and we can all catch up then. You can tell me all your news, and I expect to see some beautiful paintings from you. It's my twenty-first next month, so maybe you can do me something special as a present.'

It was a Saturday, and everyone was standing outside the front door of Robin Hill House to see her off. So many people and all so dear to her, yet she had met them all because of horrible things that had happened.

'Now, you, Cyril,' she said pointedly, but with teasing in her voice to lighten the mood, 'if you're not sure about anything with the animals, just pick up the phone. The Fenshaws have had one installed since I lived there before, so we're not cut off.'

'Well, you look after yourself, girl,' Gabriel said, stepping forward to hug her, and she noticed the moisture hovering on the lower lids of his rich brown eyes. Ralph's eyes. 'You're the only daughter-in-law we've got.'

'I will. And you, too.'

It was Mary's turn to bid her farewell next, and since Wig was at the factory, that just left Nana May and Clarrie to say goodbye. Meg's heart twisted like a corkscrew as the old lady hobbled forward on her stick. She'd been such a rock since the beginning, so solid and dependable, a wise old owl. But she was in her eighties now, and Meg was a little fearful. For what if anything happened to her while she was absent?

She hurled the thought to the back of her mind as she turned to Clarrie. They took each other's hands and for several seconds the world drifted away as their eyes locked in understanding. They had shared so much, their innermost secrets, such anguish on either side, had held each other up. Meg knew in that moment that she did truly love her. She couldn't have her mother back, but if someone was to take her place, no one in the world could have done so better than Clarrie.

Meg sniffed back a tear and spun round to Leslie who was holding the bicycle for her. Her little suitcase was strapped to the pannier rack over the back wheel, and she'd stuffed a shoe bag into the basket at the front. She swung her leg over the crossbar, since it was still the same men's bike Ralph had renovated for her. She'd already trained Thimble to run safely alongside her on the lead as she rode the bicycle. So hooking the lead about her wrist, she started pedalling down the drive, calling her goodbyes to the small crowd by the house. Then she took her other hand from the handlebar to wave vigorously, before turning out onto the lane.

And then she was on her own. Leaving one life behind to start another new one. Except that it wasn't new. She was going home. And though her vision blurred with tears, her heart swelled with joy.

Some time later, when everyone was doing what they normally did on a Saturday morning, Clarrie was standing silently by the bedroom window, staring over the grounds to the empty cottage. She'd lost her Meg. For the time being, at least. And now she'd gone, Clarrie had the feeling she wouldn't be coming back. First Rosebud and now Meg. Thank God Wig had been spared when he'd come so close to death. And Hitler seemed more intent just now on invading Russia rather than bombing Britain. And she had Penny and all the children to keep her occupied. Until the end of the war when they'd all go back to whatever homes they had left in London. She'd miss them all. But none as much as Meg. She didn't hear the light footsteps and the soft tap of the walking stick until Nana May came up behind her and placed a knowing hand on her arm.

*

'Right, you horrible lot of morons! At ease, if you can remember what that means.'
The sergeant major cast his spearing gaze over the recruits who stood in regimented lines before him on what passed for a parade ground. They'd come to him as a motley crew: cocky blackguards who'd needed the edges knocked off, ex-gaolbirds, and others who were downright thick in his opinion. He'd beaten and bullied them into shape with as much rigid discipline as he could muster – which even in his own eyes was considerable. It had still taken much longer than most intakes of raw recruits, but it was no good sending them into active service if they weren't ready. They could put other men in the unit in danger, especially where they were headed, and could make the difference between victory and defeat. If possible, that wasn't a risk worth taking when the British Army was suffering so many setbacks.
He waited while they shifted into the at ease position, despairing of the few who were still a split second behind the others. But they'd had months of training, and things couldn't be delayed any longer. They were needed now, not next year.
The sergeant major's steely eyes narrowed further as they travelled over the sea of faces. Some of them probably wouldn't last five minutes in battle, but others were more resilient. Take Green, for instance. He was a wily one. Would probably make a good corporal in situations that required stealth and cunning. He was one of the ex-gaolbirds. The army might just put him right.
'You're still a load of low-down scum, but your training's over,' the sergeant major bellowed. 'I wouldn't give you a day, but you've got a fortnight's final leave before you're shipped out. You'll be told where once you're en route. That means on the way, you ignorant bastards. But as far away from me as possible, I hope! You'll be given your passes later today, and you'll be back here by eighteen hundred hours on the twenty-second of the month. Now, do I make myself cle-ar?' he blared, raising his voice to foghorn level. And after a deliberate pause for effect, he yelled, 'Dismissed!'
The scuffling of army boots scraped through the drizzly autumn air and there was a general murmur as the parade broke up and the men turned away. Two weeks was more than they'd expected, but that could mean they were being deployed further afield where they might not get home leave again until after the war. If they survived it. But might as well make the most of it while they could.
'My missus'll be pleased to see us,' someone said.
'Mine, too. And the kids. I've missed the little blighters.'
'Well, I ain't got no missus, so I'm off to the best knocking shop I can find to get me leg over while I can!'
'Sounds like a great idea. I'll come wiv yer. Fancy a freesome, do yer?'
Bawdy laughter ricocheted about the group as they crunched towards the barrack huts. That one was all mouth and no trousers. At least, that was what they all thought.

'How about you, Green?' someone else asked. 'You got a girl hidden away somewhere?'
Nathaniel Green pinned on his face what he thought was an appropriate leer. 'Might have,' he answered gruffly. 'But I've got a bit of unfinished business to see to first.'

'What's that, then?'

'None of your bloody business.'

No, it certainly wasn't. He had no intention of telling anyone – or of seeing any of these useless idiots ever again. He'd played his part well, showing as much enthusiasm and intelligence as he could. The army would think he was a reformed character, a reliable and trustworthy soldier. Little did the fools know! He wasn't going to risk his neck for a capitalist country that had never done him any favours. If the Germans invaded, well, he'd be happy to collaborate. They'd be more appreciative than anyone else he'd ever known! The plan was easy. He'd disappeared before, and he was perfectly capable of doing so again. He knew how to cover his tracks, and was a master of disguise. The military police would never find him.

He had it all planned. When he'd been inside, he'd pretended to keep himself apart from his fellow inmates. But there'd been one other who'd responded equally to his guile, an elderly forger who would have been released by now. And Nathaniel knew where to find him. A new identity card and ration book would be no problem.

Nathaniel had his army pay in his pocket, so he could pay his way. In fact, it was the first time in ages that he had a decent amount of money to his name. Ironic or what? he sneered to himself. He'd lose himself up north, Manchester or Liverpool perhaps. Somewhere he'd not had any connections with in the past and where they wouldn't think to look for him. He was quite good at both those local accents, so wouldn't stand out in the crowd.

And he'd soon find a way of making a living. The Black Market was nothing to someone like him.

He'd give it a while, six months at least, before he made his way back down south. To Kent. Was there any way he could track Esme down? He wasn't sure. But that wasn't so important. What he wanted was to stake out Robin Hill House. With any luck, Meg bleeding Chandler would still be there. Seemed to have a thing going on with that Ralph Hillier, so that might have kept her there.

And then he could take his sweet revenge. He began to drool at the very thought.

*

'Meg, my dear, happy birthday!' Clarrie cried, rushing to open the front door. She'd been standing by the sitting-room window, watching for Meg to pedal up the drive. She noted sadly, though, that Meg didn't have Thimble with her, which probably meant that she wasn't staying overnight.

'Clarrie!' Propping the bicycle against the front wall, Meg launched herself into the older woman's embrace. 'So good to see you again!'

'Oh, come on in! We're all waiting for you in the drawing room. It's such a special occasion, we thought we'd have your party in there.'

'It's not that special,' Meg protested, hanging her coat on the hall stand.

'Yes, it is! You only turn twenty-one once in your life. Wig was just so sorry he couldn't join us.'

'Yes, I know. There's a war on!' Meg joked.

'But he said to open one of his precious bottles of champagne to celebrate.'

'Oh, that's kind of—'

But she didn't get any further. As they went into the drawing room, she was regaled with a chorus of bright voices singing 'Happy Birthday to You', followed by a rendition of 'You're Twenty-One Today', led gustily by Penny. As it was half-term, everyone was there, and she was hugged and kissed until she was breathless. Although she was really happy being at Home Farm, it was so good to be back among her friends at Robin Hill House.

Ada had done her best to produce a spread – egg and spam sandwiches, vegetable flans and a fruitcake topped with some almonds she'd found lurking in the pantry, rather than the cardboard icing that had become such a joke. Joyce and Maureen had made the most light and fluffy tarts with some of that year's batch of blackberry jam. Bunting from the village fête had been pinned along the picture rail, and the last roses from the garden adorned a huge cut-glass vase on the mantelpiece above the fireplace where a log fire burned merrily.

'We'd like you to have the vase as our present to you,' Clarrie told her. 'Take the flowers back with you, but I'll clean the vase and put it away for safe-keeping.'

'Oh, Clarrie, thank you!' Meg gasped. 'I never thought I'd own something like that.'

'Well, you deserve it.'

'And I'd like you to have this.' Nana May thrust a long, thin box into her hands. 'It was my mother's, but my wrist's got too big for it now,' she explained as Meg opened the box to find a pretty silver bracelet.

'Oh, Nana May, it's beautiful! Thank you so much!'

'And this is my and Mary's present to you, girl.' Gabriel held out a wooden object. 'Not wrapped, I'm afraid. Can't get wrapping paper for love nor money nowadays. Made it myself for you to put on the wall by your front door.'

'Oh, Gabriel! Something to hang keys on! In the shape of a key itself. Oh, my goodness, you are clever! It must've taken ages.'

'Well, you're twenty-one, so you need the key to the door!' her father-inlaw grinned.

Everyone came forward with a gift of some sort. Lively chatter filled the room so that Meg didn't hear the phone. But she didn't know that Louise had been out in the hall waiting for it to ring.

'Meg!' she called, putting her head around the door. 'Time for my present. Something I arranged for you. You're wanted on the phone.'

Meg's forehead pleated into a perplexed frown as she followed Louise out into the hall. This was mysterious. But her heart took wing as she began to guess.

'Hello?' she spoke into the receiver, her pulse leaping.

'Hello, my darling! Happy birthday!' a beloved voice came down the line. 'And congratulations on your twenty-first!'

Meg released a squeal of delight. 'Oh, Ralph, thank you!' she cried aloud. 'Oh, this is the best birthday present ever!'

Louise grinned at her, and then quietly slipped away.

Twenty-three

'Well, that's it, then.' Alan Fenshaw finally broke the shocked silence after he switched off the radio in the kitchen at Home Farm. 'We're at war with the Japs now, and all.'
'Yes.' Meg's voice was small. 'But so's America. The Japanese couldn't expect them to take such an attack lying down.'
'At least America's decided to join us in the fight against Hitler, as well. At last,' Maggie Fenshaw put in glumly. 'So that's maybe one good thing to come of it, even if they have lost half their fleet and so many brave young men, too.'
'Tell you what, I wouldn't like to be a British colonial out in the Far East just now, either,' Meg considered, her frown deepening. 'A rubber plantation owner or something. They say the Japs are ruthless fanatics, even worse than the SS, if that's possible.'
'All society parties and G and T's.' Alan shook his head gravely. 'No good can come of a life like that. But I pity the poor sods if they don't get out before the Japs get there. Lose everything, they will. And it's women and children, too. Not just the menfolk. And I reckon there won't be much either we or the Yanks'll be able to do to help them.'
'Yes, well, you'd think we had enough on our plates keeping Hitler off our shores,' Maggie sighed. 'I just wonder where our Paul will be sent when his training's over.'
Meg watched as Alan reached out and squeezed his wife's arm, and a little piece of her heart tore. Yes. It was a rare person who had nobody to fret over. A husband or sweetheart, a son or father, uncle, cousin or friend. She almost envied the twins whose parents had disappeared without trace, and the boys didn't seem to care too much. They could probably find their mum and dad if they really wanted to. They must have changed their rationing registration, and surely a few enquiries around the food shops would shed some light on the matter. Unless they'd moved right away, of course.
'Mr Wigmore's former chauffeur,' Meg said, not sure where the thought had come from, 'he's out in North Africa somewhere. Sent us a letter a little while ago which was nice. Didn't say a lot, of course. They're not allowed to. And it'd only be censored if they did.'
Alan sucked in his lips and released an enormous breath through his nostrils as he pulled himself to his feet. 'Well, we've got plenty of work to do in the morning, so I'm off to bed,' he announced. 'The way the man from the ministry's pushing us, the next thing we know, we'll be having to dig up the verge along the track to grow turnips and what have you to feed the extra sheep he wants us to have. I'm beginning to wonder if we're not going to need another pair of hands soon.'
'Hmm.' Meg gave a half smile. 'He certainly pushes hard. Anyway, I'll just let the dogs have a run and then I'll turn in, too.'
'We'll leave you to lock up, then.'
'Yes, of course. Goodnight.'
'Goodnight. Sleep well.'
As soon as Meg stepped towards the door, Thimble sprang up from toasting herself near the range. Slipping into her old duffel coat and wellingtons, Meg went outside into the raw December night and unhooked Jed, the Fenshaw's sheepdog, from his chain. Although Jed was an outside dog, Alan and Maggie had been quite happy for Thimble to live inside,

since that was what she was used to. The two dogs got on well, and mouthed each other playfully as they set off across the farmyard to the fallow field beyond.

Meg didn't follow them. She knew they'd come back as soon as she called. Instead, she went to spend a few minutes with Duchess in her loosebox. The giant mare was lying down asleep, but she was happy to rouse herself and nuzzle against the shoulder of the human she'd known for so long.

'With all this extra work and hardly any petrol to do it with, I'm that glad we kept old Duchess when we took over the farm from you,' Alan had declared to Meg on numerous occasions.

Meg had been glad, too – more than glad, more like ecstatic – when the first time Ralph had brought her back to visit her old home, she'd discovered Duchess still in the stable.

'Goodnight, old girl,' Meg said now, kissing Duchess's soft, velvety nose. 'See you in the morning.'

Shutting up the stable, she called the dogs and they at once came bounding back to her. She re-clipped Jed onto his chain and he curled up snugly in his kennel, while Thimble followed Meg back inside the farmhouse.

Upstairs, Meg changed into her nightclothes and slid into her old, childhood bed, in the room that, apart from the time spent at Robin Hill House, had been hers since birth. She missed all her friends back at the big house, but true to her word, she pedalled back there once a fortnight if Alan could spare her. And she was going back for a few days over Christmas. For Ralph had been promised some much overdue leave.

But who knew, anything could have happened by then. She just prayed Ralph would indeed be by her side on Christmas morning.

*

Meg leant forward to adjust the bunch of glossy holly that she'd placed on her parents' double grave.

So there we are, she spoke to them in her head. *The whole world's at war. Again. And as you know, I'm back at the farm. So things have gone full circle. It's only temporary, of course. When the Fenshaws' son comes back from the war, I won't be needed there anymore. And anyway, I still want my own farm. Unless Ralph really objects. I've never told him my plans, you see. I know I should have done... But he is a gardener, and that's a bit like being a farmer, isn't it? But that's all in the future. If there is a future. All anyone wants now is for the war to be over, but it's going to be a long haul, and nobody knows what's going to happen in the end.*

I hope you like the holly. At least it's got red berries. You can't get proper flowers now. Everyone's growing vegetables instead. But, if you can hear me, Happy Christmas wherever you are. I'll come again in the New Year. So, God bless, and I love and miss you both so much.

She squeezed her lips together to stem her threatening tears, and kissing her fingertips, let them linger on the headstone a moment before she stood up. It was stupid, she knew, the way she came to talk to her parents like this. But there was always the thought that maybe their spirits were fluttering somewhere near, and that they could still sense her presence, if nothing else.

She turned away, back to reality, to Thimble lying patiently, tethered to the gate. The dog got up, eagerly sweeping her tail over the frost-hard ground, as her mistress came towards her. As Meg untied the lead, she happened to spy on the opposite side of the road, a figure that stirred something deep in her memory.

'Mandy?' she called hesitantly.

The young woman stopped and turned round, a frown shadowing her face. And then as realisation dawned, she crossed over to Meg's side of the road. 'It's Meg, isn't it? Meg Chandler? Oh, my goodness, it's been years! I didn't know where you'd gone when you left.'

'Yes. Five years to be precise.' Meg at once felt a little ashamed at not having kept in contact with her old school friend. 'And I'm sorry now I just upped and left,' she apologised. 'But I was all over the place at the time.'

'Yeah, I can understand that. Your parents and everything,' Mandy smiled sympathetically. 'It's good to see you again, mind. How are you? And what brings you back here? Oh, silly me. Been to the graveyard. And… this isn't the dog you had before, is it? Gorgeous, mind,' she ended, ruffling Thimble's head.

'No.' Meg's throat closed up. 'This is Thimble. Mercury, well, he died,' she said, not wanting to relate the full horror of how her beloved pet had been deliberately poisoned.

'What, you lost him, as well?' Mandy was appalled. 'Oh, you poor thing, that's terrible! I am sorry. But… tell us more about yourself. Married, I see.'

'How—?'

'The ring gives it away. But… oh, my God, don't tell me you're…?'

'Widowed?' Meg released a wry sigh. 'No, thank God. But… who knows? RAF.'

'Bomber or fighter?'

'Neither. Special Ops.'

'Wow.'

'And you?'

'Engaged. Army. North Africa somewhere.'

'Ah.' Meg gave an understanding nod. 'I know someone else out there, too.' And then she pulled herself up short, her forehead rucking. 'Isn't it awful? We haven't seen each other in years, and the first thing we ask each other is if our other half is still alive'

'Yeah, it should be, *let's go and celebrate meeting up again. Have a girls' night out.* I mean, we can still do that, but it's not the same, is it?'

'No. We could have a great night out, and then come home to bad news. But, are you still working at the milliner's?'

'Nah. Trade dropped off. Who wants a new hat now clothes are on coupons? Got me marching orders back in September, and been idling ever since. I'll get me call-up papers soon, though, I expect. Thought I might try and join the Land Army.'

Meg's eyes stretched wide. 'Really? I'm a Land Girl. Back at my old home. The Fenshaws' now.'

'Ah, yeah, that's right. So how did that come about?'

Meg explained as briefly as she could about Robin Hill House, watching the astonishment growing on her old friend's face. Mandy could hardly believe how things had worked out for her.

'Flipping heck, that's amazing,' she gasped. 'To think you went to live with the people who caused the accident.'

'Not them, their chauffeur was to blame,' Meg corrected her. 'You saw them at the funeral. They're good people, and my new family now. And of course, that's how I met Ralph.'

'And now you're back at Home Farm.'

'Just for the duration.' Both girls smiled ruefully, and Meg considered how Mandy seemed to have grown up a lot in the intervening years. She'd always been kind and friendly, but they'd never been ever so close. But Meg had the feeling their relationship could pick up again.

'Tell you what, if you're serious about the Land Army,' she ventured, 'the Fenshaws are thinking they might need someone else, as well. The man from the ministry wants blood, and we're going to have to grow fodder on every inch of ground to feed the extra sheep he wants us to have. I can ask Alan and Maggie if you like. It's really hard work. Almost everything has to be done by hand. Look, you'll get broken nails and callouses,' she grimaced, holding out her hands.

'Hmm, nothing a nail file and a bit of polish wouldn't sort out,' Mandy grinned back. 'I've still got quite a collection from before the war. Gone a bit thick, but you can still use them. So it strikes me, if the Fenshaws are agreeable, we're on!'

*

'That, my darling, was the best Christmas present any man could ask for. Even if it was a day late.'

'Oh, you!' Meg pulled the pillow from behind her head and playfully hit Ralph with it. 'Yesterday was Christmas Day, and we were expected to be up early. And last night, you were the one who fell asleep the second your head hit the pillow.'

'Yes, I know.' Ralph's mouth was spread wide as he laughed aloud. 'How ridiculous was that?'

Meg's face moved into soft lines. 'You're exhausted,' she said, reaching up to cup his lean jaw. Certainly there were dark smudges under his eyes, and his cheeks were more hollow than ever. 'The work you do for the war is really special, but I can see it puts a strain on you. You need more than just a few days' leave.'

'I know.' Ralph's expression became more serious. 'And then I could make love to my beautiful wife over and over again. Like this.' He propped himself up on one elbow, intensity burning in his eyes as he lowered his head against her bare shoulder, kissing her skin with feather-light touch and trailing his lips down towards her breasts. Beneath the covers, his fingertips walked over her slender thighs to find that secret place, making her gasp with pleasure again. 'And like this,' he muttered, covering her mouth with his and taking her on a wondrous journey once more.

She let herself fall back into that miraculous world, a world where there were no guns or bombs, just white petals and pink roses and sunshine and the heady scent of the flowers Ralph had grown in a magical garden just for her. She floated away to a place where dreams come true, and she clung onto Ralph's strong, dependable frame as he moved slowly and leisurely inside her until she exploded with joy, crying out with elation.

'Sshh!' he chuckled. 'You don't want everyone to hear, do you?'

'I don't think I care, to be honest,' Meg grinned back. 'Just to have you here is so wonderful. I just… I just wish you didn't have to go back tomorrow,' she choked.

'So do I. But at least I've got home leave. Some poor wretches will be separated for years.'

They instantly fell sombre again, and Meg pulled her nightdress back over her head as she sat up. 'Yes. Mandy, my old friend I told you about, her fiancé's in North Africa, like Vic. And she doesn't know when she'll see him again. If ever.'

'Well, let's try not to think about it just now.' Ralph gave her that smile that melted her heart. 'Let's just enjoy the day. Pity Mr Perry and Mrs Sofia couldn't make it. They'd have livened things up a bit.'

'Yes. They couldn't manage the petrol ration, and Sofia refuses point blank to go on a train. Can you imagine her flicking her scarf about in a carriage crammed with soldiers?'

'And with Boris having joined up now, she mightn't be so jolly anymore.'

'Hmm, you're probably right there. But I'm sure dear Penny will keep us all amused. But I think it's about time we put in an appearance, don't you? Your mum and dad asked us round for breakfast, remember?'

'If we must. I'd rather stay here all day with you.'

'Ralph Hillier, you're incorrigible.'

'Oh, all right, then. I must say I'm looking forward to egg and bacon again, even if we are eating Percy Piggy,' he teased, pulling a face.

'You can't be sentimental about such things as a farmer,' she scolded him, getting up and slipping into her dressing gown. 'And there is a war on, you know.' And then she released an exasperated breath as someone knocked gently on the front door. 'I wonder who that is?' she sighed.

'I'll go,' Ralph offered, and he disappeared downstairs.

Meg recognised Gabriel's voice, but she couldn't make out what he was saying. She heard the front door close again and a few seconds later, she turned to Ralph with a smile as he came back into the bedroom. But the smile faded from her face as she saw his expression.

'Breakfast's ready,' he said absently. And then he murmured, 'Hong Kong's surrendered. It's just been on the wireless. The Japs... There's been a terrible massacre. Things couldn't really be worse, could they?'

And as Meg stared at his stricken face, her chest contracted. While they'd been lost in their love for one another, on the other side of the world, people had been engulfed in horror. Dear God, would there ever be a way out?

Twenty-Four

1942

A cold, deadening drizzle enshrouded the April night in a dank, miserable mist, but inside the lambing shed, all was warm and cosy. With a good foot of straw on the concrete floor, and twenty odd sheep in their woolly fleeces radiating heat, Mandy was surprised to find that she didn't feel the least bit cold, even though it was two o'clock in the morning. Over their trousers and thick jumpers, Mandy and Meg both wore the sort of boiler suit that Winston Churchill had made popular. And though she knew it was their turn to stay up all night for this particular group of ewes that were due to lamb, Mandy wasn't at all tired. Although she'd lived in the countryside all her life, she'd never been closely involved with lambing. It was all new and exciting to her, and witnessing the birth of lambs in the middle of the night was quite magical.

'It's so calm and peaceful, isn't it?' she mused as there was a lull in the proceedings. 'Nothing like being out in the countryside at night, is there?'

Meg gave a contented smile. 'I've always loved lambing. Delivered my first lamb when I was four.'

'Crikey.'

'Yup. But with my dad keeping a close eye on me, of course. He let me do more difficult ones by the time I was eight, but I was ten before he'd let me stay up at night. I loved it. It was so mysterious, being out in the dark. Working just by the light of a hurricane lamp. Ironic, really.' Meg paused to scoff with bitterness. 'I was always on at my dad to badger the electricity people to get us connected to the National Grid, but he said it was up to the landlord. But he did eventually get a generator so we could install the milking parlour. But now Alan and Maggie have got mains electricity, we can't use it out here because of the blackout. So we've got to grope around in near darkness yet again!'

'Better than being bombed.'

'Yes, I suppose so,' Meg agreed, shrugging her eyebrows. 'Not really had any air raids to speak of recently, though, have we? Most of the news seems to be about the Far East, what with the fall of Singapore and everything.'

'Yeah,' Mandy sighed. 'There's not been much about North Africa of late, neither. I wonder what my Dennis and his lot are up to. And you must be wondering if your Ralph's flying one of his missions as we speak.'

Meg nodded. She knew Mandy meant well, but it instantly triggered the old, strangling fear. 'I just try not to think about it,' she gulped. 'Ralph seemed a bit strained over Christmas. He tried to hide it, but I could tell. He needs a good long break. I'm worried he'll start making mistakes if he's pushed too far.'

'Yeah, that's a worry for everyone, isn't it? When you're tired.' Despite her excitement, Mandy couldn't suppress a long, satisfying yawn. 'Shall I pour us a coffee from the flask? That chicory stuff's terribly bitter, but at least it'll be hot.'

'I just want to have a look at that ewe, first,' Meg answered, tramping through the thick bedding of straw. 'She was moon-gazing earlier and she's been restless for quite a while. If you can help me catch her, I'll have a quick feel inside.'

'Righty-ho. So which one is it?'

'That one,' Meg pointed, pulling the top of the boiler suit from her shoulders and rolling up her right sleeve before quickly washing her arm in the bucket of water. 'Her blue mark's slightly longer than some.'

'Ah, yeah, I see. Ooh, isn't that the birth sack starting to show?'

'You're learning!' Meg grinned back. 'Right, let's try and corner her.'

It took a minute or so, the ewes scattering as Meg and Mandy approached. But the two girls gradually managed to separate them until the animal concerned was caught in a group of just four. Meg was able to pounce on her, skilfully twisting the mother-to-be to the floor in the position that always calms a restless sheep.

'If you can hold her down at that end,' she instructed Mandy, 'I'll have a feel and see what's going on.'

As Meg concentrated on putting all her knowledge and experience into play, the war and her crippling fears over Ralph's safety drifted away. Just now, she was Meg Chandler again, farmer's daughter, shepherdess, using all the skills she'd learnt from her beloved father since the cradle. In the dead of a still if chilly night, she was bringing new life into the world, each lamb a little miracle of nature.

'No wonder she's having difficulty,' she reported calmly to Mandy. 'It's coming head first. She can't manage it like that.'

'Oh, so what can you do?' Mandy asked in alarm. 'She won't die, will she? Oh, the poor thing. You won't have to shoot her, or anything, will you, to put her out of her misery? I don't think I could bear that.'

'Good Lord, no,' Meg reassured her. 'We might lose the lamb, but we won't lose her. No, I've just got to push the head back and try and find the front legs.'

Meg gritted her teeth, closing her eyes to deepen her concentration as she felt inside the ewe. Pushing a lamb back wasn't something she liked doing, although she'd performed the procedure numerous times in her life. But it had to be done, and she fairly quickly managed to locate one front hoof and manoeuvre it into position so that the tip just became visible. The other leg was trickier, but soon the two feet were side by side.

'How's it going down there?' Mandy asked anxiously since it seemed to her to be taking an awfully long time.

'I need to turn the head slightly… and… there, it's coming. Next contraction… There we are. Legs…' Meg answered, easing out the tiny, slippery limbs. 'Nose… and… we're out.'

'And is it OK?' Mandy's voice quivered as she watched Meg vigorously rubbing the skinny, motionless body with a good hank of straw. 'And why's it yellow like that?'

'Meconium in the birth sack. Means it was stressed. No surprise,' Meg explained as she swung the lamb gently upside down. 'Come on, little fellow.'

Mandy didn't really understand, but didn't want to distract Meg as she laid the lamb down again and tickled a piece of straw up its nostril. It suddenly gave a sneeze and then seemed to catapult into life. It weakly lifted its head, scrabbling with its feet, its breathing still unsure.

'Well, there we are. Welcome to the world!' Meg grinned ecstatically. 'And if I'm not mistaken, here comes another one.'

'What, another lot of twins?'

'Yes. And this one's coming normally.'

Relief and joy quickened Meg's pulse as she put the second white lamb next to its yellow-stained twin. She indicated to Mandy to release the ewe, which instantly struggled to its feet to nuzzle at its newborn offspring. Meg sat back on her heels to watch the double miracle, her heart spilling over with happiness that she'd managed to save both mother and baby, and a second lamb to boot.

It was what she was made for, to farm. And not just anywhere, but at this particular farm, in this very shed that had been at the heart of her life for so long. So while she gave the ewe a few moments to bond with her lambs, a tinge of sadness dulled the corners of Meg's elation. This interlude of contentment, of being back home, wouldn't last forever. And it was only courtesy of the war.

'Right, then,' she said, hurling her thoughts aside. And brusquely picking up the two tiny lambs, she carried them to one of the small, individual pens erected along the inner wall of the shed. The mother ewe instinctively followed, and Meg shut the new family safely inside. 'Well, I think we deserve that coffee now,' she announced, deliberately crushing her topsy-turvy emotions and pinning a smile on her face. 'Don't you?'

*

Clarrie strode up the driveway, her mind stimulated by her meeting in the village. She'd walked the younger children to school and gone straight to the vicarage to discuss the summer fête with the committee she still headed. She was buzzing with the new ideas that had been put forward, as well as the traditional stalls and entertainments that had been planned.

Her thoughts inevitably wandered to her Meg, prompted by the hope that she would produce some more of her lovely paintings again for both the village auction and the raffle. Clarrie's heart had been left bleeding when Meg had announced she was joining the Land Army and was going back to work at the farm that had been her former home. Clarrie's soul had felt empty and hollow, and she was so glad to have the company of Penny and Ada, Gabriel and Mary, and all the younger people under her roof.

There was plenty to keep her busy, of course. With so many mouths to feed, they had been lucky to retain Jane as a maid, but Louise had been conscripted. With her caring nature, it came as little surprise that she'd chosen to train as a nurse. It meant that Clarrie needed to undertake her share of cooking and cleaning, washing and ironing, but she had no problem with that. In fact, she relished her new role, and she continued to help the children with reading and schoolwork, or taking them on walks or arranging a picnic in the grounds – even if the filling for the banana sandwiches was only parsnips from Gabriel's store, boiled and mashed up with a drop or two of banana essence!

But if only she could still have darling Wig and dear Meggy by her side. At least Meg was safe, or as safe as any of them were. They often spoke on the phone and Meg had kept her promise to visit regularly, at which times, Clarrie fought to contain her elation.

Clarrie was able, though, to fear less for Wig these days. Hitler still appeared to be concentrating his forces against the Russians in the east, and had Rommel fighting for supremacy in North Africa. But Canterbury had been severely bombed at the end of May – the twins swore they could hear it – ironically at the same time the RAF had launched a huge attack on Cologne, followed by a massive raid on the military manufactories in Essen and the Ruhr the next night. Would the Fuhrer, as he was known, retaliate? Perhaps Wig wasn't as safe at the factory as she prayed, and that sinking feeling descended on her stomach once again.

The mood inside the house lifted her spirits, though. As she came into the kitchen, the door to the servants' hall was propped open to allow the warm, summer air to circulate, and through it came the strains of a seventyeight record of Vera Lynn singing 'Red Sails in the Sunset' being played on the gramophone. At least it made a change from 'Wish Me Luck' or 'We'll Meet Again' which always made Clarrie want to cry.

'Hello, Clarrie, ducks! How'd yer meeting go? Wanna cuppa?' Penny asked all in one breath, hoisting Bella up onto her hip and waving the teapot in the air with her other hand.

'Oh, yes, please, I could murder one.'

'Pretty weak, I'm afraid. Not much of this week's tea ration left,' Ada warned, busily grating carrots to make a cocoa-flavoured 'chocolate' pudding.

'Oh, well, there's a war on, you know,' Clarrie found herself joking. 'Where's Nana May?'

'Resting her eyes in the drawing room. Or at least, that's what she says,' Ada winked knowingly.

Clarrie nodded with a sad smile. The old lady was really showing her age recently, dozing off several times a day. Clarrie could tell she was missing Meg, too, by the way she perked up so much whenever Meg came to visit.

'I'll just make sure she's OK when I've had that cuppa. Oh, by the way, I saw an old tramp along the lane. He's got a bad limp, poor thing, but he just made me feel uneasy, somehow.'

'I could get Eric to check him out,' Jane offered proudly. 'He's calling in after his shift. He'll be here soon.'

'That mightn't be a bad idea. Never know. He could be a German spy, though what there is to spy on round here, I don't know.'

'Well, here's yer cuppa, Clarrie, ducks.'

'Thanks, Penny. On second thoughts, I'll take it with me.'

Clarrie picked up her cup of tea and wandered along the corridor into the drawing room where Nana May was napping in one of the armchairs. She felt her heart strain as she gazed down on her dear old friend. With Wig at the factory most of the time and Meg working away, how ever could she manage if she lost this other rock of her life?

The French doors were wide open onto the terrace with the sun streaming through. Trampas was lying just outside, and lazily cocked open one eye as she came to stand on the threshold. Gabriel and the twins were working out in the grounds somewhere, and all seemed idyllic. What a pity they were in the middle of a war.

*

Phew, that had been close!

Nathaniel Green breathed a sigh of relief. Thank God his disguise was so good that his own mother wouldn't have recognised him. The filthy, ragged overcoat and battered hat rammed down low over his eyes had served him well in the nine months since he'd deserted. With the long, grey, wispy wig and matching false beard, and dirt smeared over what was visible of his skin so that you wouldn't know if his face bore age lines or not, a quick glance from a stranger would assume he was an old man. With the added limp and a certain way he'd learnt of letting his mouth droop to one side, it looked as though he'd had a stroke.

It was a bit like play-acting, and Nathaniel found it all rather fun, fooling people so well, including the Military Police who'd never managed to get anywhere near him. This wasn't the only disguise he used, of course. That would be pushing his luck. And sometimes he needed to move freely, which this stupid, flapping coat prevented. If he was looting a bombed-out area in the middle of the night, for instance, he needed to be as stealthy as a cat against the darkness, black balaclava hiding the paleness of his face.

He hadn't made a bad living for himself. The old forger who'd produced documents for him in several different false identities had also given him contacts in Liverpool, Manchester and Sheffield, places that had been heavily bombed earlier in the war. The looters still had stashes of stolen goods, and with his assumed charm, Nathaniel had become the perfect middle man for selling them on, often to unsuspecting clients. He was soon involved up to his neck in black marketeering. But it could be a dangerous game working with criminals, never mind avoiding the authorities, and Nathaniel preferred to be his own man.

That was why, when Canterbury had received a pasting recently, he'd swiftly come back down south. There'd be rich pickings to be had. He'd keep to small items, things people who'd been bombed out of their houses would be so desperate for that they'd pay the earth for them. Even such insignificant things as soap, especially now that it was on ration, and stockings – if he could get hold of any – would bring in a fortune! Unless you were lucky enough to know one of these friendly GIs who were beginning to be stationed over here, a woman was reduced to wearing socks, like a little schoolgirl. Not that Nathaniel minded the idea of having a young schoolgirl in his clutches!

He'd wondered vaguely if he shouldn't try to track Esme down, now he was back in the area. But he didn't have a clue where to look. He wouldn't find her at Robin Hill House, that was for sure. After what had happened, they'd never have her back!

But… His vicious mind started whirring. It all came down to that Meg Chandler, didn't it? If she and her parents hadn't been driving that bloody horse and cart along the road, he'd have remained in his cushy job as the Stratfield-Whytes' chauffeur. Of course, at some point, he'd still have been conscripted, especially as it had been announced that petrol rations were going to be withdrawn altogether on the first day of next month, so he wouldn't have had a job anyway. But he wouldn't have had that bleeding sergeant major breathing down his neck all the time because he was an exgaolbird! And he would have had the opportunity to express a preference for which force he wanted to join. In which case, he'd have chosen the RAF, and who knew, he might have made it. As a chauffeur, he'd learnt a lot about engines and was a darned good mechanic. He could have made ground crew, and been safe throughout the war. Of course, German bombers had attacked British airfields especially in the beginning, but you stood a far better chance than if you were cannon fodder in the army!

Oh, yes. Meg Chandler had a lot to answer for! She'd ruined his life, and if he could make her pay, even in a small way, it would bring him some satisfaction. And then perhaps he could put the smouldering anger behind him and finally move on.

So, was she still at Robin Hill House? It was certainly the obvious place to start. And so, for the past week or so, he'd been spying on the place, hiding in the bushes and hedges near the house, watching through binoculars the comings and goings at different times of the day. He'd seen the cook – Mrs Phillips, if his memory served him right – walking to and from her home in the village every day. Old Wigmore – bloody stupid name – had only appeared at the weekend, but then he had his factory in the East End to keep an eye on during the week. Of the young men, damned Ralph Hillier and that Bob Whatever-his-name-was, there was no sign, but then they'd have been conscripted, the poor fools.

Nathaniel sneered pleasurably when he'd spied young Jane. She seemed to have turned into a confident, attractive young woman, and to think he'd had her in his hands! But he didn't see any of the other maids who'd been there in his time. In fact, the only other residents appeared to be kids, evacuees by all accounts. He'd seen a tubby woman pushing a brat of about three in a pushchair as she'd walked three little boys to school, presumably, since she'd returned without them.

Before today, he'd not seen anything of the aging gardener and his wife, nor of Mrs Stratfield-Whyte, or the old dear who was her companion, but she was probably kicking up the daisies by now. He'd noticed two young lads of about fifteen or so working in one of the fields on either side of the driveway, weeding some sort of flat cabbage. Nathaniel would try and nick a few of those if he got the chance. He knew a greengrocer he could sell them to. But to his extreme annoyance, Meg Chandler never once put in an appearance.

Nathaniel felt cheated. Maybe he'd simply missed her. With frustration burning inside, he'd become bolder. He'd try his tramp disguise and patrol the lane more freely. He'd just give it one last go, and then he'd give up on the whole idea. But he hadn't expected, though, to almost bump into Mrs Hoity-Toity Stratfield-Whyte as she walked along the lane in the opposite direction. It had sent an arrow of fear darting through him, but she'd passed by on the opposite side of the tarmac and hadn't given him a second glance. He'd kept his head down, but his eyes had shifted surreptitiously in her direction for any sign of recognition, but there hadn't been any.

When he felt it was safe, he retraced his steps. Hiding behind the hedge, he watched her disappear down the driveway, but she didn't look back or seem to be in any hurry – as she might have been if she'd taken any notice of him and wanted to do something about it.

Nathaniel pouted his lips as he began hobbling away down the lane. He was disappointed, but it was time to give up. Meg Chandler had moved on. He would have to accept it and concentrate on his illegal goings-on. It was like a game of cat and mouse that he rather enjoyed. Only he was always the winner, and the stupid authorities didn't have a clue.

It was a few moments later, though, that Nathaniel got the fright of his life. If the silly fellow hadn't alerted him by his jolly whistling, Nathaniel wouldn't have realised there was someone coming. As it was, after the scare of almost coming face to face with Clarissa Stratfield-Whyte, Nathaniel was a bit jumpy, and swiftly drew back through a convenient gap in the hedge.

Thank God he had! Coming round the bend was a bobby on a bicycle! Quite a young chap, and Jesus, he looked familiar, although Nathaniel couldn't think why. The constable cycled past at a rate of knots, although his mouth was curved in a smile, so it didn't look as if he'd been summoned. And even if Mrs Stratfield-Whyte had called the police about a tramp in the lane the instant she'd got inside, they couldn't possibly have got there that quickly, especially on a bicycle. Nevertheless, Nathaniel's heart quite literally missed a beat as the young copper turned in at the ever open gates of Robin Hill House.

Nathaniel sprang from his hiding place, brambles scratching at him in his haste, and raced away down the lane as fast as his pretend limp would let him. He wouldn't be back, that was for sure. And any ideas of having revenge on Meg Chandler would have to be forgotten. What a pity.

Twenty-Five

'I'd forgotten how good you are at art,' Mandy commented, looking over her friend's shoulder. Meg was adding the detail to a beautiful sunset backwash against which the bare branches of a massive oak tree were silhouetted in an intricate web like black lace. 'I don't know how you can visualise how things look in the winter when we're in the middle of summer.'

Meg glanced up at her with an easy smile. 'It's not difficult, not when it's somewhere you've known all your life. I'm doing a set of four of the same scene but in the different seasons. Spring was the hardest, trying to get the right bright green for the leaf buds but with the dark brown of the branches as well. It's not as if an oak tree has spring blossom or anything to show you when it's meant to be.'

'Oh, will you show it to me?'

'Yes, of course. I've almost finished what I wanted to get done on this today. Not in any hurry to get home, are you?'

'No. Mum was only cooking Woolton's pie, and it's no worse when it's cold than when it's hot,' Mandy grimaced.

Meg had to hide her smile. When Ada made it, the vegetable pie was actually pretty tasty, but then Mandy's mum was hardly the best cook in the world, to put it politely! So Meg bided her time, waiting for Mandy to continue.

'Anyway, I'd rather be here,' Mandy went on wistfully. 'It's so much quieter than at home. Makes me feel more at peace, and not quite so worried about Dennis. Been a lot going on in the desert.'

'Yes, I know. But you had a letter the other day, didn't you?'

'Yeah. But what's happened since he wrote it? Same thing with your Ralph, isn't it? Not rung for a bit, has he?'

Meg raised her eyebrows as the worry shot through her again. 'You just have to assume no news is good news,' she muttered, forcing her attention back to the final brushstrokes. 'There, that's done. I'll leave it to dry now.

It's pinned to the board so it won't blow away. So, d'you want to come upstairs and see the other ones?'

'Please. Don't know how you can bear to give them away, mind. I'd want to keep them all.'

'Well, when it's all raising funds for the war effort, you don't mind,' Meg answered as they went in through the farmhouse kitchen.

'You still here, Mandy, love?' Maggie Fenshaw asked in surprise.

'Meg's just going to show me some of her paintings, and then I'm off.'

'And I've got the milking to do on my own as Alan's not back from market yet, so I mustn't be long,' Meg advised her friend.

'Lovely old house, this,' Mandy commented as she followed Meg up the creaking staircase. 'Must feel really odd being back here. I mean, happy, but also sad 'cos you know it's just for while the war's on.'

'Just?' Meg answered, her voice laced with irony, and Mandy nodded.

Meg could see Mandy knew exactly what she meant. The war was dragging on without any sign of it being over, or of the Nazis being driven back. And now there were terrible tales of what was going on in Germany. They all knew that Hitler had set up labour camps for prisoners of war or those in occupied countries who'd *disobeyed*. But this was far more sinister. Jews had been systematically rounded up into ghettos since before the war, but now they were being taken by train en masse to a growing number of what were being called concentration camps. At first, the Allies hadn't believed the atrocities that were reported to being carried out in them, but now it was rumoured that it was all true.

It simply didn't bear thinking about, so up in the bedroom, Meg was glad to have something much happier to occupy her. As she spread out her drawings and paintings on the bed, Mandy was full of admiration.

'Blimey, they're all so good. I wouldn't know which to choose if I was buying one. And there's so many.'

'Luckily, Mr Perry – that's Mr Wig's brother, the famous artist – he kindly gave me a whole load of paints and special paper before the war,' Meg explained. 'You probably couldn't get them now. I'll have to stop if I run out.'

'That'd be a shame,' Mandy sympathised as her eyes went from one picture to the next. 'You know, when you've got enough for your Clarrie and her blooming fête, you ought to hold an exhibition. In the autumn, maybe. People could buy them as Christmas presents, they're so good.

Gawd knows there's not much to buy in the shops. People'd be thrilled to bits to be given something as great as these.'

    'Oh, they're not that good,' Meg protested.

'Jolly well are!' Mandy insisted. 'Anyway, I must be off now, and let you get on with the milking. And you think about having an exhibition, girl!'

'Yes, OK, I will,' Meg humoured her, and listened to Mandy's footfall as she went back down the stairs.

Meg sat for a moment, casting a self-critical eye over the papers strewn across the bed. They weren't nearly as good as Mr Perry's. But you wouldn't expect them to be. But she supposed they weren't bad. So maybe she'd give it some thought after all.

*

'Well, I think that's a splendid idea!' Clarrie enthused. 'You've got so many here. It seems a shame to put them all into the auction. Pick out which ones you think are the best. Personally, I think I'd keep back the set of the tree in the four seasons for a start. And I might have some old frames up in the loft, rather than just pinning them on card. Knowing the twins, they'd probably love crawling about in the cobwebs to see what they can find. Nobody's been up there for years.'

    'D'you really think so? I mean, that they're good enough?'

'I certainly do. And remember, Perry always said you had real talent. So once the fête's over, we'll put out heads together, eh?'

Clarrie indeed thrust her head forward as if they were literally doing that, her face shining and split in a grin. Her Meg had come *home* for a few days, and Clarrie was ecstatic. But to think they could work closely together on such a project as an exhibition filled her with joy. It was the sort of thing she could have been involved in if Meg really had been her daughter. They shared such intimate closeness, but Clarrie still felt it wasn't right to tell Meg just how deep her feelings ran. She might look upon Meg as her own child, but she couldn't expect Meg to see her as a replacement mother. No. It might tear at Clarrie's heart, but far better to keep their relationship as it was – and the past buried where it belonged. 'Meggy!'

Clarrie was grateful for the interruption to her train of thought as Doris rushed into the room and hurried over to squash Meg in a warm hug. A tide of contentment washed through Clarrie's veins. Was it another sign or simply coincidence that of all the evacuees, Meg seemed closest to Doris who, with her bright curls, resembled Rosebud so strongly?

'It's lovely to see you again!' Doris cried, pulling back from Meg. 'And you're here for a few days. Goody! I do miss you. And are these all the new paintings for the auction? Oh, let me see!'

'Well, we're going to keep some of them back,' Clarrie announced, glowing with pride. 'Meg's old friend at the farm suggested we hold an exhibition in the autumn.'

'An exhibition?' Doris's eyes grew wide. 'Oh, how exciting!'

'Everyone seems to think I'm good enough,' Meg said bashfully. 'And I suppose it'd be something different. You know, a different event for people to go to. Just something small. Might cheer life up a bit. What with the war dragging on and more and more things going on ration. Even if my efforts just make people laugh at me.'

'Oh, they wouldn't do that!' Doris protested. 'No, I think you should go ahead.'

'That's what I said,' Clarrie concurred. 'We could hire somewhere in Tunbridge Wells—'

'Oh, no,' Meg protested. 'I wouldn't want anything as big as that!'

'Really? Oh, all right, then. The village hall, and we could make a few posters. Even put an advert in the local paper. And then people from Tunbridge Wells might like a trip out into the countryside if they had a specific reason. Ada could work her wonders with grated carrots and make some cakes. And we could have cucumber sandwiches. By then, it'll only be this National Loaf they're talking of bringing in in the autumn, but it'd be better than nothing.'

'That's ever so kind,' Meg murmured, 'but you shouldn't go to all that trouble.'

'Nonsense. It'll be fun. But first,' Clarrie declared, getting to her feet, 'we have the fête the day after tomorrow. So I'll leave you two to sort through the paintings and decide which ones to keep for the exhibition.'

Her mouth stretched in a broad, happy smile as she left the room, and the two girls exchanged bewildered glances.

'Looks like it's a fait accompli,' Meg uttered, still thrown off balance by Clarrie's enthusiasm. 'And how are you, Doris? Summer holidays not too boring? Have *you* been doing any painting recently?'

'Time's never boring here!' Doris grinned, and Meg was pleased to note that Doris was making a big effort to get on with her life after the tragedy of her mother's death. 'There's always plenty to do in the house or outside. And if we give the boys a hand, they have time to do things with us, as well. We sometimes go on long rambles together and take a picnic. And I have done some painting. I'll show you later. And I got a letter from Daddy yesterday, so that was good. Have you heard from Ralph recently?'

Meg opened her mouth but didn't get the chance to reply as the halfopen door swung open the rest of the way and little Bella trotted into the room, holding up her chubby arms to Meg, while a flustered, red-faced Penny panted behind her in pursuit. Meg and Doris caught each other's eye and both burst out laughing. The peace was over!

*

'There you are, Mr O'Leary,' the café owner said, putting the plate of egg, bacon and sausage in front of his customer. But as he did so, he gave a surreptitious jerk of his head and his eyes shifted downwards for a split second.

'Sure I'm thanking you, so I am.'

Nathaniel Green had discovered he could slip into a convincing southern Irish drawl as easily as he'd mastered the Liverpudlian accent. It sounded even better with the drooping, lopsided mouth he'd adopted from his tramp disguise, although he'd dropped the limp to make his 'Irishman' that much different. And of course, everyone knew that conscription didn't extend to Eire, despite the connections it still had to Britain. So as long as people believed he was Irish, nobody would suspect he was actually a deserter.

As it was, he was pretty sure the café owner in Southborough just north of Tunbridge Wells had no idea he was no more Irish than the Queen of Sheba. Without the long, grey wig and beard that gave the impression of his being an old man, he looked totally different and very ordinary in a nondescript suit and coppery wig over his own dark hair. Not a bright ginger that would have attracted attention, but enough to make people believe his Irish heritage.

But if the café owner did have any suspicions, he kept his mouth shut. But then he would. Nathaniel had been blessed with good luck since he'd come back down south. The old forger had even more contacts in the area than up north, and it wasn't long before all sorts of goods had come Nathaniel's way. He didn't ask questions as to where they'd come from; looted, stolen, he didn't care. People were so desperate, he found he could sell things on so easily even to law-abiding citizens who in normal circumstances wouldn't have dreamt of buying illicit goods.

That night, Nathaniel was going to be delivering a couple of cans of petrol round the back of the café. The payment was slipped beneath the plate. He dealt regularly with the owner, and they trusted each other. Soap, parachute silk for making underwear, proper coffee, sugar, stockings. All relatively small stuff, but Nathaniel wasn't greedy. That was when you drew attention to yourself, and he didn't want that. In fact, he was beginning to think he'd been around long enough. He'd been there since June and it was coming up to the end of October. It could be pushing his luck to stay much longer. Get rid of what he had, and then time to move on.

He glanced round to check that none of the other customers was watching, and slid the money from beneath the plate and into his pocket. He'd keep his side of the bargain, even if he was about to disappear. The café owner had been good for him, and Nathaniel considered he still possessed some honour.

He picked up his knife and fork and began to tuck into the meal. A wellthumbed local newspaper sat on the table next to him. He might as well flick through its few pages. Paper was so scarce nowadays that publications were severely restricted, and each page was so wafer-thin that the ink was inclined to bleed, making the print semi-illegible.

There was the usual stuff about the war on the front page, the push in Egypt, but Nathaniel took little notice of that. It didn't affect him, after all, did it? A bit more inside, with the usual casualty notices and grieving families mourning their dead loved ones. A missing cat, a couple of jumble sales and an art exhibition in a local village hall.

Huh, who on earth would be interested in that crap? Nathaniel sneered to himself. And then his eyes bulged in their sockets. The name of the artist was Marguerite Chandler. Nathaniel nearly choked on his mouthful of bacon. Everyone thought of the bitch as Meg, but he remembered from the court appearances that her real name was Marguerite. So she *was* still in the area! Ho, ho, ho! Perhaps Nathaniel mightn't be leaving quite yet after all!

Twenty-Six

'Oh, crikey, my insides won't keep still,' Meg moaned as she stood back to contemplate the display so far.

The deserted village hall felt strange and musty especially in the near darkness. The windows were high up and it needed a long pole to draw the heavy curtains, but it simply wasn't possible to put up blackout blinds. So, just in case, anyone using the hall after dusk was obliged to grope their way about by shielded torchlight.

'If only we'd been allowed access earlier,' Clarrie sympathised. 'But the school were using it for PE, they're so crammed with all the evacuees.'

'I know,' Meg sighed. 'We'll just have to get here at the crack of dawn tomorrow to get everything ready.'

'Well, you get done as much as you can. I'm off to the vicarage to discuss the last bits and pieces for the catering. Penny's going to load the pram up with everything in the morning. Thank goodness we kept it after Bella went into the pushchair. And we can all carry something as well. But it's going to be easier to make up the sandwiches in the vicarage kitchen and just carry them across.'

Meg turned to Clarrie with a grateful smile. 'Oh, Clarrie, you've been a brick organising all this!' she cried, and gave the older woman a hug.

Clarrie closed her eyes, and just for a second or two, breathed in the scent of this girl who had become like her own flesh and blood. The sweet smell of motherhood wafted intoxicatingly inside her nostrils, almost making her giddy. What she should have had with Rosebud. She savoured it, wanting to hang onto it forever, empty and bereft when Meg finally pulled back, the grin still lighting her face.

'It's what I do best, organising,' Clarrie said, dusting off her reluctance to let Meg go, and putting on her efficient tone instead. 'I'll wait for you over in the vicarage. You're all right to lock up, aren't you? Take your time.

It's your big day tomorrow.'

She picked up her handbag and trusty, dimmed torch, and stepped out into the darkness. As she made her way over to the vicarage, she didn't notice the figure lurking in the shadows.

Left alone in the hall, Meg nervously drew in her lips. What would people really think of her paintings and drawings? Along the side wall of the building was a dado rail, deep enough for her to be able to prop her exhibits on it. There had also been a few pictures already on the wall above, which she and Clarrie had taken down and stored carefully in a cupboard, so that Meg could hang some of her own from the picture hooks. These were the ones that had been put in the old frames the twins had searched out in the loft of Robin Hill House at Clarrie's behest.

Overall, Meg was pleased with the display – as much as she could see in the glimmer from her masked torch. In pride of place was the drawing of Mercury that Mr Perry had borrowed from her to create for her the stunning oil painting of her beloved dog after he'd been poisoned. The original sketch wasn't for sale, but Meg wanted it there, as if her past was presiding over the entire affair. As if through it, her dear mum and dad would be watching.

The thought made Meg's heart clench with a mixture of sadness and pride. She remembered the day when she'd come home from school to learn that her mother had suffered yet another miscarriage. Meg had only been about ten at the time, but she was a farmer's daughter and understood all about having babies.

To cheer her mum up, she'd started on a picture of a daffodil, and her father had suggested that she was so talented that she could become a famous artist. But even back then, all she wanted to do was farm. She had, however, signed the painting – as she had continued to do with all her pictures since – with her full maiden name, Marguerite Chandler. Just like a professional artist, she mused, or an actor or a writer. Goodness, what would her dad have thought if he could have seen all this now, each item duly signed and dated.

Well, the only other thing she could do in preparation for the event the following day was to put out the cups and saucers and tea plates ready for the refreshments. She and Clarrie had already put up the folding tables, and somehow the action of laying out the crockery had a calming effect on her nerves.

So engrossed was she in the task that she didn't hear the outer door open and close quietly, and it wasn't until the inner door clicked that she felt aware of another presence. Clarrie come back for her because she was taking so long.

But Clarrie would have spoken by now. Meg's heart began to hammer as she felt instinctively that something was wrong. Slowly, cautiously, she turned round, pulse crashing at her temples.

The gasp lodged in her throat. The featureless form of a man was silhouetted against the gloom inside the hall. She couldn't see his face, but she knew instantly who it was. The way his shoulders moved, hunched in anger as he threatened her across the courtroom. The image had been seared into her memory forever. An image she never thought she'd see again. So, what in God's name was he doing here?

Hatred spewed up into her gullet like bile, but she stood still, tamping down her rage. Waiting. She was fully aware that she was alone with him in the silent, empty hall. Clarrie was waiting for her in the vicarage at the far side of the church. It was doubtful that anyone would hear her if she screamed.

She watched, holding her nerve as he stepped forward. She was able to see his face now, lurid in the jaundiced glow from the torch. Don't be afraid. Stand her ground.

'Remember me?' he sneered at her.

'How could I ever forget you?' she snarled back through bitter, clenched teeth. 'Murderer, abductor—'

'Huh!' he laughed back. 'Depends on your point of view.'

Meg held her tongue. There was no good trying to argue with him. She just wanted him to go away. Her hands balled into fists so tightly at her sides as she fought to control her emotions that her fingernails dug into her palms. She stood stock-still, her skin slicked in a cold sweat, as he paced around her, taunting her, but she didn't move, following him only with her eyes, every nerve taut and ready to snap.

Nathaniel wrinkled his nostrils as he passed behind her. His plan had been to break into the hall and slash all the paintings with the penknife in his pocket. He hadn't reckoned on finding Meg Chandler all alone like this. But now, delight beat in his heart at the thought of making her suffer. Of witnessing terror in her eyes. He drooled at the idea of beating her to a pulp, but he'd have to contain his lust for physical violence. He didn't want her to have any reason to set the police onto him. And that would put the Red Caps on his trail, too.

But she wasn't showing any fear, and she wasn't rising to the bait, either. So what could he do to wreak his vengeance? She'd know it was him now, so he didn't want to do anything that was really criminal.

Irritated with himself that he hadn't waited until she'd gone so that he could simply carry out his original plan anonymously, he began swaggering down the row of pictures, but without turning his back on her. A heavy-duty torch was placed strategically on the table near her, and he didn't want her coshing him over the head with it! But if only he could prompt some reaction from her, torment her in some way, he'd be happy. Then his eyes alighted on the drawing hanging in pride of place above the others.

'Huh, think you're really good, don't you, you stuck-up bitch?' he growled, pointing at the exhibits. 'But these are rubbish! A two-year-old could do better. And, ah diddums, look at that,' he jeered, poking his finger towards the sketch of Mercury. 'If it isn't the mangy mutt I dispatched to doggy heaven. Well, this is what I think of it!'

In a flash, Nathaniel pulled the folded knife from his pocket and flicked open the blade. Huh, that'd teach her! He'd just slash the one drawing which clearly meant a lot to her, and leave her crying. And then he'd disappear out into the darkness, never to be seen again. It wouldn't be magnificent revenge, but she could hardly set the police onto him for that. So it would have to do, and he lifted his arm.

Meg's jaw had clamped more and more tightly. She was stronger than that. She could resist all his vicious taunts. But when she saw the steel blade flash in the torchlight, her heart reared in her chest as unleashed rage shot through her limbs. No! She wouldn't let the devil who'd killed her parents and her dog desecrate the picture that meant so much to her, the very essence of her being before he'd destroyed her life.

Madness swirled through her brain as she launched herself at his raised arm. It seemed to take him by surprise, and his fingers opened, releasing the knife which clattered to the floor. But he wasn't going to let her get the better of him, and using all his might, he hurled her downwards.

She landed with a thud on her back, the wind knocked out of her so that she could hardly breathe, let alone move. An instant later, caution flung to the wind and blinded by a red fog of anger, Nathaniel was astride her waist, pinning her to the floor. Terror roared in Meg's head and she managed to lash out at him, hitting and scratching. But he merely laughed at her, and then his cruel grin changed into a delirious smirk.

'Oh, what have we here?'

Anger spiked through Meg's heart as she saw him wave aloft a small envelope. Damn it! The letter must have slipped out of her pocket when she fell.

'Flight Sergeant R. Hillier,' Nathaniel chortled gleefully as he read out the address while avoiding her attempts to snatch the letter back. 'Oh, I see you're wearing a wedding ring. So, you married the bastard, did you? And he's in the RAF? Air crew, is he? Oh, what a pity it's a central address. I'd have liked to know where he's stationed. But no matter. It'll probably happen anyway, but I can pray every night that his plane crashes and he burns alive.'

His face screwed up like a demonic gargoyle, and Meg glared up at him, horror blazing through her in a tidal wave. Her anguish was so intense, it turned to white-hot rage, and she bent one leg to brace her foot against the floor, bringing her other knee up to slam it into Nathaniel's back with all the force she could muster.

For a split second, he seemed to falter, so she did it again and again, ramming her knee into his back. Other than irritating him, it seemed to have little effect. But all she had suffered because of him – the loss of her parents, her dog and her home, and now his vicious curse towards Ralph – burned through her in an inferno. She gathered saliva to spit in Nathaniel's face. The surprise might just give her the chance to get away.

But just as she was about to launch the gobbet of spittle at him, he suddenly let out a yelp of pain and rolled sideways from her, crashing onto the floor at her side. Her gaze flicked upwards. Standing over her, with a rounders bat raised in the air ready to strike again if necessary was the figure of a tall, elegant woman dressed in a smart, tweed suit. Clarrie. Just for an instant, Meg slumped with relief, but then with Nathaniel's cruel words ringing in her head, she scrambled to her feet. While Clarrie stood guard, Meg grabbed some of the thick string that had been tied round her packaged paintings. Repulsed by the physical contact, she nevertheless grasped hold of Nathaniel's wrist. But instead of resisting, he squealed like a stuck pig as she pulled his arm behind his back and bound both his wrists together. Throwing Clarrie a warning glance not to let down her guard, she dragged Nathaniel to his feet, almost relishing the pain she was evidently causing him. Grabbing her coat and her torch, between them, they frogmarched him across to the vicarage.

*

The vicarage kitchen was a warm, cosy oasis as Meg and Clarrie sat sipping hot tea at the table. It wasn't until the vicar had called the police and Nathaniel had been taken away in a police car that both of them started to shake as what had happened across the way in the village hall began to sink in. Nathaniel's vicious curse still swirled in Meg's brain. It was just that, a curse, nothing more. She was stronger than that and wouldn't let his hatred hurt her anymore. But it had certainly unsettled her, and thank heavens Clarrie had come along when she did.

The same inspector who'd been involved when Green had been arrested previously had rolled his eyes at discovering the same culprit yet again. He'd taken statements from Meg and Clarrie, but he also had some other news for them.

'He's on the Military Police's wanted list, too,' he'd explained. 'Deserted about a year ago, so they're delighted to have recaptured him, and are most grateful to you.'

Knowing of Eric's connection with Robin Hill House, he'd also drafted in the young constable who'd arrived a little later on his bicycle. The inspector had left, but now Eric was sitting at the table with Meg and Clarrie, and the vicar and his wife.

'I think the inspector explained that you don't have to press charges with regard to the assault,' Eric said gently. 'But you can go away and think about it. The thing is, as a deserter, he'll have a good sentence to serve in military prison. And then he'll probably be sent out to the Far East to serve in the army, and if he tries to desert again out there, well, heaven help him. Now, we suspect his collarbone's broken, but it was in defence of someone being attacked. Mrs Stratfield-Whyte is a pillar of the community, and nobody's going to doubt her word. But if you press charges, it'll go to court, and you'll have to go through all that again.'

Eric pursed his lips with a sympathetic sigh. 'If it were me, I think I'd let the military deal with him. But the assault on you, Meg, will remain on record. So, sleep on it. And you can always discuss it with the inspector if you want further advice.'

'Thank you, Eric,' Clarrie said gratefully. 'Meg?'

Meg looked from one to the other, then lowered her eyes. 'I'll think about it,' she murmured. 'But I'm inclined to agree with Eric. I just want the blackguard out of my life, and put an end to it forever.'

'I think you're right,' Clarrie nodded. 'I know we're all in shock still, and maybe it'd be natural to want to make him pay for what he did tonight. But he's going to pay for his desertion well enough.'

'I agree,' the vicar put in. 'It's not exactly Christian forgiveness, but as he's going to be punished anyway, I'd be inclined to leave it at that. But, how are you both feeling now? And what about tomorrow? The exhibition.
Will you be up to it, Meg?'

To Clarrie's immense pride, Meg lifted her head almost in surprise.
'Of course, vicar. I'm not letting that devil ruin all our plans. And if people do get the bus all the way out here from Tunbridge Wells, we can't let them down. And I'm not just doing this for me. I'm doing it in memory of my mum and dad.' Meg's gaze travelled to Clarrie's face, and she squeezed the older woman's arm. 'And for all the people who've been so kind to me since my parents died.'

Her blue eyes deepened to sapphire as she caught Clarrie's glance, the tension on her face moving into soft lines of love and affection. *Oh, Clarrie. You saved me*, her look said silently. And inside Clarrie's heart, such an intense warmth of emotion wafted hither and thither that she could have burst. For a brief moment, she and Meg had shared a terrible fear, but they had fought it together, united as one. Bringing them closer than ever, their souls entwined. And when Meg leant forward and encircled her in an embrace so charged with feeling, Clarrie could have sung with joy.

Twenty-Seven

1943

'Well, I hope he bloody well rots in hell!' Ralph fumed, turning to Meg with incensed rage burning in his eyes as they walked through the woods with the dogs. 'And why the hell didn't you tell me before? It's been months, all through the winter! All you told me was how well the exhibition went, and that you sold all but two of your paintings.'

Meg raised her eyes to her husband and her heart broke. She'd never seen Ralph so angry, even when they'd discovered what Green had been up to on previous occasions. She knew why, of course. The strain of all those secret, night-time missions was showing. He'd aged, his eyes sunken and with deep crow's feet at the corners from peering into the darkness. What he needed was sleep, but when they went to bed, sleep wouldn't come. He was too used to being up and alert at night, flying into enemy territory. And Meg would hear him get up and creep downstairs, not returning to bed until dawn was approaching.

She'd waited until, with the calm of the countryside soothing his nerves, he'd at last managed a few good nights' sleep. It was why he'd been sent home on two weeks' leave. His commanding officers had seen the signs, the way his hands would suddenly start shaking as they were now. Other people's lives, whole operations, could be put at risk if he made a mistake, to say nothing of the loss of an aircraft, equipment, and information. The Resistance was of vital importance, disrupting German movements, uncovering intelligence. Things sometimes went wrong. As they had done on Ralph's last mission. Not his fault, but his superiors could see that his nerve had snapped, and he must have that much-needed – and overdue – leave. He and his pilot, Neville, had both been sent home.

Meg had brought Ralph into the woods at the deepest part of the estate, on the pretext of giving all the dogs some exercise. She wanted to take him somewhere quiet where they shouldn't be disturbed, to tell him what Nathaniel Green had done back in the autumn, the evening before the exhibition. Guessing how he might react, she'd almost been tempted not to tell Ralph at all, but he was bound to hear it from someone, and she wanted to get in first.

'Pity the bluebells have gone over,' Meg had said in an attempt to put Ralph in a relaxed mood before she spilt the beans.

'Yes,' he'd answered, his voice flat and dull.

Meg tried again, taking Ralph's hand as they walked along the path. 'It was so kind of Alan and Maggie to have Cyril take my place at the farm again so I could spend these two weeks here with you. He doesn't have my experience, of course, but he's so willing.'

'Yes.' Ralph gave another monosyllabic grunt, and Meg gritted her teeth. There was only one thing for it.

'I don't think I told you,' she began tentatively, her pulse starting to gallop. 'I saw Nathaniel Green again. Back in the autumn.'

'What!'

Meg's words had prompted an animated response this time, and she knew she had to go on. So she told Ralph briefly what had happened and how Green had been a deserter, which angered Ralph even more. Meg deliberately left out, however, how Nathaniel had discovered they were married, and how he had virtually put a curse on Ralph that had kept her awake at night, even though she tried desperately to rationalise the situation. All the devil had learnt was that Ralph was in the RAF. On its own, it was useless information. It would be impossible for him to use it to harm Ralph in any way.

'So why didn't you press charges against the bastard?' Ralph demanded when she'd finished, glaring at her almost accusingly.

'Because he didn't really hurt me, and I really didn't want to go through all the court process again,' Meg explained as patiently as she could. 'I just wanted to forget it had ever happened. And I knew if I'd told you before, you'd have been worried about me. But it happened so long ago now, that as far as I'm concerned, it's all in the past. But I don't want there ever to be secrets between us, which is why I've told you now. And anyway, the Military Police were dealing with him. And it looked as if Clarrie'd broken his collarbone, so I thought that was enough.'

Ralph was staring at her darkly. But then she saw him take a deep breath as if to calm himself. 'Good for her,' he said vehemently.

'She was going to hit him over the head,' Meg went on, 'but realised in that instant that she could kill him, and she didn't want that. Wasn't that clever of her to think that?'

'Certainly was,' Ralph agreed, and then he surprised Meg by pulling her towards him and crushing her against his chest. 'Oh, my love, I just couldn't bear the thought of anything happening to you,' he murmured brokenly into her hair.

A deep frown creased Meg's forehead. Ralph was holding her so tightly that her head was pressed hard against him and she could hear his heart beating hard and fast. Her stomach clenched, for what had he seen that had cut into him so deeply?

When she at last felt him begin to relax a fraction, she gently pulled away enough to be able to cup his hollow cheeks in her palms and bring his face down so that she could place a lingering kiss on his lips. She could feel the tension pulsing out of him, and when she glanced up, his eyes were softly closed, though the tiny muscles in his brow were still twitching.

'Let's sit down on that fallen log over there,' she suggested quietly, taking his arm. 'I think you need to tell me what happened on that mission,' she said, raising her eyebrows questioningly at him.

For a moment, his mouth clamped in defiance, but then he lowered his eyes and nodded slowly. He didn't utter another word until they had sat down, and then he seemed to be concentrating more on watching the dogs sniffing about in the undergrowth. Clarrie's three were quite elderly now, and Thimble was quite comical as she tried to get them to play more boisterously. But Ralph didn't look as if he was finding it amusing.

'So?' Meg prompted him softly.

Ralph's elbows were resting on his spread knees, hands clasped together, and he dropped his gaze as if concentrating on them would give him the strength to relive the horrific scene. Meg was beginning to think that perhaps he wouldn't say anything after all when at last he began to speak.

'There was a clearing,' he said, his voice so low that Meg could only just hear him. 'We'd used it before. But not often. You don't. It was nine months since we'd used it last. It was a landing, not just a drop. We had an agent to pick up. It's only a tiny clearing, but the Lysander's built for that and Nev can land it on a pinhead. We were coming in low. Lights dimmed, wheels down. Guided by a couple of flashlights. And then...' He broke off, choked. And his head drooped even further. 'All hell suddenly broke loose,' he barely whispered. 'Even above the engine, we heard the shots. Nev immediately began to abort the landing. But from the ground, you probably wouldn't have realised. And then the girl...' Ralph paused again, pinching his upper lip between his forefinger and thumb before forcing himself to go on. 'Jeanne her name was, if I remember rightly. Code name, that is. Instead of running off into the woods to try and save herself, she ran out into the clearing, waving her arms at us to warn us. I suppose she thought that was more important. That they'd see she was a girl and wouldn't... But they mowed her down with a machine gun. She was no older than you.'

Meg could hear the sharp catch in his voice that brought him to a halt. She'd let him speak without interruption, her own heart sickened by his words as she imagined the darkness of the woods at night, the plane coming in low and stealthily, the secrecy. And then the horror of the German guns tracing through the pitch black. The girl being hit, several times, her body shuddering as each bullet tore into her flesh as she went down.

Meg gulped down her nausea, her hand closing on Ralph's arm. She went to speak but her own words stuck in her throat before she could make her voice work. 'So… what happened next? Did the others get away?'

Ralph took his time, taking a deep breath before releasing it with a shake of his head. 'There's been no radio contact since. The girls at our end, they can recognise the touch of the operative. And… nothing. The Germans strafed the plane, but Nev pulled us out so quickly. But we were bloody lucky they didn't hit anything vital. I think they realised we'd got out of range, and they went after the poor sods on the ground instead. So we don't know yet if anyone got away. Managed to lie low. And anyone who was caught… They'd all been issued with cyanide pills. But it makes some people instantly sick so it doesn't get a chance to work. There's obviously no way of knowing beforehand,' he concluded bitterly.

He was still staring at his joined hands, and Meg tightened her hold on his arm. She could feel him shaking, and she was aware of her own blood pulsing nervously.

'I'm so sorry,' she croaked. 'It must've been dreadful. But you mustn't keep these things to yourself. It's good to talk. Get it off your chest.'

Ralph nodded, his eyes still lowered, but then he suddenly turned to her, his face alight with anguish. 'Oh, Meg, I love you so much,' he muttered.

Meg knew he was going to break down as he reached out for her, and she spread her arms to wrap him in her embrace. He shuddered against her, and she tried to soothe him while she had to bite back her own tears.

She waited patiently for his wrenching misery to pass. God knew she'd had enough experience of her own to know that these moments didn't go on forever. You became so saturated in your own sorrow that you couldn't absorb any more, and the tears would eventually dry.

Sure enough, Ralph's shoulders slowly ceased heaving, and he drew back, knuckling at his wet cheeks. 'Sorry,' he mumbled. 'I feel such a fool.'

'No, love, don't say that,' Meg answered softly. 'You've been flying these missions for too long. You need a break.'

Ralph nodded, sniffing. 'Yes, I suppose so. It gets to you after a bit. But,' he smiled awkwardly, 'I shouldn't have brought it to you. And I promise I won't again. I really want to enjoy this time with you.'

Meg returned his smile. 'So do I. But you can always tell me things, you know. A problem shared, and all that. And things are starting to turn a bit with the war, aren't they?' she said optimistically, trying to lift their mood.

'Maybe. And the Yanks are bringing more and more troops over here. There's a lot coming in via Plymouth, I think. I reckon they're gradually building up to something big. Even if not for a long while. And what Nev and I do will be more important than ever. Information, preparation, supporting the Resistance.'

'What, for invading France?' Meg's eyes opened wide.

'I can't see that we're anywhere near it yet. But I reckon the time will come. Not for ages yet. Maybe next year, I don't know.'

Meg blinked at him. The war had been going on for so long, it almost felt as if it would never end. But it couldn't last forever, could it?

'Meg! Ralph! Oh, there you are!'

They both looked up as a slight figure hurried towards them, weaving its way through the trees. Meg saw Ralph hastily wipe the back of his hand across his mouth, relieved that the tearing moment when his tense emotions had broken out had passed before someone had come looking for them.

It was Doris, her red curls tied in bunches that streamed out behind her. 'Oh, good, I'm glad I found you!' she panted as she came up and stood squarely before them, her face a jubilant smile. 'Thought you'd want to know the news. Your pals in Bomber Command, Ralph, overnight they destroyed two big dams on the Ruhr and damaged others, knocking out their electro-power stations. So they won't be able to make any more bombs or anything there for ages. And it's messed up the water supply to their canals so they can't use them for transport, either. Great news, isn't it? Maybe it'll all be over soon, and my daddy can come home!'

As she skipped away, Meg's smiling glance snagged on the ironic look on Ralph's face. 'Sadly, just one small step,' he sighed. 'And it'll take more than that to stop Hitler. Remember how quickly Wig got the factory going again after it was bombed. The Germans will repair the damage in no time.'

'Surely it'll take them months if it's as bad as that? It's got to make a difference.'

'To an extent, I'm sure. But what about the Japs?'

Meg bit her lip. Yes, Ralph was right. And there were bound to have been innocent civilians drowned when the dams were breached.

'Well, let's try to feel encouraged, anyway,' she said optimistically, calling to the dogs as she rose to her feet. 'And let's enjoy the rest of our walk while it's still nice.'

She held out her hand to Ralph and he took it, standing up with a playful smile. 'Yes, miss,' he teased. 'And by the way, I don't think I said, but I think you look rather fetching in short white socks. Reminds me of the little girl you were when we met.'

'Ralph Hillier!' Meg laughed in mock horror, and laced her arm about his waist.

Twenty-Eight

Up in her room at Home Farm, Meg took the photograph of Ralph from the bedside table, stroked her fingers across his cheek and kissed the glass before setting it back in its place. The popular song, 'I Just Kissed Your Picture Goodnight', by the American artist, Phyllis Jeanne, went round in her head as it did every night, making tears of fear and sadness well up in her eyes as she snuggled down between the sheets.

She hadn't seen Ralph again for months, though he had managed to ring the farmhouse on occasion. He told her that things were all right, but she could sense the tension in his voice, and their conversation was stilted. Dread still inched its way into her heart. For how long could Ralph's luck last?

The shrill tone of the telephone ringing down in the hallway of the silent farmhouse sent a barb of terror darting through her chest. Oh, dear God. Who would be calling at this late hour? Ralph. Her thoughts at once shot forward, crippling her, cramping her stomach so that she was ready to vomit. A burning plane falling from the sky. Oh, Christ, no!

She held her breath, pulse cracking inside her skull, as she listened to Alan Fenshaw padding down the old stairs. The familiar creaking. *Oh, please God, no.*

When Alan came back up and tapped on her door, the pain in her chest paralysed her, and she felt herself swoon.

'Meg? Meg, your Clarrie's on the phone. You'd better come.'

Clarrie? Nothing to do with Ralph, then. They'd have rung Home Farm, not Robin Hill House. She felt giddy with relief as she shot out of bed, grabbing her dressing gown. But if not Ralph, what...? Oh, Lord, she hadn't heard anything in the distance, but had there been another unexpected raid on London? The factory? Wig?

She nodded at Alan, flying down the stairs to the phone, and hearing Thimble's claws clicking on the bare wood steps as she scampered down after her. 'Clarrie?' Meg said as she picked up the receiver, her stomach turning sickening cartwheels. 'What is it?'

'Oh, Meg,' she heard Clarrie's faltering voice at the other end of the line. 'It's Nana May. I'm pretty sure she's had a stroke. I've called the doctor, but she seems bad to me. You couldn't come?'

'Of course.' The words tripped off Meg's tongue without a second thought. 'I'll get there as quickly as I can.'

She replaced the receiver in its cradle, pausing for a second or two to gather her emotions together. Dear, *dear* Nana May. It was strange, but she'd always felt as if the old lady would be there forever. She'd been in Meg's life for so long, a stalwart rock when Meg had lost her parents and come to Robin Hill House as a rebellious stranger, having to make her own way in a hostile world.

'It's Nana May,' she told Alan briefly as she regained the top of the stairs. And now Maggie joined her husband on the landing. 'It sounds bad. I must go.'

'Of course. If only I had some petrol, I'd drive you there in the lorry.' 'Well, I've got the bike,' Meg said, her thoughts racing ahead of her.

'You'll take care of Thimble for me?'

'Least we can do. But you take care, love. Don't really like the idea of you cycling all that way on your own at night, but there's nothing else for it.

Give us a call when you get there so we know you've arrived safely, eh?'

'Yes, I will,' Meg promised, disappearing into her room to throw on some clothes. Five minutes later, she set off into the October night, pedalling through the darkness as fast as she could by the glimmer from the slit in the cardboard over the bicycle's front light. Damn Hitler and his bombs! There weren't many nowadays, but you still couldn't break the blackout rules, not even for Nana May.

When she finally flew up the driveway at Robin Hill House, the doctor's motorcar was parked outside. Exhausted from pedalling so quickly through the pitch-dark lanes and yet fired by anxiety, Meg propped the bike against the wall of the house. Finding the front door unlocked, she slipped swiftly inside, opening and shutting the door in a split second. At once, she bumped into Clarrie who was showing the doctor out.

'I'm so sorry, Mrs Stratfield-Whyte,' he was saying. 'There's nothing much more I can do. It's in the lap of the gods now, but it doesn't look good. I'll call again in the morning, but I must warn you, I'm not sure she'll make it through the night. Just keep her as comfortable as you can.'

Clarrie nodded, and Meg saw her lips twist as she clamped them tightly against her anguish. In the pale glow from the veiled table lamp, the older woman's face looked white and strained as the doctor stepped out into the darkness.

'Oh, Meggy.' Clarrie slid into her arms, gulping down her fears. Just for a second. She needed this young girl, her Meg, in order to force the next breath into her lungs.

'Wig?' Meg ventured, feeling tears pooling in her own eyes.

'I've phoned him. He's going to the station to see if there's any way he can get back. If only he still had the car. As it is, he probably won't be able to get here until morning. But… you heard what the doctor said. It might be too late. But you go on up,' Clarrie said, forcing a smile as she rubbed Meg's arm. 'Mary's sitting with her. Penny's just put the kettle on in the kitchen. I'll bring you up a cuppa when it's ready.'

'Thanks,' Meg nodded. 'But I'll just give Maggie a call before I go up, if that's OK? She wanted to know I'd got here safely.'

Clarrie nodded, and then wandered off towards the kitchen, running her hand distractedly through her hair. Meg watched her go, and then, after quickly making the telephone call, she hurried up the servants' staircase.

But when she reached Nana May's room, she hesitated outside the door. She suddenly felt herself falling into the deep, dark hole where she'd been once before. It had all happened so quickly that she'd never had the chance to say a proper goodbye to her parents after their tragic accident. Now she suddenly felt that if she was about to say farewell to the dear old lady who was part of her family now, it would feel as if she was bidding a final adieu to her parents at the same time.

Grief surged through her as she girded up her failing courage to open the door. A row of nightlights flickered on the mantelpiece as if echoing the life that was draining away from the figure in the bed. A comforting log fire glowed in the small grate, and Meg's mother-in-law was sitting in the armchair pulled up to the bedside. Mary stood up as Meg came in.

'How is she?' Meg whispered.

Mary shook her head. 'I expect you'd like a few minutes with her on your own,' she answered. 'I'll just go down to the kitchen for a while.'

As Mary left the room, Meg lowered herself into the chair. The ache she'd felt so many times before ripped through the back of her throat, and her vision blurred with moisture. Nana May was propped up on a mound of pillows, her skin sallow in the glimmer that cast eerie shadows on the walls. She was utterly still but for a slight, irregular rise and fall of her chest, her mouth partially open and drooped to one side.

Meg reached out and stroked the back of her wrinkled hand. It already felt cool, the skin paper thin. And Meg felt her own mouth clench in an ugly grimace as she battled against her tears.

'Thank you for everything, Nana May,' she croaked. 'You've been so good to me. To everyone. We all love you so much.'

She bowed her head, sniffing back the tears that were starting to trickle down her cheeks and drip onto their joined hands. In the still silence of the night, she gasped when she suddenly felt movement. Nana May's finger tapped almost imperceptibly on her hand, and when she glanced up, the old lady had managed to lift her eyelids a little.

'Cla-rrie,' she rasped almost inaudibly through her drooping lips. 'Daugh-ter.'

The two words had clearly cost her a huge effort, and Meg's heart fractured. 'Don't talk now, Nana,' she said, trying to sound as normal as possible but knowing that her voice seemed strange. 'Save your strength. And yes. I know. Clarrie's been like a daughter to you. And she loves you like a mother, too.'

She paused, choking on the brutal pain that raked her throat. Her entire being. Were those to be Nana May's last words? Would she be the last one ever to hear her voice? And then those kind eyes were forced wide open as the dying woman looked at Meg, her gaze burning and intense.

'No!' she spoke determinedly, her voice strong even though her mouth wasn't working properly. 'Clarrie. *You*!'

Meg blinked at her, taken aback. Nana May was trying to tell her something, but what? She shook her head, brow pleated in a desperate frown. She *had* to understand!

'W-what?' she questioned. And then a torch of light burst inside her. 'You mean... Clarrie thinks of *me* as *her* daughter?'

The old lady's eyes shone brightly and she gave the tiniest nod. But there was something else, something fiercely questioning on her face. And suddenly Meg understood.

'Yes. And she's like another mother to me, too. I really will let her be a mother to me. I promise you.'

She saw the half-paralysed mouth move into a lopsided smile, and the old head nodded, relaxed back onto the pillow, eyes closed. Face content and peaceful. Meg sensed that she'd said what she needed to say. And that now she was ready to go. And watching her, Meg was blinded by her tears.

Later, Nana May's breathing became more laboured, chest rattling rhythmically with each gasp. She didn't speak again. Nana May Whitehead, faithful servant and companion, slipped away peacefully at five o'clock in the morning with Clarrie and Meg, who she looked upon as her daughter and granddaughter, by her side, and Mary Hillier standing at the foot of her bed. Wig arrived shortly after nine, devastated that he'd been too late to say goodbye to the dear woman who'd taken care of him since the day he'd been born.

For a long time, Robin Hill House was a very sad place. And yet it would grow in strength and love. Because Nana May had shown them all the way.

Twenty-Nine

1944

'Good luck, then, both of you. Take care of yourselves. And I hope, well, you know.'

'Thanks, Maggie. And thanks for coming to the station with me.'

'Least I could do.'

'Well, we'd better get on this train before it goes without us.'

Meg dragged herself away, and she and her mother-in-law, Mary, climbed up into the crowded carriage, each with her little suitcase and gasmask box. There were whistles and a few catcalls from a group of soldiers as Meg forced her way down the packed corridor – instantly muted by the fierce glare of the older woman obviously travelling with her!

They managed to squeeze into a compartment with mainly civilian passengers, and Meg tripped over their feet to get to the window in order to wave to Maggie Fenshaw as the train lurched and began to move forward. She was anxious to get going, and yet she reared away from this journey she'd prayed she'd never have to take. Maggie had been a rock over the last few hours, and tears stung at the back of Meg's eyes as she threw her friend a watery smile and gave a little wave of her trembling hand.

As the train gathered speed, the other passengers moved along so that Meg and Mary could sit down. It was a bit of a squash, which led to some smiles and light-hearted chatter, but neither of the two women was in the mood for conversation. They were both nervous about the journey, the longest either of them had ever made. But the main thing on their minds was exactly what they'd find at the end of it.

Meg had felt sick ever since she'd received the telegram the previous day. The flimsy paper shook in her hands and she'd stared at it, numb with shock, unable to tear it open. It was Maggie who'd helped her find the courage. The letters had danced before her eyes, refusing to make sense until Maggie read them aloud. And then Meg's stomach had cramped so tightly that something inside her collapsed and she sank to her knees.

Ralph's plane had crashed and he was in Plymouth's Royal Naval Hospital. It was all the telegram said, and Meg's mind had been turning wild circles ever since. Ralph had survived so far, but Meg imagined his injuries must be severe. So as Meg and her mother-in-law boarded the train, they had no idea if they'd find him still alive when they got there.

There'd been so much to organise. Meg had telephoned Robin Hill House straightaway. Jane, blossoming since she and Eric had recently become engaged, had answered at the other end. She was equally shocked by her friend's news, and had run off to find Clarrie all in a fluster.

As Meg waited, she suddenly yearned desperately to hear Clarrie's voice again, and Nana May's dying words echoed in her head. Yes. Kind as Maggie had been in the last ten minutes since the dreaded telegram had arrived, it was Clarrie that Meg wanted to turn to. They'd helped each other through so much in the past, but it ran much deeper than that. Clarrie seemed so fragile at times, yet when it came to helping others, she could be so calm and collected. Could it be that Meg recognised the same balance of emotions in herself? Did they really share some affinity that almost made them like mother and daughter, just as Nana May had intimated in her dying breaths?

Gabriel was in bed with 'flu and a raging temperature, but of course Mary was desperate to see her son and had arranged to meet Meg at the station. Clarrie herself wouldn't come down to Plymouth. She had her responsibilities at Robin Hill House, and would also need to take care of Gabriel and their young evacuee, Ed, in Mary's absence. Though dear Penny would be willing enough, Clarrie felt it would all be too much for her to cope with. To top it all, they were about to have poor old Topaz put to sleep, and Clarrie knew Doris was going to be devastated and she wanted to be there for the young girl. And besides, it was fitting that Meg and Mary, as Ralph's wife and his mother, should go alone.

As it was, Meg and her mother-in-law were both so lost in their own anguish that they barely exchanged a word until they came into London. The ticket man at Tunbridge Wells had advised them to take the Plymouth train from Waterloo rather than the one from Paddington, as it would mean less time trying to travel across London. Also, once past Exeter, the train from Waterloo took a route around the north of Dartmoor and then down its western side, which he felt would probably suffer fewer interruptions than would the train from Paddington which followed the south coast.

Despite his assurances, Meg lost count of the unscheduled stops along the line and delays in the stations, although she and Mary were glad of the opportunity to nip off to the ladies'. They'd both brought welcome thermos flasks with them and some provisions, but Meg gagged every time she took a bite of her sandwich. Her stomach was aching from hunger, yet churned so viciously that her throat closed up and she had a job to swallow the tiniest morsel. She shook inwardly, and looking across at Mary, her motherin-law was suffering exactly the same loss of appetite. Their eyes met, and they gave each other a wan, supportive smile.

It was dark when they finally arrived in Plymouth, and bitingly cold. Groping along unfamiliar pavements in the blackout was a nightmare, but by asking passers-by on the street, they were told how to get to the naval hospital by bus. It seemed that the wartime spirit of comradeship was as strong here as anywhere. After all, Plymouth had suffered as badly as London in the Blitz, and all around, ghostly ruins tottered among acres of rubble that had once been homes, shops and offices.

Meg was so exhausted she could hardly stand by the time they finally discovered their destination, her head swimming and dazed, and she was sure Mary must feel just as bad. She was Ralph's wife, but Mary was his mother, and the gruelling journey must have been even harder for her with her advancing years. But they both felt they would be tormented until they *knew*.

Their identity cards were checked, of course, when they arrived at the hospital and Meg produced the telegram. It was a massive building, and they were taken along a maze of corridors. Heaven knew how they'd find their way back. But Meg didn't really care. All she wanted to know was that Ralph was still alive.

After they'd walked what seemed miles, they were eventually asked to wait in a small, stark, windowless room that boasted no more than a few austerely upholstered chairs. Meg sank onto one of them, her pulse trundling, the silence reverberating in her ears. It felt like a bad dream. Couldn't be happening. She and Mary sat next to each other, instinctively holding hands as they waited for the news.

'Ah, Mrs Hillier junior and senior, I believe,' the naval doctor who entered the room a while later greeted them. 'You must be tired after your long journey. But I'm sure all you want is to know about your husband, son. Well, the good news is that he's stable.'

Meg knew that she swooned and she struggled not to sink into the deep chasm that seemed to open up around her. She lost the doctor's next few words, but she was in control of herself again by the time he'd sat down opposite them, clasping his hands between his spread knees.

'The plane came down a week ago—'

'A *week*?'

'Yes. It takes time to set the wheels in motion, contact relatives. Not my department, of course. Treating your husband *is*. All I can tell you is that the plane came down over western Dartmoor, and he was the sole survivor. Now...' The doctor paused, pulling in his chin and regarding them darkly. 'He was badly burned. Not his face, I'm happy to say,' he put in quickly, 'but one arm from the elbow upwards and across the shoulder. It might've been a lot worse, but he had the sense to roll on the wet grass to put out the flames. As it is, provided we can stave off any infection, he should make a full recovery. There'll be scarring, of course, and possibly some surgery. Skin grafts, that sort of thing. But overall, there's no reason why he shouldn't lead a normal life in the future. And he wasn't in the smoke long enough for it to have affected his lungs at all.'

Meg didn't know whether to laugh with relief or burst into tears. In truth, she didn't know what she felt. She could see Mary's eyes were glistening, and made an effort to pull herself together. She must be strong for her mum-in-law's sake.

'Can we... see him?' she faltered in a small voice.

'Through a window, yes.' The doctor's face was still grave. 'Thirddegree burns aren't as painful as you might imagine. They go deeper than the nerves, you see. But he is mildly sedated, and he's sleeping just now. We're barrier nursing him to prevent infection, so it's not worth you gowning up. So what I'd suggest is that you come back tomorrow. He should be able to talk to you at some point then. So, if you're ready, come with me.'

Meg exchanged glances with Mary, and together on wobbly legs they followed the doctor down a corridor. He stopped by an internal window, inclining his head. Meg's heart was in her mouth. She couldn't bear to look, and yet she knew she must. Nathaniel's curse flashed across her mind but she forced it to one side.

When she brought her eyes to peer through the glass, Ralph just looked asleep, peaceful and calm, a sheet turned down over a blanket across his chest. Over one shoulder Meg could see a dressing the doctor explained was something called tulle gras, but other than that, Ralph appeared perfectly normal. Most importantly, he was alive, and their love would bring them through, Meg was sure.

'D'you have somewhere to stay?' the Royal Navy nursing sister who took over from the doctor enquired some minutes later.

'No, we don't,' Meg told her, suddenly dropping with fatigue. 'We thought we'd find a boarding house, although we've no idea where.'

'We've a couple of places we recommend,' the sister said. 'We do this often, you see. Wait here while I make a couple of calls, and I'll give you directions.'

Meg nodded her thanks, then turned back to gazing at Ralph through the glass. She willed him to get better, pouring every vestige of her strength into his body. He was alive and he was *going* to stay that way. She was damned well going to make sure he did.

*

'Meg?' Ralph's voice was frail, as if it was taking a massive effort for him to speak.

Meg could feel her heart breaking, and forced a smile to her face. 'Yes, it *is* me under all of this,' she told him from behind the mask. She wanted so much to touch him, but the doctor had instructed them not to, despite the sterile gloves, gown and cap in which both she and Mary had been dressed. With deep burns, infection was the enemy, they'd been told. There were drugs called prontosil and M and B powders, but prevention was better than cure.

'Your mum's here, too,' Meg said gently, watching as Mary came up on his other side.

'Hello, love.'

Ralph turned his head. 'Mum?'

'Yes, it's me. Not exactly glamorous, these outfits, are they?' Mary tried to be light-hearted. 'Dad sends his love. He's got 'flu, so he couldn't come.'

'Where are we?' Ralph frowned as if trying to focus his thoughts as well as his glazed eyes.

'Plymouth.'

'Plymouth? And you came all that way?'

'Of course. We didn't know how you were, so we came straightaway. But they say you'll be fine. It'll just take time.'

Ralph nodded, and then his eyes flew wide open. 'The agent? Neville?' he asked in panic. Meg held her breath. The doctor had said Ralph was the only survivor, hadn't he? But surely it wouldn't do Ralph any good to know, not yet at least.

'I don't know,' she lied.

'I don't remember…' Ralph screwed up his face in agitation. 'It's all a blur. Flames…'

'I think that's enough for today,' the doctor interrupted. 'Say goodbye while I go and write him up some more sedation. And once you've ungowned, I'll have another word with you.'

'Thank you. Hear that, Ralph? We'll see you again tomorrow, darling.'

Meg yearned – how she yearned – to kiss him, hug him. The sister coming in with the medication saved her from breaking down in tears, and a few minutes later, she and Mary were talking to the doctor again.

'I am right that you came all the way from Kent?' he was asking, to which they both nodded. 'Well, I'll see what I can do, but when he's well enough, I'll try and have him transferred to the Queen Victoria Hospital in East Grinstead. That'll be better for you, won't it? They have a specialist burns unit there. Doing pioneering work with plastic surgery to rebuild men's faces. Your husband, er, son, might get away without any skin grafting or suchlike, but if he does need anything, he couldn't be in a better place. But whatever happens, I'm sure they'll recommend that he's not

returned to active service when he's recovered.' 'I should

think not, too!' Mary declared.

'Sadly, very often it's a case of patching them up and sending them back,' the doctor explained sympathetically. 'If they don't have a physical disability, which your son won't. But his recovery will take many months. I believe he was a very skilled navigator, so perhaps he can return as an instructor rather than flying himself. I reckon he's done his bit, don't you? Besides, it's going to be a long road to recovery, and perhaps the war will be over by then.'

'Pray God it will be,' Mary agreed fervently. 'Things do seem to be on the turn, don't they? In Europe, at least. The Far East's probably a different matter.'

Meg clamped her lips. The old bitterness against fate swooped down on her again. They were talking as if they were pretty certain Ralph would survive. She wanted to believe them with all her heart, but she couldn't rest until he was definitely on the mend. After everything she'd been through in her life, she simply didn't think she could go on without him.

Thirty

'You will be all right on your own?'
Meg looked into Mary's anxious face and smiled reassuringly as they stood together on the platform. 'Of course. I'll write at least once a week to keep you up to date.'
'You take care, then, girl,' Gabriel nodded. Having recovered from the 'flu, he'd come down to join his wife and daughter-in-law, but now, with Ralph making steady progress, he and Mary were returning home. 'And make sure that son of ours behaves himself.'
'I'll do that, all right. Now you get back safely and I hope you don't have all the delays we did coming down.'
Mary nodded, and after some brief hugs, the elderly couple climbed into the railway carriage. Meg didn't see them again as they were swallowed up among the hordes of passengers, even though she walked alongside the train, searching every window, as it puffed forward. Nevertheless, she stood waving at the end of the platform until the train steamed out of sight.
It was only then that it hit her how alone she felt in this unfamiliar, bombed-out city. It was early morning, and visiting wasn't officially until the afternoon. So how could Meg spend the intervening time? She took a walk down to Sutton Harbour and the quaint Barbican Quay which dated back nearly four hundred years. She vaguely remembered from her history lessons at school that this was where the Pilgrim Fathers had set sail for America at the start of the seventeenth century. Now Meg tried to imagine how the place would have been as a busy trading port. There were still fishing boats and other vessels as if nothing had changed so much, but just behind the wharves, the winding Elizabethan streets had been devastated by German bombs and would never be the same again.
With a deep sigh, Meg made her way round to the Hoe where she and Mary had taken several bracing walks in the winter wind that seemed constantly to come off Plymouth Sound. She stood for a while, gazing out over the water. The view across the bay was breath-taking, but the barrage of ack-ack guns everywhere and warships and other naval craft coming to and going out of Devonport base were a bleak reminder of the war. Meg shivered, and continued her brisk walk.
She eventually turned her back on the sea and dragged herself up through what had once been the centre of the city, but was now a swathe of flattened buildings and devastation. Much had been cleared away since the major Blitz of three years before, but it was still one extensive bomb site with vivid reminders of the past horrors. It brought back cruel memories of the destruction Meg had seen on the trip up to London for Doris's mum's funeral when they'd been caught in an air raid. Now the ruins provided eerie monuments to the people who'd been killed or injured. Here in Plymouth, there'd apparently been a few air raids the previous year, Hitler just letting people know he hadn't forgotten this important naval base, and Meg prayed there wouldn't be another while Ralph was still here. For who knew what new menace Hitler would come up with to terrorise the people of Britain with again?
Meg made a mental effort to pull herself together. She mustn't think like that. They'd suffered so little in the Kent countryside, even though there'd been one or two incidents,

and now Ralph should pretty well be out of the conflict. Meg should feel relieved, but uneasiness still churned in her stomach.

The war was far from over. Tragically, they'd only recently learnt that Wig and Clarrie's former chauffeur, Vic, had been killed out in North Africa. Whilst at Home Farm, Meg had made sure she didn't mention it since Mandy's fiancé had also fought in the tank regiment at El Alamein. He'd only just come home on leave after all that time, and yet he'd already been recalled, to Italy this time, so Mandy had only been reunited with him for a very short period. Poor girl had been distraught when he'd had to go back so soon.

Meg gritted her teeth and moved on. It was almost noon, and she knew of a little café on her way to the hospital where she could grab a bite. Ralph would be longing to see her, she knew. Boredom and restlessness were the enemies as much as infection now, and physical progress was painfully slow. Time lay heavily on Ralph's hands, despite his still being kept lightly sedated.

'They told me this morning, about Nev and the agent,' he couldn't wait to tell her the instant she arrived, his agitation so great he'd scarcely said hello. 'And it all came back to me. We were coming back from a night mission to pick up the agent outside St-Brieuc. We were raked by some bullets, but we seemed OK until we'd crossed the south coast. We get back over Britain as quickly as possible, you see. But the engine started spluttering as we flew over Dartmoor. There was no way we'd make it back to Suffolk, so we tried diverting to the nearest airfield, RAF Harrowbeer. But we didn't make it.'

He paused, drawing in Meg's gaze. She didn't want to hear this. She didn't want to look at the anguish riven deep in his face. She just wanted to wallow in the joy that he was alive. She'd been through so much horror of her own that she felt saturated with it. But if Ralph needed to unburden himself, she must listen. She must be strong for him even if she didn't feel it. That was what love meant, wasn't it? Sharing everything together, everything fate threw at you. Being part of that person just as they were part of you.

'I know, my love—'

But Ralph hardly seemed to have heard her. 'We were almost there. Just a few miles. Then there was smoke and we lost height. There wasn't time to bale out. Nev did his best, but… I must've blacked out for a few seconds. I don't remember crash-landing. When I came to, there were flames in the front cockpit. Nev was unconscious. I tried to drag him out, but his legs were trapped. I couldn't budge him. Then I realised my arm had caught fire. The flames inside were spreading. I knew it was about to blow. I didn't know what to do. I didn't want to leave Nev, but I knew I couldn't save him. So I saved myself. I got out just in time. The force of the blast knocked me off my feet. I rolled in the grass to put out the fire on my sleeve. I don't remember any pain, just lying there watching the plane burning with Nev and the agent inside it. I just pray to God they stayed unconscious.'

His words ended in a desperate sob, and Meg felt her heart rip. It was as if Nathaniel's curse had been granted but in a different way from the one the devil had meant. Meg knew herself there was nothing anyone could say to ease Ralph's pain. It was something you had to fight on your own.

'You did your best,' she whispered, since she knew that was what you did. Blame yourself.

'I know. There was nothing wrong with our navigation or Nev's flying. But I *feel* as if it was my fault. I knew you'd understand. That's why I had to tell you. I couldn't save Nev any more than you could save your parents.' Meg had averted her gaze as he'd described his own personal horror. But now as she looked back at him, his eyes were glistening, and she realised that tears were trickling down her own cheeks. She'd never felt as close to him as she did now.

'I wish I could hold you,' she choked. 'But I'm not allowed to get near, and your getting better is the most important thing now. You owe it to Neville to survive. I never met him, but I know that's what he'd have wanted.'

To her utter relief, Ralph sniffed hard and nodded. 'Yes. One day, when the war's over, I'll maybe go and visit his wife when I can. She's up in Scotland somewhere. And when I'm well enough, I'll go up on the moor and thank the farmer and his family who came out to help. Pencarrow their name was. Without them, I might've died.'

Yes, Meg could imagine. The day they'd arrived, she and Mary had watched out of the window as the train skirted the north and then the western edge of Dartmoor. Dusk had been closing in, and the moor had taken on a frightening bleakness as it disappeared into total darkness. Now Meg shuddered as she imagined Ralph lying out there, injured, in the bitter January night. If it hadn't been for the good people at the remote farm, whoever they were, she mightn't have been sitting at Ralph's bedside now. Even if they knew the moor like the back of their hands, there must have been some danger for them, trekking over such wild terrain in the pitch black.

But that was what the war had done; brought together people, strangers, in one united spirit. A spirit Meg had witnessed among the Londoners sheltering from the Blitz down in the underground station. A spirit Adolf Hitler, to say nothing of the Japanese, of course, had yet to break. And Meg had become aware of the growing number of Yankee troops amassing in the area. There was a sense of anticipation slowly building that was almost palpable. She had the distinct impression that the United States had yet to show its mighty power to the full. That, between them, the Allies were planning something tremendous.

And when it came, who knew…?

*

'I'd say the easiest way to get to Peter Tavy is to get the train into Tavistock,' Meg's landlady had informed her, 'and then walk. You take the main road north out of the town, same direction as you've been on the train,' she explained, indicating a straight line with her hand. 'And after a couple of miles, you turn off to the right, go over an old bridge and then follow the road into the village. About another mile or so, I think it is. I'll draw you a map.'

'That's very good of you,' Meg had answered. 'Thank you.'

'The least I can do, my lover. I'm afeared I doesn't know the place very well. You'll have to ask when you gets there. But what I can tell you is that you've got two trains to choose from. One goes up the side of the river and across the Bere Peninsula. Very pretty it is once you gets past Devonport. That one arrives at Tavistock North. The other one goes round the edge of the moor, see, and goes to Tavistock South. That must've been the way you came down from London, from what you said.'

'Yes, I think so,' Meg confirmed. 'It was pitch dark by the time we got there, though, so we couldn't see a thing. So I think I'll go that way. I'd like to see the moor in daylight.'

She didn't add that something inside her wanted to see the sort of ground where Ralph's plane had come down. The better she could understand what he'd been through, the better she could help him work through his anguish. So now, as the train chugged its way northwards, Meg's eyes searched the wild uplands of Dartmoor's rugged landscape. Its open, seemingly infinite terrain sloped up to high, craggy outbreaks of granite that she'd learnt were known locally as tors. Barren and unforgiving, Meg had the feeling that under other circumstances, the moor could hold immense savage beauty. A place to get lost inside one's own thoughts, find oneself again as you were soothed by a sense of nature at its most primitive. But it had been a black, bottomless hole on her journey to Plymouth with Mary a few weeks earlier. A vast nothingness. And all Meg could think of just now was how it would have been a hostile desert of loneliness and terror as Ralph's plane had plummeted earthwards.

She got off the train as her landlady had indicated and made her way down into the attractive town of Tavistock. She'd been told that the place had once been wealthy due to the abundance of copper in the area. Or at least, the land and mine owners had amassed fortunes, although a succession of local dukes had been most philanthropic towards the miners and their families. When the mines had closed, Tavistock had become a sleepy market town existing mainly for the local farming community and the usual commercial services to support it.

Now though, at the start of February 1944, it was anything but sleepy. And there was good reason for that. Troops. British, but mainly American. The place was heaving with them, and people were excitedly lining the streets as well, as if waiting for something. The atmosphere was electric.

'Excuse me, but please can you set me on the right road for Okehampton?' Meg asked a woman standing on the kerb with two small children. 'I need to get to Peter Tavy.'

'Doesn't you want to see what's going on first?' the stranger asked in almost affronted surprise.

    'Going on?'

'Why, yes. They say General Eisenhower hissel's coming to inspect his troops in Bedford Square. Big things be afoot, if you asks me.'

Meg was a little taken aback, and she remembered the conversation she'd had with Ralph when he'd been home on leave the previous May. He'd felt preparations for something big were starting even back then, and after all, the Allies had been whittling away at Hitler's domains ever since. Could it be that something really was stirring, if not immediately, then in the foreseeable future?

'Oh, I'd have liked to see that,' she told the woman with genuine disappointment. 'Eisenhower, eh? But I've got to get up to a farm near Peter Tavy, and then all the way back to Plymouth by tonight.'

'You'd best get going, then,' the woman agreed. 'You wants to go down that road there,' she pointed out, 'and just follow it for a couple of mile, and then you turn off right as the main road bends slowly left. No signposts, of course, so you might have to ask.'

Meg thanked the woman, elbowing her way through the thickening crowds until she eventually got out onto the main road where she was able to lengthen her stride. She was walking along a wide valley, but it seemed the road was frequented by American troops in jeeps and all sorts of other military vehicles.

    'Can we give you a lift, missie?'

Meg's heart thumped in her chest as she turned to look at the driver of an open jeep that had pulled up beside her. A lift? He must be joking! But he was an older man with a trustworthy face, and there were a couple of other GIs in the vehicle with him, all in their smart uniforms. And there were so many other personnel on the road that surely it would be safe?

'Just to the turn-off to Peter Tavy, if you know where that is,' she said cautiously.

'Sure thing, miss.' The soldier gave a half salute. 'Been stationed here a while, so I know my way around. Hop in. Take you all the way to the village if that's where you're headed.' Someone else's hand extended to help her climb aboard, and she perched warily on the seat as they rejoined the road.

'Lucky we're going this way,' the driver continued, changing gear. 'Most of us are required for the ceremony with Old Ike,' the chap went on with affection in his voice. 'You sure not going to watch, then?'

'No. I'm...' Meg hesitated, but there was no harm in telling him the truth, and in a way, she'd feel safer if they knew she was a married woman. 'My husband's in the RAF. His plane crashed on the moor a few weeks ago.'

'Jeez, we heard about that. He OK?'

'He was the only survivor. Recovering in Devonport Hospital. Only they're going to transfer him to a hospital nearer home when he's well enough. I'm going to try and find the farmer who came out and saved him, and thank him on my husband's behalf as he won't be able to do so himself.'

'Oh, wow, ma'am, we're mighty sorry to hear about all that.'

'Sure hope he gets better soon.'

'Here, Chuck, you got any of them stockings on you for the little lady? I've got some chocolate about me somewhere.'

It only took five minutes to reach the turn-off, and another five to cross the old stone bridge over a small but gushing river, and then follow the lane that ran more or less parallel to it on the left, with the moor rising up on the right. Climbing out of the jeep when they reached the village, Meg found herself waving goodbye to the GIs, her coat pockets stuffed full of little gifts. Overpaid, oversexed and over here was the general grumble about the Yanks, but that hadn't been her experience. She supposed she had taken a bit of a risk accepting the lift, but it had been an interesting experience as well as saving her some time.

Peter Tavy was a tiny, intriguing place with a couple of farms with their barns in the actual village itself. The church, with the pinnacled tower that Meg had noticed was typical of the area, was set at the end of a wide grassed area flanked by tiny cottages that she guessed were some sort of almshouses. A woman with a scarf over her curlers was heading for the large graveyard that surrounded the church, and Meg hurried to ask her the way. She was directed out the far side of the village and up onto the moor proper.

The view as Meg walked briskly along was spectacular. The track led partway up one side of a steep valley so that she was looking across to the rolling moor opposite. She crossed her arms over her chest, for the further she walked, the more exposed it became to the biting wind. A group of wild ponies stood on a flat outcrop of rock on the far side, long manes and tails shifting in the moving air, and Meg could see a patch of white in a hollow. She shivered. Beautiful though it was, the landscape would be inhospitable in the middle of a January night, and Meg's gratitude went out to the people she was trying to track down. If they hadn't braved the elements, Ralph would very likely have died.

The substantial farmhouse was the only one around so it was easy enough to find. Meg called out as she rounded the building into a farmyard behind, suddenly feeling somewhat nervous. And then she stood still, bowing her head in submission, as two dogs ran out, barking furiously. But the barking was friendly, and a few seconds later, an elderly man appeared from one of the barns.

'Mr Pencarrow?' Meg called.

'Yes?' he answered, fixing her with chocolate brown eyes. He was tall, his back straight despite his years, and Meg could see he must have been an exceptionally handsome man in his youth.

'I'm Meg Hillier,' she announced. 'Wife of the airman you rescued a few weeks ago.'

The fellow's creased face at once moved into lines of concern. 'How's he doing? He is… OK, then?'

'Yes, thank you. Thanks to you, that is. If you hadn't gone out onto the moor like you did in the middle of the night, I'd probably be standing here a widow. So… I've come to thank you from the bottom of my heart,' she concluded in a rush to get the words out before she burst into tears.

'Oh, there, there, cheel, it was nothing, like.' Meg suddenly felt workworn hands clasp hers. 'Come inside and meet the wife.'

'It was such a brave thing to do,' Meg gulped between sobs. 'I can see what it must be like out there in the dark.'

'Not when you're born and bred to it,' Mr Pencarrow told her as he led her towards a door at the back of the farmhouse. 'Born on this farm, and die here I will. Know this land like the back of my hand. And my son came with me that night, too. He's a farmer above the age for conscription, see, so we didn't lose him to the forces. So going out to see what we could do to help was a sort of thank you for that. Out on the moor our son is today, so you won't see him, I'm afeared. But I'll pass on your thanks. Good of you to come all this way. From Plymouth, is it?'

Meg found herself being welcomed into a warm, spacious kitchen by Joshua Pencarrow's wife and a younger woman who was introduced as their daughter-in-law. Meg was ushered into an armchair next to a large range that was throwing out heat, and a mug of weak tea was pressed into her hands.

'Ralph's not well enough to travel yet,' she explained when she managed to gather herself together again. 'And as soon as he is, they're going to transfer him to a hospital nearer home. So he won't get a chance to thank you himself. Not for a while, at least. So I've come instead.'

'Well, he'll be welcome here any time,' Mrs Pencarrow beamed. 'Both of you will. Maybe when the war's over.'

'D'you think it ever will be?' Meg sighed.

'Oh, yes.' Joshua spoke without looking up from filling his pipe. 'All over the country they are, but the amount of Yanks we've got hereabouts, the camp up on Plaister Down, they're planning something all right.'

'And your husband's coming on all right? And where is home?'

'Slowly, but yes, thank you. He is improving. And home's Kent.'

'Ah, a long way, then. And you have the look of a country girl.'

'Yes. Farmer's daughter.'

'Ah, I knew it. So what sort of farming are you into, then?'

Within minutes, they were all chatting away, comparing notes. Meg was invited to stay to lunch, and found herself telling them all about Robin Hill House and how she'd ended up working as a Land Army girl back on the family farm. In return, Meg learnt how Rosebank Hall had been in the Pencarrow family for generations. They were yeoman farmers, owning their own land and also a couple of smaller farmsteads that they rented out. They were well respected in the area, yet Meg could see that they weren't the sort of people to put on airs and graces.

'Went through hard times back along did my parents,' Joshua told her, sucking on his pipe. 'My mother, now, she were the village wise-woman and herbalist. Many a tale she and my dear old dad could've told you if they'd still been with us.'

Meg could imagine Joshua could talk in his own quiet, self-effacing way forever, and she'd have been interested to listen. But it was time she left for the journey home. She gave them some of the chocolate the GIs had given her, and they extended an invitation to visit at any time. She felt she was among friends, wrapped yet again in that wartime spirit that seemed to pervade everywhere.

'Walk with you to the village, I will,' Joshua announced, as they both shrugged into their coats. 'Need to call into a friend.'

A minute later, they were out in the raw February afternoon, and Meg was waving goodbye to the two women. As they set off down the track, Meg's eyes travelled over the craggy landscape. Once again she couldn't help imagining what it would have been like for Ralph, in shock, watching his friend and their passenger die in the burning plane, badly injured himself, all alone and lost out on the desolate moor in the pitch black of a freezing winter's night. A glacial chill ran through her. The kind, selfeffacing man by her side truly was an unsung hero.

'Where… did it happen?' her tongue seemed to ask of its own accord.

'Oh, over the other side of the valley.' Joshua waved his arm vaguely. 'Can't see the spot from here. We heard the crash, see. And we knew where it was because of the flames.'

Meg gulped, and then nodded briefly. 'It… was a long way for you to go. I'm so very grateful to you. So thank you once again, you and your son.'

'Got to stick together against that Hitler, haven't we? Now, you take care, cheel,' Joshua said as they came into the village. 'And I hope we'll see you again one day, you and your Ralph.'

'Yes, I'm sure he'll want to thank you himself in person.'

Meg shook Joshua's hand firmly, and then turned to wave back as he waited on a corner until she was out of sight. The wind blew hungrily about her coat, and she hurried on as quickly as she could. She wanted to be back in Tavistock and on the train before dark, and she hoped she could call in to see Ralph as well, and tell him all about her experiences of the day, and the wonderful people who'd saved his life.

And she also wanted to tell him about what she'd seen in Tavistock, Eisenhower's visit, and the growing sense of hope she felt she could almost touch.

Thirty-One

'Welcome home, Ralph!'

Clarissa joined in the chorus of joyous greetings as everyone surged forward into the hall. But the lady of the house kept back, waiting her turn, holding her emotions in check. She'd been to visit Ralph several times at the hospital in East Grinstead once he'd been transferred, and had watched the haunted expression gradually fade from his eyes. And as he'd recovered, Clarrie had noticed how Meg had blossomed again, her gaunt, strained face filling out once more and her body taking on more womanly curves.

Clarrie watched now as Meg's eyes gleamed with happiness, and her own heart lifted with elation. Because Ralph had come home, so had Meg. *Her* Meg. She'd missed her so much when she'd been away working in the Land Army at Home Farm. The beloved young woman had come back to visit every few weeks, speeding up the drive on her bicycle. The children under Clarrie's care were a great comfort to her. She felt like a surrogate aunt, and then dear old Penny was such a scream, lifting her spirits since Nana May had passed away. But it was only Meg who made Clarrie feel like a mother again. And now Meg had returned to Robin Hill House to be with her hero husband, and Clarrie rejoiced.

As everyone trooped through the house, Glenn Miller's 'Moonlight Serenade' was playing on the radio. It had been left on permanently since the Allied invasion of France the previous month, in case there was any sudden news. It was going to be a long, dangerous haul, but steady progress was being made. One of the big worries now, though, were these new flying bombs, or V1s as they were known, that had been attacking London to devastating effect over the last few weeks. The recent Allied bombing of the storage depots in France had drastically reduced the problem, but it was bound to start up again. Hitler wasn't going to give up without a fight.

But Clarrie wasn't going to let morose thoughts spoil Ralph's homecoming which was going to be held out in the gardens – or what remained of them since Gabriel and his band of young helpers had dug up so much of the lawn to grow vegetables. It was turning out to be a cold, wet summer, but today the sun was making a rare appearance in the July sky, and a celebration picnic was set out down by the lake. Ada and Penny had worked wonders with the ration books, and everyone was in party mood.

'Good to have you home, Ralph,' Wig told him in a quiet aside as plates were handed round and Ada, Penny and Jane carried out pots of tea.

'D'you know what I want more than anything?' Ralph said, arching his eyebrows.

'What's that, love?' Meg asked anxiously.

'To get this ruddy uniform off.'

Ralph gave a bitter grunt, to which those near to him replied with a forced chuckle, not wanting to upset him. It wasn't like Ralph to be churlish. Perhaps his mind wasn't as healed as his body, but surely that would come in time.

'All your clothes are waiting for you in the cottage. So come on.' Meg held out her hand and Ralph grasped it tightly as they made their way through the orchard. 'I expect it feels weird to be back,' she said, slightly unnerved herself. Ralph felt… not exactly like a stranger, but she knew they'd need time for their emotions to settle down. She supposed they were both still in some deep-rooted shock.

'To be honest, I'd rather it was just you and me,' he answered, and Meg noticed him glance wistfully about him as they entered the cottage. 'This is a nice little place and I'm very grateful to have it, but I wish we had somewhere that was really our own. This just doesn't feel right anymore. I suppose it's because I don't feel quite the same person I was. Not with *this* to remind me all the time.'

They'd reached the bedroom and Ralph had stripped off as Meg went to the wardrobe to fetch one of his old shirts. She'd seen the awful, twisted scarring up his arm and across his shoulder on several occasions at the hospital, but it still made her wince. But it could have been so much worse. When she thought of the patients, airmen mostly, she'd seen at East Grinstead being treated for appalling facial burns, she thanked their lucky stars. She took Ralph's hands and squeezed them. 'I know. But we'll get through this. Together. For now, just relax and enjoy all the goodwill. And when the war's over, then we'll see.'

Ralph nodded, and as Meg watched him don his civvies, she felt a little something jump inside her. She was going to fight back in more ways than one. She knew exactly what she was going to do. Always had done, ever since she'd been turned out of Home Farm after her parents had died because, back then, legally she had been too young to carry on the tenancy. The *plan* that had been simmering for so long in the recesses of her mind was going to burst out in glorious light. But first she must restore Ralph to his old self.

'The invasion seems to be going well, doesn't it?' she said as they returned to the homecoming party. 'I know so many of the Allies were killed in those first few days which was *awful*. And poor Boris was so terribly wounded. But they seem to be really pushing forward now.'

'Yes, poor young bugger. At least they got him back to Blighty, but his injuries sound pretty serious. I can only think of him and Max as unruly kids racing round the place like lunatics when they came to visit.'

'Mr Perry and Mrs Sofia must be worried sick about Boris. When I think of Sofia and her sense of fun, even if she is a bit eccentric, it just doesn't seem right.'

'Yes. Knowing Hitler's days are numbered isn't going to help her at all, is it? It's going to take time, but we'll get the bastard in the end. Even if he is trying to fight back with those bloody V1s.'

'Hmm,' Meg grunted grimly. 'I told you, didn't I, that Bob and Sally were both slightly hurt when one landed in their street? And Poor Clarrie's worried the factory'll be hit again, and that Wig won't be so lucky a second time.'

'That line of anti-aircraft guns and barrage balloons they set up along the North Downs doesn't seem to be working very well, so perhaps she's right to worry. But best not mention anything about it for now, and I promise to enjoy this little party in my honour.'

He actually grinned down at Meg, filling her with optimism. Dear, good Ralph was still there beneath the hurt and suffering.

During the afternoon, he duly joined in all the chatter, didn't even mind answering Leslie's probing questions about his injuries. Nobody took any notice when Wig was summoned to the phone because Peregrine was on the line.

Meg was among the first to see him walk slowly back across the terrace and down the steps, his head bent. Clarrie must have seen Meg's frown and followed her worried gaze. Then she sprang forward to meet her husband.

'Wig? Is something wrong?'

'Yes, my dear. I'm afraid there is,' Wig answered solemnly. 'Boris... died of his wounds this morning.'

Meg's hand went over her mouth. Oh, dear God. Poor Boris. And poor Sofia. Because she'd take the news harder than anyone.

Meg didn't notice Clarrie turn silently away. Pain jerked through the older woman's body. Dear, irritating, adored Sofia would be stricken. She was one of the few people guarding the secret of Clarrie and Wig's tragic loss. And now she, too, was to know the agony of a mother's grief. Clarrie was blinded by a grey fog of anger and sorrow as the old, helpless emptiness opened up inside her once again. How was Sofia to cope with the same misery that had dogged her own life for all those years? How cruel fate could be! And Clarrie's hands balled into furious fists at her sides.

*

'You're not going to cry on me, are you?'

Meg looked up into Ralph's teasing face and tossed her head to quell her threatening tears. 'No, of course not,' she answered determinedly, grasping the lapels of his uniform overcoat and pumping her hands against his chest as if to emphasise her resolve. 'Why should I cry? You're well enough to be going back to your base. And this time I know you'll be coming home, no matter how long it takes. No more missions, just training others.'

'It's still going to be a while before I'm home for good. Hitler's losing the game, but he's not giving up yet by any means.'

Meg's shoulders dropped in a sigh. 'Yes. But it's got to be over some time next year, hasn't it? Surely?'

'I sincerely hope so. And then you and I can begin a proper married life together. Ah, hear that?' Ralph tilted his head at the distant whistle. 'Train's coming. Give me another hug. And no tears, remember?'

Meg laced her arms about his neck and their mouths clung in a hungry, desperate kiss. Meg closed her eyes as the train rumbled in beside them, wishing it would just disappear. Ralph's arms about her waist crushed her to him, but at the last minute, he pulled back and leapt onto the carriage step just as the guard came along to slam shut all the doors.

'I'll write to you tonight.'

'Take care, my darling!'

She blew him a kiss and hurried alongside as the train lurched forward. She was beginning to hate stations. She stopped at the end of the platform, waving, and her hand dropped limply to her side as she turned away.

She mustn't be sad. Ralph had recovered from his dreadful injuries, and he was going to be safe. And Meg had something to keep her happy until his return. As soon as Ralph had been transferred to the hospital in East Grinstead, she'd gone back to her work at the farm, the place she still thought of as home. But when he'd come back to Robin Hill to convalesce, she'd gone to live there again, although she'd still helped out at Home Farm whenever she was needed, pedalling to and fro on her bicycle. But now she was returning to her Land Army work full-time. Until the war was over.

Guilt clawed at her. She wanted the war to end, and she wanted Ralph home safely in her arms. But it would mean the wonderful time she'd spent working for the Fenshaws at Home Farm would be over. Even if their son, Paul, didn't survive the rest of the war and she was still needed, Meg couldn't continue there. Her place was by Ralph's side, and it was simply too far to travel back and forth daily to the farm on an indefinite basis.

The autumn wind lifted the hem of Meg's coat as she turned out of the station. She felt upside-down inside. But whatever happened, she vowed to put her *plan* into action. Something Ralph had said the day he'd returned to Robin Hill had stuck in her mind, so she knew he'd approve. But in the meantime, she wanted to continue working at her old home for as long as possible.

Deep in thought, she took her bicycle from where she'd left it propped against the wall. And then, remembering that Ralph would be home for Christmas, her heart squeezed with happiness.

Thirty-Two

1945

He gave in at last, the treacherous little man with the stupid moustache. Disappeared. There were rumours he was dead. Committed suicide. Who really cared, so long as he was gone? Many said it was the blanket bombing of Dresden that finally did the trick, others that Hitler was beaten anyway. But now it was over, in Europe at least. And, God willing, peace would come to the Far East as well before too long.

Everyone had known it was coming, especially in those last few weeks. There was going to be a national holiday, and people were making preparations for the celebrations. It had even been announced that you could buy material off coupons to make bunting. And yet somehow, after nearly six years of war, of bombings, losing loved ones and homes, scraping by on rations of food, soap, clothing and so forth, so many items almost impossible to get hold of, and no private petrol at all, it seemed unreal that peace could ever come.

The hardships would go on, of course. Such things couldn't right themselves overnight. But knowing that the towns and cities of Britain would no longer be attacked, that the men and women serving in Europe would be coming home safe and sound, was such a phenomenal relief that the enormity of it was too much to comprehend.

It was late afternoon on Monday 7th May. Meg and Mandy were out in the fields at Home Farm, checking on the progress of the season's lambs. Meg could almost feel her blood pumping expectantly through her veins, her stomach knotted as excitement simmered inside her. Was she dreaming? Could the peace everyone had craved for so long really be becoming reality? Or was it all a cruel trick? Would their desperate hopes be shattered?

Only one ewe that spring had given birth to triplets, and as it was always unlikely that the third would survive, Meg and Alan between them had succeeded in tricking another mother with only one lamb into fostering it. Meg was just making sure all was still going well when she thought she heard someone calling. She and Mandy caught each other's eye as they both looked up. Maggie was running towards them, shouting and waving her arms. They'd never seen her move so fast.

And then she drew near enough for them to start making out her words. 'It's over!' she was screaming. 'It's over!'

The world stopped turning, and Meg's senses dropped away as she straightened up. It couldn't be true. Could it? She wanted to believe it, but surely she was imagining it. Oh, Mum. Dad.

And then a bullet of white and brown fur hurtled after Maggie, barking crazily in this unexpected game. For when had the farmer's wife ever found such speed before? Thimble raced past her and came to leap about Meg instead, scattering the sheep in all directions.

The taut string snapped, and Meg burst into tears of joy as she caught Thimble's collar and, for a second in which her emotions untangled themselves, buried her face in the dog's thick coat. But she was instantly standing up again. Maggie's puffing, beaming face. Mandy's dangling jaw closing as it turned into an ecstatic grin, a thousand stars dancing in her eyes.

A fountain of joyful abandonment spiralled up inside Meg as the news sank in. The three women grasped each other in elation, jumping up and down and squealing with an exhilaration such as they'd never felt before.

'Ssh!' Meg suddenly shushed them. 'Listen!'

They did. And across the fields chimed the distant peal of church bells. A sound they hadn't heard in years.

'It's true, then!' Meg cried through her tears. 'I can't believe it!'

'Was on the radio just now, my dears.' Maggie, too, was choked with emotion. 'They've surrendered to Eisenhower in France. And tomorrow they'll be signing something in Berlin. Tomorrow's going to be VE Day. And they say both Churchill and the King'll be making speeches tomorrow, as well.'

'Oh, I can't wait till then to celebrate!' Mandy exclaimed.

'I don't suppose many people can. You two get off home to your families.'

'But don't you want—?'

'Alan and me can manage for a day or two. Our Paul's not been hurt at all, so he'll be coming back to us safe and sound. That's enough celebration for us. Now off you go before I have to chase you!' Maggie laughed.

Meg hesitated, her euphoria interrupted. She was already home. But she supposed Clarrie was her family now. And she could feel her heart being pulled towards Robin Hill House as if by a thread.

Back at the farmhouse, she clipped on Thimble's lead, and giving Mandy, Maggie and Alan a final hug, set off down the track on her bicycle. Thimble was nearly eight now, and had long learnt to run alongside the bike on the lead. In the village, people had run outside, and were cheering and hugging each other, and Meg waved merrily to them as she passed before setting out towards Robin Hill House. She couldn't remember how many times she'd pedalled the same route. But never had she done so with such joy in her heart.

When she reached Robin Hill, she cycled straight round to the back of the house. Propping her bike against the wall, she let Thimble off the lead and the dog at once went in search of old Trampas and Sunny who were both on their last legs now. Meg laughed as she watched the younger dog scamper off. The animal would hardly know why all its human friends seemed so happy.

As she came round the corner, all three sets of French doors that led onto the terrace from the dining room, corridor and drawing room respectively were hooked wide open. Music was blaring out from the gramophone, and everyone was outside, dancing, whooping in unleashed delight and generally giving way to unbridled joy. Penny had her three plus Ed in a circle doing a raucous *Hokey Cokey* in competition to the Vera Lynn record being played, and everyone was laughing and joking as Meg had never thought possible.

'Meggy!' Doris cried, racing across with her freckles stretched across her cheeks in a huge grin. 'Isn't it wonderful! It means Daddy will be coming home!' And then Doris proceeded to pull her round in circles until they both collapsed in a breathless heap.

'Oh, where's Clarrie?' Meg finally panted.

'Trying to get through to the vicar on the phone,' Doris puffed. 'To make the last-minute arrangements for tomorrow. They've had everything ready and waiting for the celebrations, but just didn't know when they'd be. Only everyone's trying to use the phone at the same time.'

Meg gave Doris a broad smile, but in her head she was thinking that she would, too! All she wanted was to hear Ralph's beloved voice, but she knew she'd never manage to get through to his base.

When she stepped into the hall, there was Clarrie, speaking efficiently into the receiver. But when she saw Meg, such an expression of serene contentment came over her face that she appeared to glow like an angel. Meg's heart lurched as she recalled Nana May's words, and she almost felt giddy as her love for Clarrie rushed through her in a whirlwind.

'Just a moment, please, Vicar,' Clarrie spoke down the phone, and an instant later, the two women embraced like mother and daughter, their souls entwined as one.

Meg felt Clarrie's reluctance as she dragged herself away. 'I'll be with you in a minute,' she whispered to Meg, and Meg went back out to the terrace, the world suddenly bright and brilliant in a kaleidoscope of happy colours.

Later that evening, with Gabriel and Mary happy to stay with Penny as she babysat Bella, everyone else tripped into the village. Despite all the fêtes and celebrations Clarrie had organised over the years, Meg had never seen anything quite like it. The green was heaving with everyone from babies to the aged. Bunting was already up and fluttering from lamp post to lamp post, tree to tree. Tables had been placed outside front doors with any food and drink people could lay their hands on. At one end, a piano had been dragged outside and someone was thumping out *Knees up, Mother Brown* for gyrating revellers. Big band music or Vera Lynn's patriotic tones were crackling from open windows, all blending and weaving among a cacophony of human voices raised in rejoicing. Children were playing games, enthralled to be out in the gathering darkness. And at midnight, when hostilities were officially at an end, a match was put to a huge bonfire in front of the church, sending joyous flames and sparks high into the night air.

Meg suddenly spied Jane hurrying across to her and Clarrie, arm in arm with Eric, still in his uniform. 'We feel we can get married now!' she cried, and before anyone had a chance to congratulate them, the happy couple waltzed off into the crowds.

'Ah, I'm so pleased for Jane,' Clarrie sighed. 'Eric's perfect for her. Strange to think they met because of that devil who will be nameless. Hope we never hear of him ever again!'

'So do I! But I'm not going to think about him tonight!' Meg declared determinedly. 'I just wish Ralph was here now.'

'And I wish Wig was. But we'll have them back soon, and things will get back to normal. In the meantime, you and me, we have each other.'

Moisture suddenly collected in Meg's eyes again as she looked into Clarrie's face. Yes, they'd grown so close. And Meg had to choke down the desire to hug her tightly and call her… Mum.

*

A week or so later, however, the joyous atmosphere at Robin Hill House was tempered with sadness.

'It's going to be so quiet without you all,' Clarrie moaned, trying to put on a brave face as they all gathered outside the house with their suitcases at their feet. It was a repeat of the scene six years previously when the evacuees had arrived – except that nobody carried a gas mask, and instead of nervous faces, bittersweet tears glistened in each pair of eyes. Clarrie glanced around the ring of friends about to set off to the village and the bus that would take them to the station. From Tunbridge Wells, they would all be travelling together to London Bridge Station where Ed's mother would be meeting him. At sixteen and fifteen respectively, Joyce and Maureen would be completing their journey alone, but their father had sent written directions in case they didn't recognise their way around after so long, especially with the bombings having changed everywhere. Since leaving school, Joyce had been working at the village bakery, and Maureen had taken over Louise's role at Robin Hill House. But back home in London, the shop next door to their parents' bakery was empty, and their father was hoping to be able to take it on and turn it into a tearoom where the girls would work, with a view to taking it over completely when they were old enough. So, much as they had loved their time at Robin Hill, they were really excited about going home. Clarrie was so happy for them that their future seemed assured, but she would miss them dearly.

As for Penny, her brood had grown and were capable of making it to the village on foot, and the twins were going with them to help carry their luggage. Just as well since Wig had no petrol for the car, the jolly woman had declared with her wobbling laugh.

'When Daddy comes home, we've nowhere to live in London,' Doris had voiced her thoughts when the days of celebration had finally subsided. 'He'll be going back to work at the office, I expect, but there's such a shortage of places to live, he'll probably find it easier to find some digs or something without me. So, could I possibly stay on here, please, Clarrie? I like it at the grammar school, but I only want to stay on until next year. And then, I love it here so much, I'd love to work for you, Clarrie.'

Clarrie's eyes had stretched wide with surprise before a contented smile crept onto her lips. As the brightest of the three girls, Doris had passed the scholarship for the nearest grammar school and was doing well. But with Cyril hovering by the doorway pretending to look nonchalant, Clarrie guessed that fifteen-year-old Doris had another reason for wanting to stay. And Clarrie had no objection. In fact, she couldn't have been more pleased! She was a lovely girl, and Clarrie had another reason, too. One she needed to keep close to her heart. Doris's resemblance to Rosebud.

'If your father agrees, of course you can! You could be my new lady's maid!' she said, clapping her hands. 'Now wouldn't that be fun!'

But now her heart was heavy as she was saying goodbye to so many of the people who had been staying under her roof and become her good friends over the last six years. And she'd been watching the children growing up as if they'd been her own.

'And I'm gonna miss you all so much, too!' Penny was replying, bobbing her head up and down so that her double chins danced. 'And Ada, dear, you've taught us so much about cooking, my Archie's stomach won't know itself. London's only a train ride away. Gawd knows what sort of mess Archie's let the house get inter. But who can blame him, working fulltime on the railways and being an ARP warden ter boot? But soon as I'm straight, I want you all ter come and visit.'

'Of course we will. And our doors are ever open, too,' Clarrie told her, her voice catching on the lump in her throat. 'Now you'd better get going, or you'll miss the bus.'

There was a surge of last-minute hugs. For six long years, they'd yearned for the war to be over so that they could all go home. But they'd become a special little community at Robin Hill House, forming bonds that were likely to last a lifetime. And now that the moment of departure had finally arrived, nobody was sure they wanted to leave, after all.

'Blooming lucky, you lot, ter have homes ter go back ter,' Leslie broke the tension in his inimitable way. 'Not that me and Cyril wanted ter go back ter London. But it would've bin nice if our mum and dad hadn't buggered off ter pastures new without letting us know where the bloody hell they've gone.'

'We can do well enough without them,' Cyril put in, puffing up his chest. 'Got totally new lives now. We should be grateful.'

'Course I am, but—'

'We really must get going!' Penny called. 'Come on, you lot. Best foot forward!'

With that, all the travellers picked up their cases and set off down the drive, Penny leading the way with her little tribe, Joyce, Maureen and Ed following, and the twins bringing up the rear with an assortment of bags. Clarrie stood with Doris, Ada, Gabriel and Mary, and Jane, waving off the little troop and calling their goodbyes. Clarrie's eyes misted over until she could barely see the last of her charges disappear out of the drive. So that was it. The end of an era. She wished so hard that Wig had been at her side to support her. But, just like Meg who'd had to go back to her work at Home Farm, Wig had said his farewells a couple of days previously when he'd returned to London himself. There would have to be huge changes at the factory, and he needed to make massive decisions about its future. Clarrie sighed as they turned back into the house. But, as the saying went, as one door closed, another one opened. She had a new future to look forward to, as well. Ralph would be demobbed soon, and her Meg would be coming home.

And Clarrie's heart rejoiced.

Thirty-Three

Back at Home Farm, Meg was getting Duchess ready for a day's work out in the fields. Thank goodness they'd kept the strong, willing animal, Alan had said on so many occasions, with there being little or no petrol for the tractor or the lorry. But Duchess wasn't young anymore, and Meg was hoping that petrol supplies would soon start to trickle through again before too long.

Meg sighed as she led Duchess out of the loose-box, the familiar plodding of her hooves tearing into her heart. None of this was going to be for much longer. All the evacuees at Robin Hill House, apart from Doris, Cyril and Leslie who were staying on permanently, had gone back to their London homes. Men were already being demobbed as they gradually returned to Blighty, but thousands were still fighting in the Far East, of course. There were also many who'd continued to serve in Europe in order to sort out the chaos the war had created and to help the liberated countries get back on their feet.

Ralph was still instructing others. The RAF wasn't going to disintegrate just because the war in Europe was over. But it wouldn't be long before he returned to civvy street, and Meg would go back to Robin Hill House. Besides, Paul Fenshaw had been demobbed, thankfully unscathed, and had been home for nearly a week, so neither Meg nor Mandy would be needed for much longer.

Meg's brain was shrouded in confusion. She yearned for Ralph with an unbearable ache in her belly like a hunger. Yet she knew his return wouldn't entirely bring her the peace she craved. It was time to put her plan into action.

She'd already approached Mr Briggs, the land agent, when she'd seen him at market recently. He'd shaken his head sympathetically. There was nothing, no hint of a tenancy coming up anywhere, but he'd let her know if anything cropped up. It was the same everywhere she enquired, many frowning at her sceptically. She screwed up her mouth into a mutinous knot.

Things hadn't changed much, had they? The Land Army girls had worked their guts out, but they still weren't good enough to be in charge of their own destinies!

Meg let out a despondent sigh. She couldn't be patient forever. Being Ralph's wife meant everything to her, but her dreams would come true if they could run their own farm together, as well.

'Ah, there you are, Meg, dear.' Maggie's kind voice broke into her tumult. 'The others, well…' The woman glanced back at the open door to the farmhouse, her brow in an uncomfortable frown. 'They've sent me to break the news to you.'

Meg held her breath. This was it. The agonised wait was over. In a way, it was a relief. 'It's all right,' she muttered into her boots. 'I've been expecting it. I've always—'

'I don't know what your plans were,' Maggie went on, seemingly unaware that Meg had spoken. 'But we're going to give notice. Alan and our Paul want to work together. I know my Alan's not as young as he was, but there's many a year left in him yet, and this farm isn't big enough to support two men and any family that might come along. We've found somewhere bigger over in Sussex. It's just perfect.'

'Oh.'

Meg's heart dropped like a lead weight. She'd known she'd no longer be needed, but she wasn't expecting this! At least she could always have come to visit, but what if the new tenants weren't as accommodating? Oh, Lord…

'I'm sorry. I should've broken it to you more gently. But you must've…' Maggie stopped as Meg's face blanched. 'You all right, my dear?'

Meg stared at her, thoughts lurching drunkenly inside her head. What if…? What if the new tenants…? What if… *the new tenants…?*

She grasped Maggie's arm in an iron grip. 'Maggie, promise me you won't give notice just yet?' she said urgently. 'And can I use the phone?'

Her eyes flashed like steel and Maggie nodded in astonishment. 'Of course you can, my dear. But...?'

But Meg had already abandoned Duchess and ran across the yard and into the house as if Beelzebub himself were after her. Thimble, by her mistress's side as ever, cavorted after her, but when the door swung shut in her face, the animal trotted back to Maggie with doleful eyes.

'No good asking me,' Maggie told the dog with a bemused shake of her head. 'I know no more than you.'

Inside, Meg charged up the stairs to rummage in the drawer in her bedroom for her little address and telephone book. Would she be able to get through to Ralph at the base? Even if she couldn't, well, she'd have to take a chance. It was an enormous step, but she knew from things he'd said... Most importantly, the person she needed to speak to was Mr Chillcott, Wig and Clarrie's solicitor who'd always taken care of her money as well.

*

'Can I have everybody's attention, please?'

Ralph banged gently on the kitchen table that had been carried outside the cottage into the September sunshine. It was laden with sandwiches and cakes, and anything they could lay their hands on. The war might be over – out in Japan as well now, thank God, even if it had taken those two horrific bombs to end it – but rationing was bound to last for some time. Not that anyone at Robin Hill would starve with all the fruit and vegetables Gabriel grew with the help of his full-time apprentice, Leslie, and also Cyril when he wasn't tending the animals.

The little gathering fell silent as Ralph's words percolated the happy chatter. When all was finally quiet, Ralph took a deep breath and smiled.

'First of all, I have to say how wonderful it is to be back among you all, and especially my darling wife.' He turned to Meg for a moment, squeezing her hand with a deep, affectionate smile before continuing more solemnly, 'But this isn't just a celebration of peace. Nor is it just a homecoming for Bob and Sally and yours truly. It's something else as well. Meggy and I have an announcement to make.'

A soft murmur rippled among the gathered guests, and Ralph saw Leslie dig his twin in the ribs with a little snigger. 'No, Les,' Ralph chuckled. 'It isn't the patter of tiny feet. Not yet anyway. It's something entirely different. But I think Meg should be the one to tell you.'

He gestured for Meg to step forward, his eyes gleaming with ineffable love. Meg felt her cheeks suddenly burning. She wasn't expecting this.

'I'm sorry,' she said, shaking her head with a flustered laugh. 'I thought Ralph was going to tell you. Now... you know we both love you all dearly,' she began hesitantly. 'Always will. But sometimes it's time to move on. We wanted to start afresh. To begin a new life together. But on our own. We won't be far away, mind, so we can still see you often. The thing is...' She glanced at Ralph for reassurance, and her heart filled up as she felt his love pouring into her. 'The thing is, the farm where I was born, where I grew up, and where as you know I've been working as a Land Army girl, is being vacated. And Ralph and I, well, we're not just the new tenants. We're the new owners.'

A gasp ricocheted about the little crowd, everyone frowning and murmuring. Meg's heart gave a little jump, a mixture of both joy and sadness. Her eyes travelled over all these people she'd come to love so much, and she held up her hand to silence their voices before she went on, 'I can tell you now that when my parents were killed, I received substantial compensation. With Wig and Clarrie's help, I invested it, and over the years it grew to enough for me to be able to buy the farm. At least with a mortgage as well. And Ralph's put in his savings, too. It is our joint future, after all,' she added, turning to him with a loving smile.

For a few seconds, everyone was stunned as the news sunk in. It was Leslie who broke the silence.

'Bleeding hell, so yer a farmer now, Ralph?'

Ralph threw up his head with a broad laugh. 'Apparently so!' he grinned. 'But I'm told it's not much different from being a gardener. And I'll have a good teacher.'

'Can I come and help with the animals?'

'Course you can, Cyril. Expect we'll be glad of your help while we're getting started. And Meg's old friend, Mandy, wants to work for us, too.'

Surprised, delighted conversation broke out among the group who'd been thrown together by fate, and endured so much. They surged forward one by one to congratulate Ralph and Meg, hugs, kisses and handshakes heartily exchanged.

Nobody noticed that one person hung to the back, biting her lip. Clarrie supposed she should always have expected Meg to leave one day, but when she and Ralph had married, Clarrie had basked in contentment, believing they'd remain at Robin Hill forever. Looking at them now, Ralph's arm about his wife's waist in such a natural fashion, and Meg beaming up at him so adoringly, Clarrie felt she should be delighted for them.

But she wasn't. Rosebud was gone, and soon Meg would be, too. Clarrie would always have her darling Wig by her side, but she still missed Nana May so much. She would have dear young Doris, of course, a lovely girl who physically resembled Rosebud so closely. She should feel grateful that her future would be surrounded by so many people that she loved. But it was still Meg who had filled that place in her heart that Rosebud had left so hollow and empty.

Tears of sorrow and rekindled grief swam in Clarrie's eyes and threatened to run down her cheeks. She mustn't let them. No one, not even Wig, must see her distress. She'd lost her child, and the grief would remain with her every day until she died. Her dearest, darling Meg had closed the yawning chasm in her soul for, what, nine years now. But the wound was breaking open again.

Clarrie sniffed hard. Breathed in deeply. Then strode forward with a beaming smile on her face.

'Congratulations, both of you! And when do we get our first invite?'

She opened her arms wide. And suddenly all her fears dissipated as Meg hugged her as if she would burst.

'Never!' Meg crowed ecstatically. 'Not officially anyway. Because I want you and Wig to come whenever you like!'

'Do you really mean that?' Clarrie faltered as a fountain of joy sprang up inside her.

'Of course! That's what's so wonderful about it, not being that far away from you all! And I couldn't believe it when I spoke to Mr Briggs and he said that the landowner actually wanted to sell. Thought he could make more money investing the capital elsewhere now the war's over.' Meg shook her head in joyful bewilderment. 'Thank God you and Wig helped me pursue that compensation, or I'd never have been able to afford it. So now, because of you, I'm going to be living forever in the place I really do call home. So wishes do come true sometimes, don't they?'
'Well, this really calls for some celebration,' Wig said, coming up behind them, wielding a bottle in the air. 'Been keeping this for something really special,' he winked. 'Now who's for some bubbly?'

Thirty-Four

1946

'Hello, you two!' Clarrie beamed, opening the front door. 'I was in the sitting room and heard the car. Come on in, it's freezing outside.'
'I'm just popping down to Mum and Dad's,' Ralph said apologetically. 'But then maybe we could all have a cuppa together, Mum and Dad as well, if that's OK?'
'Yes, of course.' Clarrie's brow twitched in a tiny frown as she beckoned Meg inside. 'You go in, Meg, and I'll go and ask Ada to rustle us up some tea. We weren't expecting visitors on such a miserable day. Won't be a jiffy.'
Meg stepped inside the sitting room where a jolly fire was blazing in the grate. She slipped off her coat, holding her cold hands out to the flames. Meg guessed they weren't heating the spacious drawing room on such a raw, January day. It was a waste of fuel with so few people in the house.
It did seem so very quiet nowadays, after the bedlam that reigned when Penny Higginbottom and everyone else had been living there. Wig was doubtless at the factory, Doris would be at school, while the others were possibly in the kitchen having a well-deserved cup of tea. Bob and Sally had moved into the cottage, but both were working for Wig and Clarrie again. Meg would want to see them all later, but first she wanted a private word with Clarrie. More than a word. She had something to tell her, and her pulse was racing with anticipation.
'Oh, it is good to see you,' Clarrie declared as she came back into the room and settled opposite Meg in the other armchair, her face aglow. 'And tell me, how is life down on the farm?'
'Yes, everything's going very well. Ralph's taken to it like a duck to water.'
   'Well, he was already halfway there,' Clarrie chuckled.
'Yes, he was.' Meg returned her smile. 'And I think the challenge of pastures new has helped him recover mentally from the war. And physically, well, apart from the scarring, he's absolutely fine.' She glanced briefly around the familiar room, waiting for the right moment. She was itching to tell her the news, but somehow didn't feel she could launch into it straightaway. 'How's Jane finding life at the Police House?' she asked.
'Oh, brilliant!' Clarrie exclaimed. 'She has to answer the phone and take messages when Eric's not there, and see to people who call in. I was so pleased for them when Eric was

promoted to our village bobby. But I have to say I was a little concerned that Jane mightn't be able to cope with everything it would entail for her. But I needn't have worried. She's coping incredibly well. And it's given them a nice little home now they're married.'

'I'd like to call down and see her afterwards. Oh, it's so wonderful to have petrol to get around with again, isn't it? Even if it is strictly rationed. So I'm afraid we won't be able to stay too long if we're going to do that as well. We'll need to get back for milking and… well, we did want to see you,' Meg faltered, beating about the bush. 'All of you.'

Clarrie tipped her head, raising one inquisitive eyebrow. 'Well, it's always wonderful to see you, but… is there something special you wanted to talk about?'

Meg felt the peachy hue that warmed her cheeks. And it wasn't just because of the fire. 'Well, yes, there is actually. I… that is we… we're having a baby.'

Delight spun round inside her as she watched joy gradually blossom on Clarrie's face. The older woman's mouth slowly opened before it lifted in a grin. But somehow there was a strange little movement at the corners of her eyes.

'Oh, that's fantastic news!' she cried. 'Oh, come here, you clever girl!'

Both women stood up and met in a long hug, holding each other tightly for some seconds before sitting down again.

'Oh, so how long have you known? When is it due?' Clarrie asked excitedly.

Meg felt herself relax now she'd delivered the news. 'Well, I suspected over Christmas, but I wasn't sure. But I saw the doctor this morning, and he confirmed it. I'm about three months. So due about mid-July.'

'Oh, but what about the farm?' Clarrie asked, suddenly horrified. 'You can't go on farming while you're pregnant.'

Meg threw up her head with laughter. 'I'm only having a baby! There are certain things I shouldn't do, but I have got Ralph, and Mandy, of course. And you know Cyril cycles over once a week to help with any really heavy work that needs doing.'

'Well, you take care of yourself,' Clarrie frowned. 'A baby is such a precious thing. You… you mustn't take any risks.'

There was a strange catch in her voice, and a look of such concern and sorrow came over her face as she lowered her cornflower blue eyes that Meg felt something jerk in her own chest. A sudden weight like a fog drifted down, and Meg slid on her knees in front of Clarrie, taking her hands as she turned her head away, her lips thinned to a fine, anguished line.

'Clarrie?' Meg whispered, compassion creasing her face. 'Clarrie, what is it?'

She waited, confused, as Clarrie twisted her neck as if she would throw something out of her head but couldn't. Her eyes were screwed shut, but after a tearing sigh shuddered from her lungs, she slowly opened them again. Meg could see tears collecting on the lower lids as she met Clarrie's gaze.

'I… I maybe should have told you before,' Clarrie finally croaked, her voice broken. 'But… it's always been too painful. I never wanted to speak to anyone about it other than Wig and Nana May. So we always kept it a secret so that I'd never have to.' She paused, gulping in air. 'I… I told you we never had children. Well, that wasn't true. We never had any *more* children. We wanted them. Desperately. But we had a child. A beautiful little girl. With red hair and freckles. A bit like Doris.'

Meg stared at her, all sorts of emotion chasing around inside her head, ripping at her heart. Clarrie. The nursery. Certain things that had been said.

'Oh, Clarrie,' she breathed, her words more like air. 'What... what happened?' she asked so softly, since she knew really, didn't she?

'She... she wasn't even two,' Clarrie murmured into her chin. 'She had all the symptoms of meningitis.'

Meg breathed out slowly, letting the horror and the grief and the sadness settle into her soul. Poor Clarrie. Poor Wig. Nana May who must have suffered with them.

Meg waited. In silence. For ... for what she didn't know.

'What... was she called?' The words slid from her mouth, wanting to soothe, to show she *understood*. She knew what grief was. But a *child*... Clarrie slowly raised her head. And stared straight into Meg's eyes.

'Her name was Marguerite.'

A little gasp snatched at Meg's aching throat. Marguerite. Her own full name. Of course. It all made sense.

She couldn't speak. And as the tears rolled down from Clarrie's eyes like glistening pearls, so Meg's own vision was misting over. Nana May's dying words slid inside her head. That's what the old lady was trying to say, wasn't she? All that time, all those years, Clarrie had been holding that inside. But Nana May knew the only way Clarrie could mend was by admitting the truth.

'Oh, Clarrie, I do love you so much!' Meg choked, enfolding the older woman in her arms, rocking her, crooning to her. 'And what I haven't said is that Ralph and I want you and Wig to be grandparents as well as Gabriel and Mary. Just as if you were my real mum and dad.'

She felt Clarrie stiffen, and then draw back slowly from her embrace.

'Do you... really mean that?'

A smile of pure, unadulterated elation flooded into Clarrie's face like sunshine.

'Oh, yes. Mum,' Meg whispered back, and the word felt good on her tongue.

*

'So sorry I couldn't get back from London any quicker,' Wig apologised as they came into the farmhouse kitchen.

'But you're here now,' Meg beamed. 'And you, little man, are going to meet your other grandparents now. Grandma Clarrie and Grandpa Wig.'

Meg carefully lifted the tiny bundle from the carrycot and stepped around the table. Clarrie had settled herself in one of the chairs ready to take the newborn child, her heart overflowing, and gazed down proudly at the minuscule creature Meg slipped into her arms.

'Your grandson,' Meg whispered.

Their eyes met — and that was enough. No words were needed; they both understood.

"I wish Nana May had been here," Wig said softly, leaning over to stroke the baby's cheek. The tiny mouth kept moving even in sleep, and the sight filled the room with quiet wonder.

Meg swallowed the lump in her throat. "Maybe she is. She'll always be in our hearts — so she must be here."

"Yes," Clarrie agreed gently, her eyes returning to the sleeping infant in her arms. Her heart was overflowing with love and joy. Never in all her years had she imagined feeling this — the incredible happiness of being a grandmother. She might not have been one by blood, but it didn't matter. The bond was just as real.

"Oh, he's perfect," she murmured, sliding her finger into the baby's tiny palm. Instantly, the little hand curled around it, holding tight. "And how are *you*, Meggy?" she asked, finally looking up.

Meg smiled faintly. "A bit sore, but not too bad. You know how it is."

The two women exchanged a knowing glance — one of ease and understanding built on shared pain and trust. Clarrie had told Meg she'd confessed everything to Ralph. She had believed that honesty was the only way forward, and to her surprise, telling the truth had lifted a weight she hadn't realised she still carried.

"Shall we sit in the parlour?" Clarrie said. "You'll be more comfortable there."

"Yes, I think I will. And can you carry Thomas for me?"

"Of course."

"You two make yourselves comfortable," Ralph said warmly. "I'll put the kettle on."

"Well," Wig declared, tapping his pipe against his palm, "if you're going to chatter about baby nonsense, I'll enjoy a smoke outside." He winked at them both, then stepped out through the door and crossed the yard toward the garden Ralph had been tending behind the house.

As Wig filled his pipe, the image of Clarrie and Meg sitting together with the baby stayed in his mind — such a peaceful, tender sight. He'd never thought his dear Clarrie would find this kind of happiness again. She'd been through so much, yet she had become a source of strength for everyone around her — even for poor Sofia. It was all because of the love between her and Meg.

Strange, he thought, how it had all begun — in tragedy for Meg. Wig often wished they'd met under different circumstances, but life rarely offered such choices. What mattered was where they had ended up: together, as family.

He had some news for Meg, though he wouldn't share it just yet. She still worried that **Nathaniel Green**, the man who had once caused her so much suffering, might one day return. But Wig had learned the truth — Green had been captured in the Far East and forced to work under horrific conditions on the Burma Railway, where he'd died like thousands of others. A grim fate, but no one deserved such cruelty — not even him. Still, Wig knew Meg would sleep easier when she finally heard. For now, he'd let her keep her peace.

He wandered to the edge of the lawn, content. His wife was happy, the factory was thriving again, and life — after years of chaos — had found a quiet rhythm. What more could a man ask for?

Beyond the garden, the fields glowed gold under the setting sun. Cows grazed lazily in the fading light, and as Wig lifted his eyes, a smile touched his lips. High in the pale blue sky, a single star was already shining — clear and silver.

For a moment, he fancied it was **Nana May**, watching over them all.

He smiled up at the sky and gave a small, gentle wave.

Manufactured by Amazon.ca
Acheson, AB

30863922R00101